A VINE

Gay Biddlecombe was born in South Shields but lived in Battersea, south London, for the first twenty-two years of her life. After leaving school she started a career in journalism and worked on newspapers for over twelve years. She met her husband, Peter, when they worked on the same provincial newspaper and they continued to live in London after they married. Peter eventually started his own international business consultancy and soon afterwards Gay joined to help him with the business.

Gay now runs one of England's most famous and successful vineyards producing a range of wines including her own champagne-method sparkling wine. She exports her wine all round the world and supplies some of the top tables in the country. Her vineyard is open to the public and Gay now also has a substantial shop and restaurant and organizes shows and exhibitions throughout the summer. She runs a wine club and still writes for magazines and journals about English wine. She is also the BBC Radio Sussex wine correspondent.

GAY BIDDLECOMBE

A Vine Romance

PAN BOOKS

LONDON, SYDNEY AND AUCKLAND

First published 1993 by Pan Books Limited
a division of Pan Macmillan Publishers Limited
Cavaye Place London SW10 9PG
and Basingstoke

Associated companies throughout the world

ISBN 0 330 32767 4

1 3 5 7 9 8 6 4 2

A CIP catalogue record for this book is available from
the British Library

Typeset by Cambridge Composing (UK) Limited, Cambridge
Printed and bound in Great Britain by
Cox & Wyman Limited, Reading, Berkshire

TO ELSA, MY GREATEST FRIEND

CONTENTS

ACKNOWLEDGEMENTS

I would like to thank all my family for their support and help, and particularly my husband Peter, whose idea this book was. At the same time thanks are due to all the people who have helped me along the way and, of course, to all those who have enjoyed and still are enjoying my wines!

CHAPTER ONE
A Taste of English Wine

23 APRIL, ST GEORGE'S DAY

6 a.m.   'Come on, girls – let's go!' I call to Elsa, Honey and
Blue, my three golden retrievers, who rush past,
almost knocking me over in their hurry to get to the
door first.

What a day! Crystal clear with a solid deep blue
sky. The sun is shining and it's great to feel the
warmth after the winter months. It's just great to be
alive.

6.15 a.m.   As I walk through the farm gate towards the cowhouse the vineyard lies ahead, glistening with dew.
Everything smells so fresh. The village church clock
strikes – it's always late.

The dogs are already rushing past Hilda, who is
running to greet me. Up she goes. She likes to sit on
my shoulder like a parrot but, being a cat, I suppose
it's because she likes to look down on all the other
animals. By now the dogs are all rolling on the wet
grass.

Lady, one of my oldest sheep, says hello and waits
patiently by the gate to her field for a friendly pat
behind the ears. She must be one of the oldest sheep
in Sussex!

6.45 a.m.   I turn into Lodge Field vineyard where it all began.

Elsa's caught the scent of a rabbit and the three of them are off.

The vines will like this sunshine. Their buds burst three weeks ago and already the vineyard looks alive and healthy. I only hope we're not caught out by a late frost. So far we haven't had one but there's always a first time. It would be disastrous.

The dogs collide with the fence that the rabbit has obviously escaped under and their barking disturbs a pheasant who protests loudly and takes flight. Blue thinks it's worth chasing.

As I reach the top end of the vineyard I look back over the estate across the top of the vines towards the farm and the house to the church beyond. Who would have thought that one day I would be a wine producer – in England!

The grass was cut yesterday and the smell is wonderful.

7 a.m.   I can hear the horses neighing as Peter, my husband, is getting their morning feed ready. He's late. Probably been chatting to an early morning rider passing by. He always does.

Come-on, another of my cats, appears, talking continuously. She thinks she is a Siamese. Hilda jumps off my shoulder to greet her, licking her face, and I leave them to discuss the night's adventures.

7.15 a.m.   Into Barley Gratton, our largest field, which we use for grazing cows. I like this field. It slopes in several directions and is surrounded by trees of oak, ash, chestnut, birch, lime and holly. From the top you can see the South Downs rolling in the spring sunshine. The dogs are off again. There are lots of rabbits

in this field, which is also home to 'my' badgers and
fox family. It would make a great vineyard because it
mainly slopes deep to the south. All around me is a
wonderful promise of abundant growth. Everything
has either just burst or is about to. It's the best time
of the year.

Primroses are everywhere – pick a bunch for the
cowhouse and witches will stay away! I can see the
blue-green leaves of wild strawberries and the pale
lilac cuckooflower which heralds the cuckoo and is
supposed to mean the soil is rich in metals. The
delicate white flowers of the blackthorn say a farewell
to the winter bleakness and the small white star-like
flower of the garlic mustard – more picturesquely
known as Jack-by-the-hedge – are among the first
flowers in the hedgerow followed by the brassy,
glossy yellow, star-shaped flower of celandine.

I like the celandine because the name is Greek for
swallow and its appearance coincides with the return
of 'our' swallows who come back every year from
their long travels to nest in our great tithe barn, in
the winery and even in our shop. Every spring I
breathe a sigh of relief when they first appear. It's
great to be in Sussex. And it's great to be walking
around my vineyard and farm. I still can't believe it.

7.30 a.m. 'Come on,' I call to the dogs, 'I've got work to do –
let's go!'

I walk back up Great Meadow. Perfect for a
vineyard with its slopes and good aspect. But not
yet. As I walk towards the cowhouse with three
panting, wet dogs my sister-in-law Ruth is unlocking
the gates. The vine against the cowhouse wall is well
ahead. It won't be long before the flowers appear if
this sun keeps shining.

[3]

8.30 a.m.   All the animals have been fed. Peter rides out on Laddie, his handsome bay gelding.

'I won't be long,' he calls, knowing once he is in the woods he will forget the time.

A quick breakfast, if you can call it that. The telephone starts to ring. Are we open today? Today of all days!

9 a.m.   Mum and Dad arrive to help. Honey is barking by the vineyard gate. It's the florist with the red roses I ordered specially – one for everyone who comes to see us today.

Ruth is checking we have bottles chilled ready for tastings. And plenty of glasses cleaned and polished. Adrian, my brother, is getting the red and white umbrellas out and placing them among the garden furniture I bought so visitors can sit and enjoy not only the wine but the peace and quiet of the countryside. I must get changed into my new red sweatshirt I had specially printed with our name and logo. Everyone else is wearing theirs.

9.30 a.m.   About thirty minutes to opening time. Open the great tithe barn doors and put the lights on. Check there are plenty of brochures on the information desk. We've just had them printed and they tell our story in brief.

Peter has rushed back on Laddie, both of them all hot and sweaty. He has to hoist the English flag – the Cross of St George – above the tithe barn doors. Check the loos.

9.45 a.m.   Open the gates. Put our new 'Open' sign out. The shop is open and Ruth is giving it a final once-over.

The garden is tidy and although it's early in the year the red geraniums make it look colourful. The vineyard is bathed in sunshine. Everything is looking good.

10 a.m.   We're open. Welcome to St George's!

Although I am now a Sussex wine producer, I grew up in Battersea just after the war when it was very much on the wrong side of the river and not the best part of south London. My parents, my older brother Adrian and I lived in three rented rooms until the council gave us a flat and we moved up in the world.

Battersea in those days was full of character and atmosphere. I remember the market with its gruesome jellied eel stall alongside the Cockney fruit and vegetable sellers, and the marvellous shop, wood-panelled and covered in sugar, whose owners smelt deliciously of the hard-boiled sweets they made. We used to take tram rides up the Junction and spend Saturday mornings in the local flea-pit, playing cowboys and Indians afterwards in the streets and on the bomb sites.

My first school was dark, all panelled in oak, and the teachers had navy bloomers and powder-caked faces. Then there were the glorious days at the 'big' school, where I avoided saying I lived in Battersea because my fellow pupils came from Wandsworth and Clapham. In those days, going to the countryside meant climbs up Red Hill in Surrey and walking by the river at Richmond and Hampton Court.

When I left school I joined a non-union local rag in Tooting, where the conditions were Dickensian. A year later I joined the big boys on the union paper in the same area. I was the only girl in what seemed a racy world of news stories, beer drinking, eye-shields, smoke, excitement – and swearing. It was while I was training to be a journalist that I met Peter, the one reporter on our paper who was obviously destined for greater things and who didn't swear.

Peter and I married in 1965 and moved into a rented flat in Streatham. After five years of working hard and saving we bought our first house there. And at last I had a garden. Those were the days when Sunday mornings meant lying in bed till 9.30 reading the papers.

It was on one of those lazy Sunday mornings four years later that I spotted a private advertisement for a timber-framed house in Surrey. The country was the last place I wanted to live – all that mud! Besides, I loved my work, the theatre, restaurants, art galleries, shops, concerts. I just loved being a Londoner.

'Why don't we go and have a look?' I said to Peter.

'Okay,' he yawned, 'though I don't know why.'

Within two hours we were there. Within three hours I wanted to live in the country. We had arrived to find the owner up a tree trying to catch a swarm of bees. Some ducks waddled up to us and lost interest when they realized we had nothing for them. Suddenly I decided this was the life for me. Peter had given me a book on self-sufficiency as a joke. Now I wanted to live the book. At thirty-two I wanted to change my life.

We didn't buy the house in Surrey, which was riddled with dry rot, but we did find Oaklands, a large rambling Victorian house set in a beautiful but neglected garden near Edenbridge in Kent. The house looked as though it had not been touched for centuries. Everything about it spelt expense and hard work but it was going cheap and we loved it.

By the end of 1975 it was ours. For the first six months we camped there at weekends. While we were working in London during the week the local family building firm were re-roofing, re-plumbing, re-wiring, revealing oak panels and oak floors. It became a major campaign and every week something else was added to the list of things to be done.

We began to live for Friday evenings when we would drive down straight from the office near Piccadilly Circus. The air was fresher in the country, the sun brighter. It was quiet and peaceful. And gradually the house and garden were coming into shape.

Then in spring 1977 I had my first taste of English wine. Peter and I were driving through Penshurst when I asked him to stop so I could buy an ice cream! He pulled up outside a dingy little shop in the village. Like all village shops, its small window was crammed full of faded packets and tins and a ginger cat. Their selection of ice cream was limited. As I was waiting for change I glanced at a shelf which had one solitary bottle of wine on it. It was a bit dusty but I could see the word 'Penshurst' on the label.

'What is that?' I asked.

'Some wine that's been made in the village. We have our own vineyard you know. It's not bad stuff,' said the fat, elderly woman in a floral apron, 'though I'm not a connoisseur, mind.'

I bought it. The label said English wine.

'Can't imagine it will be any good,' said Peter. 'It's probably some home-made fruit wine.'

'No, it says here it's from grapes grown in a vineyard in Penshurst.' I was reading the very small print at the bottom of the label.

'A vineyard!' Peter scoffed. 'It's probably someone's greenhouse.'

That evening, the bottle having been duly dusted and chilled, we opened it without any reverence.

'Not bad,' said Peter.

'What do you mean, not bad?' I challenged. 'It's bloody good!'

I didn't know then that that bottle was going to change my life.

★

I kept the phone ringing a long time – that's one simple rule you soon learn living in the country. It's usually much further to get to a phone.

'Yes? 'Allo?' An Australian voice was gasping for breath. I thought I might have misdialled and ended up somewhere in the outback.

'Is that the vineyard at Penshurst?' I asked.

'You bet it is.' The Australian sun shone straight through the phone.

'I hope you don't mind my ringing but I had a bottle of your wine last night. I never knew there was such a thing as English wine and I liked it.'

'Thanks.'

'I would really like to know more about it – or rather about the vineyard,' I went on.

'Well come on over,' was the welcome but unexpected reply.

Taken slightly aback by the warm response I asked: 'When, and where are you?'

'Any time you like and you can't miss us.'

'How about now?'

'Sure, why not? I'll be working in the vineyard.'

'Thanks. Sorry, I didn't catch your . . .'

The phone was down.

'Come on, Peter, we're going out,' I shouted upstairs.

'But I . . .'

'Come on. You're in for a surprise.'

The Land-Rover was moving before Peter closed the door. Just fifteen minutes later I saw them. Vines – row after row of vines.

'That's an English vineyard,' I said, just as amazed as Peter.

'Are you sure? I can't see any leaves let alone grapes.'

As we swung into the drive up to the house, Bob Westphal, the cheerful Australian, was getting off his small tractor. He was bronzed and rosy-cheeked with jet black hair.

'G'day,' he said to Peter, shaking hands. 'Wana have a look round?'

Although it was late March it was sunny and warm. Bob took us into the field we had seen from the road. It contained row after row of pruned vines, looking more like dead young trees, threaded along row after row of wire fixed to big wooden posts. It didn't exactly look like the vineyards we had been to abroad but it was certainly neat and well organized.

'There's not much to see yet,' Bob said, 'but the buds are about to burst. All this fine weather.'

He talked proudly and excitedly about the small vineyard he'd just started, having bought the place as an orchard producing apples for local shops.

'One or two people are growing vines here so I thought I'd have a go. Might as well. Keeps me busy, though. Come and taste some of the wine.'

He invited us into a converted garage with boxes of wine piled high and two large tubs of water with bundles of vines crammed into them.

'What are these here for?' I enquired.

'They're surplus. I'll probably put them up and sell them,' Bob said, more interested in selling the end product. An hour later we left with two cases of wine and 250 vines in the back of the Land-Rover!

'What on earth are you going to do with that lot?' Peter laughed. 'You realize what you've just spent – over two hundred pounds.'

'I'm going to plant a vineyard,' I said.

Easter wasn't far away and we had decided to take an extra day off work. The whole family were coming for the weekend because the two guest rooms at Oaklands were now completely finished. And besides, I thought, they can all lend a hand with planting the vines.

I had prepared the site, according to Bob's instructions, in the middle of the orchard where conveniently there were no trees. All the Bramleys and Coxes were in a semi-circle around the outside but there were still lots of bumps and holes.

I hired a rotovator from the local do-it-yourself shop and after almost two hours of struggling to get it started I managed to bump my way around, churning up the soil.

While Peter explained to Mum, Dad, Adrian and my sister-in-law Ruth that the whole idea was mine, I handed out the second-hand and new wellies.

'I thought we had come to sit by the log fire, eat, drink and chat,' said Mum.

'I thought I'd wander down to your local,' said Adrian.

'Oh come on,' said Ruth, 'the quicker it's done the quicker we can sit by the fire.'

It was very cold and the sky was that muddy grey which warns of snow. As we started digging, the first flakes drifted down.

As we progressed the snow was swirling all around us and settling on the ground except where we were digging.

'This is crazy,' said Peter.

'Keep digging,' I said.

'He's right,' everyone rallied.

'We've only a hundred and twenty-seven vines to go,' I tried jollying them along.

Two days and a full-scale blizzard later all 250 vines were planted.

While most of them flourished that summer I tried to learn as much as I could about vines and wine. There were no books apart from amateur gardening books which were not very informative. Through Bob I got the names and addresses of some other vineyards and visited them when I could. I hadn't realized that there were quite a few people growing vines to make commercial wine. Most of them were fruit farmers who knew a lot about land, soil and fruit but not much about wine.

'Did you know,' one of them said, 'that England had plenty of vineyards when the Romans were here?'

''Course it's one thing growing the damn things,' said another, 'it's another making the wine . . . and I can tell you it's not easy to sell.'

Having looked at his wine label, which depicted a farmyard scene with chickens and pigs and had the word Farm writ large across it, and having tasted the wine, I could see what he meant.

Another potential wine producer said when I asked for his advice: 'I won't have any problems selling. They'll be queuing at the gates. I only need to sell one bottle to everyone in the village per month and I'm laughing.'

He's not laughing now. I could have told him at the time that life is never that simple. In fact, the one thing I noticed every time I met a grower was that they knew nothing about selling or marketing. It was essential to make good wine – and that would come from good growing – but the marketing was of equal importance.

And what struck me most was that while the growers were, in a sense, pioneers, few seemed confident of the future and those who had just started producing wine were apologetic about it. All except Bob who, in his flamboyant Australian way, was confident about everything.

By the following summer I had been bitten by the wine bug. I knew little, I had no experience and I couldn't train since, unlike other countries, Britain did not have colleges or even universities teaching and giving qualifications in viticulture and viniculture. But I knew what I wanted to do. If all these men were having a go without any experience surely a woman could do as well – maybe even better!

Oaklands, our house in Kent, was finished. We were happy there, Peter and I. We had even started taking riding lessons. And we were building a tennis court.

'I want to plant a big vineyard,' I said, 'and produce wine. We can't buy any more land around here, so we'll have to sell.'

'But you haven't produced any wine yet from the vineyard you've got,' Peter pleaded. 'And let's face it, you've no real experience.'

'I'm thirty-five,' I argued. 'A vineyard takes three to five years to establish. Bloody hell, I'll be forty before I can produce wine. There's no time left. So I haven't got experience . . . what the hell!'

Back to the estate agents.

'Okay,' Peter resigned himself. 'You fix it. But it will mean you'll have to give up London.'

I visited every type of house and farm you can imagine, from big arable farms to tiny, barely self-sufficient patches of dirt in the middle of nowhere. I saw one farm just outside Crowborough in East Sussex which made all its money by allowing the local water board to spray raw sewage on the land for one half of the year then renting it out for shooting to the National Union of Mineworkers for the other half. I saw one house in Chiddingly, also in East Sussex, which had its own ballroom!

Just outside Sevenoaks we came across a farm with a sixteenth-century farmhouse which looked perfect. It had over two hundred acres, lots of wonderful sloping fields to catch the sunshine, plenty of farm buildings which could be converted into wineries, store rooms, tractor sheds. And it was on the main road which would be good for future business.

'Let's make them an offer,' I suggested to Peter.

'Well, if you are going to make them an offer, make certain it's a serious offer,' he replied.

'I know,' I said. 'You don't have to tell me about selling houses. Didn't I sell the Streatham house for a good price?'

I made them an offer but when, after three weeks, we still hadn't heard from either the farmer or the agent we decided to continue looking. Didn't really like it anyway!

CHAPTER TWO
On the Move Again

As soon as I saw Cross Farm, I knew it was perfect. It just felt right. I felt it was a happy place. It had the right atmosphere.

'Can you feel it?' I asked Peter.

'Nonsense,' he said, 'but it is nice. And I could have a horse.'

We had received the details about three weeks earlier. When I looked it up on the map we both agreed it was a little off the beaten track, too far from a station and, for that matter, too far from London. So I put the estate agent's details to one side.

One Saturday we had decided to look at a farm near Tunbridge Wells. As we drove in it looked like a municipal rubbish tip.

'Oh my goodness,' said Peter, 'let's turn round now.'

We hurriedly looked round and, although I like a challenge, the land told me all I wanted to know. It was thick heavy clay which had been rutted over the years by tractors and animals. Leaving, rather dismayed, we decided to drive on down to the coast. We had travelled south for about twenty minutes when –

'Stop,' I shouted.

Peter slammed down the brake and we both lunged forward.

'What's the matter?' he asked.

'That's it,' I said. 'Didn't you recognize it?'

'What? Have I run over something? There could have been a car behind . . .'

'Reverse back up the lane,' I said.

'Now what?' he asked wearily.

'It's that house – the one you said it was no good looking at.'

He reversed up two hundred yards and we both peered at it.

We got out of the car.

'It's lovely,' I said.

'It's not on a main road . . . no good for selling wine,' said Peter.

'It's perfect,' I said. 'I hope it hasn't gone yet.' I knocked on the door but there was no reply.

The following Monday I rang the agent at 9 a.m. It had not been sold.

'But there is a lot of interest in it,' said the agent, as all estate agents do.

We arranged to see it on the Wednesday. Everything about it felt right.

The large house was built in the seventeenth century by one of the old Sussex ironmasters, a man called John Hammond. There was a big courtyard and lots of old farm buildings. We went into one large barn and although the only light came from the door and several cracks and holes in the roof and walls, we could still see its magnificent beams. It was, as we discovered, an eleventh-century tithe barn, reputed to be the oldest in Sussex.

We began to get excited.

'You'll be able to get a horse, Peter,' I encouraged him, 'and ride on your own land.'

There were fields all around us and the farm was in the middle of the small village, right opposite the church and churchyard.

'John Hammond and his family are buried over there,' Mr Mobbs, the owner, said.

I rather liked the idea that he would be watching over us.

Twenty years before I would have thought it a reason *not* to buy the farm!

Between the farm and the church was a small country lane which came from nowhere and led to nowhere. Further along was a pub, a few houses, a village shop and the village hall.

'It's not a main road and it's very pretty. It'll be good for business,' I said. 'This is it. It just feels right.'

But we hadn't had a thorough inspection or looked around the house yet. White-haired Mr Mobbs explained that he and his wife found the place too big since their children had grown up and left home. There were tears in his eyes as he said they had only just decided to sell but didn't want to leave.

The front of the house was slightly Georgian but inside and at the back it was definitely old Sussex farmhouse. There were oak beams in some of the rooms, but not in others. We found out later that they had all been covered in. In the front living room was a wonderful old inglenook fireplace with John Hammond's initials on the original iron fireback. There was a smaller one in the back lounge with an old bread oven. There was a newer extension alongside the house, an enormous room that could have contained my first home in Battersea and our council flat combined. In one corner was a grand piano.

'This is the music room.' Mr Mobbs was obviously proud of it. 'We sometimes have concerts here for the church. It used to be a library.'

I asked about the land.

'We only use the land for walking the dog,' said Mrs Mobbs.

On many of the old beams in the house and barns you could see the original builder's marks and instructions. The tithe barn still had its old earth floor with the threshing platform in the middle. The original doors had been replaced but you could see where the big old cart-horses had pulled the wagons in to the threshing floor and then out to the courtyard on the other side.

The horses had been kept in a brick building which at first we thought was an additional cottage. The date of 1748 was carved above the door which also had a very ornate and elegant carved surround.

'Got it from the Hudson Bay building in the City of London,' said Mr Mobbs who turned out to be an interior designer.

Inside were stone walls, an earth floor and arched beams. At the very top, underneath the roof, were some old planks and a door to where, we found out later, the groom used to sleep above the hay and the horses.

'You see, Peter, you could keep your horse here,' I said.

'I might have to sleep here too,' he groaned, 'if we can't afford the house.'

There was a second, smaller barn which was open on both sides and several outbuildings, all piled high inside with rubbish. Further on we came to a cottage. It was more modern, smaller but with lovely views over the land.

'The children use it for parties,' said Mr Mobbs. 'I've been meaning to do it up but never got round to it.'

'What about the fields?' I asked.

There were five fields altogether and the total acreage was nearly thirty-six. To us it was enormous. There were three fields behind the house stretching back up to a ridge with a boundary of oak trees down the middle. Across the top of the ridge, and forming a natural boundary with another farm, was a long line of established trees – oak, ash, chestnut and holly. To the south of these three fields were two much larger fields, at the top of which you could see the South Downs. We were later to buy three more fields, bringing the total acreage up to over fifty.

'I rent the fields to the local farmer. If you're wise you'll do the same,' said Mr Mobbs.

'But I want to plant vines,' I said.

'Vines?' he said. 'Vines, here at Cross Farm? I don't know whether that's wise. You'd better talk to the local farmer. He'll be able to advise you.'

Walking back I saw an old iron sign half buried near a heap

of rubbish. Mr Mobbs was way ahead talking to Peter. I pulled it out. It read 'The Hunum Herd of Pedigree Jersey Cattle. Owner: Lady Blunt.'

I found out afterwards that Lady Blunt had taken her prime Jersey herd and moved to Kent, leaving Lord Blunt with his mistress.

I would love to have met Lord Blunt. He was, by all accounts, flamboyant, elegant, a womanizer and a heavy drinker – which probably explained all the empty whisky bottles we found over the years! He was also stinking rich and it was he who rebuilt the top floor of the house for his servants, the library for all his books and the cottage for his mistress. He lived at Cross Farm for several years in the late 1960s and there are still people in the area who remember him well and talk about the 'goings-on'.

'Um . . . cattle,' I thought.

As we drove back to Oaklands I was getting excited with plans.

'But it is off the beaten track,' Peter kept saying.

'I know,' I said, 'but that's its charm. And if our vineyard is successful and if we sell good wine that won't matter. Look how many French vineyards are in the back of beyond.'

'Okay . . . as long as I can have a horse.'

As soon as we got back to Oaklands, I telephoned Mr Mobbs.

'We'll take it,' I said.

We agreed a price and I posted a cheque to his solicitors as a deposit. At the same time we put Oaklands on the market. Within a week it was sold.

My main worry about moving was how our cats would react. We had four: Come-on, Eustace, Hilda and Squeaky.

Come-on adopted Oaklands first, then us. She was the prettiest thing I had ever seen. A tortoiseshell kitten with four

white paws and a large white bib. She used to visit the builders
at lunchtime from an adjoining farm whose owner had some
funny ideas on how to look after cats and kittens. She shared the
bricklayers' sardine sandwiches and the carpenters' milky coffee.
When we were there she would stand on our new wellies while
we were trying to work on the garden and sneak into the house
in the evenings and share our picnics. When we had a Chinese
takeaway sitting on the bags of cement and using bricks for a
table, she was our first dinner guest.

'Why do you call her Come-on?' I'm always asked.

'Because that's what we first said when we saw her. "Come-
on. Come-on." And she did.'

Eustace was a real gent. When we first met he was a bit down
at heel but you could see he liked the good things in life. He was
gentle and had impeccable manners, a big black cat with a white
bib and white spats that made him look as though he was always
about to dine out at his club. Hilda was the opposite: mousey,
bossy and only interested in the practicalities of life.

They had arrived one Friday night at the kitchen door. It was
bitterly cold outside and had been snowing all day. As soon as
we reached Oaklands from London, I rushed to the kitchen to
put up the temperature control of the central heating and heard
their pleas at the door. I opened it and Hilda raced by without
any introduction. Eustace acknowledged my gesture and glided
in.

I gave them some warm milk and some of Come-on's food.
She had disappeared to her favourite place after looking disdain-
fully at our guests. They curled up together on a chair by the
new Aga, the warmest place in the house, and went straight to
sleep purring loudly as if to say, 'We found our home . . . we'll
be no trouble.'

The following morning, while Eustace was still asleep, Hilda
was scratching at the door to get out. The wind was fierce and
the whole garden was covered with at least three to four inches
of snow. I opened the door and she shot out, so full of purpose

that I followed her. I didn't want to lose my new friend. She ran round the front of the house, along the driveway and down past the vegetable garden towards the orchard. She moved so fast that she barely left paw marks in the snow. I had forgotten to put my wellies on and my feet were beginning to get wet through my slippers. Just outside an old shed, where I was keeping my brand new garden tools, she skidded to a halt. There was a very small window that was only slightly open. She jumped straight through the gap and disappeared inside.

Well at least I know where she is, I thought as I got closer. Funny, I hadn't noticed any sign of her in there before, but she obviously treated it like home.

Just as I turned to go back to the house she jumped out again on to the snow and started running back towards the house with what looked like a rat in her mouth. I gave chase but in my wet slippers I couldn't keep up with her. All I could see as I followed was this furry thing swaying as she ran. As I got back to the kitchen door she was there waiting to be shown in. It wasn't a rat, it was a little black kitten, son of Eustace. She had obviously been sheltering it in the shed. Now she had found a better home she was bringing it along as well. She dropped the squeaking ball by the Aga then looked at me with her huge green eyes.

'Okay,' I said, 'you win. One more isn't going to make any difference I suppose.' She started licking her cold, hungry and squeaking baby.

After I had made sure there were no more kittens around and realized that poor little Hilda, who was only a kitten herself, could not have coped with more since she was skin and bones, we all had breakfast. For the next week I virtually fed the kitten by hand with Hilda watching to make sure I was careful. Eustace just slept through the whole thing, obviously dreaming of all those elegant clubs in St James's.

'That's men for you, Hilda,' I joked.

Very soon, and after a visit from the vet, all three were doing well. They had been wormed and treated for ear canker. Their dirty coats were shining and their purring was even louder – apart from the kitten who did nothing but squeak like a mouse so I called her Squeaky. Eustace and Hilda had been given their names because they matched the characters in L. P. Hartley's book of that title which I was reading at the time.

At first the little family wouldn't leave the Aga except for the briefest of necessities. They were probably still thawing out after all that time spent fending for themselves in arctic conditions. Then gradually all three would pop out together to play. By the spring they were gambolling about all over the house and garden.

One day, as we turned into the drive, we saw Hilda heading straight for the kitchen door. In her mouth was Squeaky. A wringing wet, squeaking Squeaky who'd obviously fallen in the pond.

'So if we move what do we do about the cats?' Peter said as I dried her out by the Aga.

'We'll take them with us,' I said.

'But we can't. They're not ours, they adopted us.'

'They're ours now,' I said.

'But how do you know they'll stay? Everything will be different. They'll probably get lost,' he persisted.

'I'll find out,' I said.

'Put butter on their paws,' an old lady in the next village told me. 'Put butter on their paws. When they start licking the butter off then you know they're at home.'

'Now there's nothing to stop us,' I told Peter. He nodded.

All I needed to do now was make a phone call.

'Hi,' I said. 'How's things?' It was a dismal Saturday afternoon in December.

'Okay,' said Ruth, my sister-in-law. She and my brother lived in a semi-detached house on a modern housing estate in the boring countryside of Wickford, Essex. Adrian commuted to London where he worked as a printer for *The Times*.

'I'm just off out to a neighbour's with the kids to have some tea and a chinwag. Adrian's watching the football on the box.'

'We're going to buy a farm and I'm going to plant a vineyard. Do you want to help?' I asked. I never beat about the bush.

'What!' Ruth shouted. 'Adrian, turn that down. You're not serious . . . You are serious.' She was beginning to know me after ten years. 'You've already got a vineyard. We helped you plant it. Remember.'

'I mean a real vineyard, a big one. And I'm going to make wine. We've seen just the place and it has another house. How about it? It will be a whole new life. A new adventure.'

'I just don't know,' she laughed, 'the things you do. I'll call you back.'

In less than an hour the phone rang. It was Ruth.

'When can we see it?'

CHAPTER THREE
Butter Paws and Strawberries

Well there we were. At Cross Farm with the contract about to be signed. But we needed a small mortgage and the Agricultural Mortgage Corporation, or AMC for short, seemed the best bet. Trouble was they had to make sure we were going to put the land to good use.

I decided to seek advice from the Ministry of Agriculture. In any case they might know something about planting a vineyard.

'Vines, you say,' said the man from the Ministry of Agriculture, in his heavy tweed suit and wellies. We were standing together in the middle of one of the fields at Cross Farm.

He stuck his chest out, stood taller and said: 'I wouldn't if I were you.'

'Why not?' I asked politely.

'Well because . . . well this is England. They wouldn't grow. Waste of money. Now strawberries – you could grow strawberries. Set up a PYO.'

'What's a PYO?' I asked.

He looked reassured. 'You see what I mean? I wouldn't grow vines.'

We had called in the local Ministry man to ask his advice. After he'd left, I was even more determined. To do the opposite.

Young Mr Day was a different matter. He was an agricultural consultant – a red-faced young man in a tweed jacket, knitted tie and corduroy trousers. At first, however, things did not go too well.

'Did I hear you right? You want to plant a vineyard?' he asked incredulously.

'Yes, I want to plant a vineyard,' I repeated.

'But where?' he asked.

'In Sussex.'

'But you can't. Not in Sussex.'

'Oh yes I can. And I will. Now will you help us to get the mortgage?' I was beginning to lose my patience.

'But no one plants a vineyard in England. Now, strawberries . . . how about strawberries?' he beamed.

'They have. They are and they will,' I said, trying to recall the famous Vita Sackville-West quote about growing vines in England ('We did. We don't. We can. We could. We should.') without much success. But the meaning was still there. 'Vineyards have been planted in England for centuries. They are being planted now and there will be lots more. It's the future of agriculture. And I don't want to grow strawberries.' I had lost my patience.

I glared at the hapless Mr Day who sat in his office surrounded by copies of *Farmers Weekly*, agricultural manuals and graphs of profit potential in different forms of land and stock management. He smiled and leant forward in his chair. He looked at my husband Peter first, with pleading eyes, then he looked at me and said: 'With all due respect what on earth do you know about planting a vineyard in England? For that matter what do you know about farming and horticulture? You are, after all . . . and with respect . . . a Londoner.'

He saw that I was about to leap out of my seat and said, almost like a doctor calming a patient: 'But I can advise you about strawberries. Now strawberries . . .'

'A Londoner!' I shouted. 'What has that got to do with it? I can buy a pair of green wellies and a tweed jacket too, you know.'

He didn't like that.

'What I meant was, farming, horticulture, working the land is hard work for people who don't know what to do, haven't had experience or been to agricultural college. But . . .' he hesitated. He went very red.

'Okay.' I calmed down. 'I admit all that. But I can try and I will succeed. I don't need a university degree.'

After we had convinced him we were serious he had to help us convince the Agricultural Mortgage Corporation to give us a loan to make up the difference between the cost of Cross Farm and the money we made on the sale of Oaklands.

'But it will have to be with strawberries,' he said.

'Oh God, how many more times?' I moaned.

'No, what I mean is, you can plant your vineyard but we will have to go for the loan for strawberries,' he said.

'The AMC will think you're mad planting vines . . . well, you're getting used to that,' he smiled. I smiled.

'So we will prepare a viability report for strawberries.'

'PYO,' I said.

'Yes, of course, PYO,' he said. 'Once the AMC agree to lend you the money you can go your own sweet way. Leave it to me.'

Within two weeks a report had been written and a meeting arranged. The day the Agricultural Mortgage Corporation manager was coming I could have entered *Brain of Britain*, *Mastermind* and *Gardeners' Question Time* on strawberries and walked away with a shelf-ful of awards. The man from the AMC wore a new Barbour, a tweed hat and green wellies and arrived in a Volvo estate. Peter and I showed him round, with Mr Day in tow.

'The soil is good here,' I began. 'Good Tunbridge Wells sand and Wadhurst clay. Ideal drainage. Good growing conditions.'

He grunted and made some notes in a little red notebook.

'Strawberries, you say,' he said.

'Er . . . well yes,' I said.

'Very good idea. Sound and sensible. PYO?' he asked.

'Er . . . well yes,' I hesitated.

'How do you propose to manage it?' he asked.

'Very well,' I said.

'No, I mean what management proposals are you making? The land management, the varieties, the crop maintenance, a shop, a car park for visitors,' he said.

'Yes, of course. Yes.' I looked at Mr Day who came to the rescue with a well-rehearsed delivery of facts, figures, proposals and forecasts.

An hour later as the AMC man got into his Volvo and shook hands with Mr Day I thought I heard him say: 'Save us from townies.'

Two weeks later our mortgage had been agreed. And we were moving again. This time it was in the middle of a raging blizzard on St Valentine's Day, 1979.

We'd already removed from the garden all the cuttings, plants and shrubs I had wanted to keep. We'd even built a big trailer to take them. Now all the furniture was ready to go. Even the old billiard table that we had had to buy with the Streatham house was dismantled. All the books were in packing cases. But no cats.

I had prepared two tea chests for them with their cushions and blankets in the bottom. I also had ready a plastic jug full of cream, two tins of their favourite food – and a big slab of butter. But could I find them?

The removal men packed the first furniture van. Still no cats. The men packed the second. Still no cats. As they finished packing the third, the cats arrived. It was almost as if they had been making their final tour of inspection, saying goodbye to all their old haunts. Eustace came into the kitchen first. He sniffed and walked straight up to the tea chest, for all the world like an elderly colonel boarding the QE2 – first class, of course. Hilda came next, looking a little nervous as if she knew she should be travelling tourist but hoped nobody would take much notice of her because she wasn't as well dressed as the other passengers. Then Squeaky, who looked as if she was just going for the fun. Finally Come-on, who always behaved as if she was different from the other cats and probably, deep down, resented their presence in any case. For her, I had a chest all of her own.

I put the wire netting over the top of the tea chests, carefully carried them to the back of the Land-Rover and we were off.

As we travelled the twenty-five miles from Oaklands to Cross Farm the wind and snow grew worse and we got slower and slower until it seemed more like a hundred miles. We had to stop twice because we couldn't see where we were going and once the wind blew off the green tarpaulin we had tied down over the top of the trailer.

Unlike the move to Oaklands – all sunshine and smiles – this move was getting more and more grim with each passing mile. The removal men kept moaning that they would be late and while Eustace and Squeaky had decided to sleep the journey through, Hilda and Come-on were beginning to complain.

When we arrived the blizzard was going full blast. Everything got soaked being brought into the house and the removal men did nothing but moan. The snow was even drifting into the house. Instead of putting everything in its proper place straight away we had to pile it into the former music room or library, the largest room, to dry out. By the time we had unloaded all three vans the room looked like a warehouse. Finally I brought the cats in. Eustace and Squeaky were still curled up fast asleep in the bottom of the tea chest, totally oblivious. Come-on and Hilda were demanding to be let out.

'I'll put them in a room upstairs,' I said. 'Come-on I'll put in the bathroom. Then tomorrow I'll try the butter.'

For the next four or five days, as we gradually started unpacking, putting things into place and moving them again because I wasn't satisfied, I kept buttering their paws. But no luck. At first they seemed to resent it, especially Come-on who behaved as if this was yet another indignity she was being forced to suffer. Eustace just agreed – anything for a quiet life.

'How much longer are you going to try it?' Peter asked me as we moved his big partner's desk into his study.

'Just one more day,' I said, collapsing in a heap on the floor. 'One more day.'

The following morning, of course, they were all licking their paws like mad.

'So what do you do now?' Peter asked.

'Let them out,' I said. 'Once they start licking their paws they know they're at home. They'll come back.'

'You're certain?'

'Of course. That's what the lady said.'

I opened the kitchen door and out they ran. You could almost hear them shout 'Freedom!', apart from Eustace who was probably mumbling something about getting a quick snifter at the nearest hostelry.

There was not much time left if I wanted to start on my project this year. I'd already arranged for some drainage contractors to come and inspect the fields and give me estimates. In the middle of all the mess I was beginning to wish I hadn't. But at least the blizzard had stopped.

Two men in old yellow waterproofs and muddy boots arrived in a small van.

'I'm planting a vineyard,' I said.

They looked at each other and smiled. They said nothing.

'I need advice on draining the water off the fields.'

'Vines don't like to get their feet wet,' Bob Westphal had told me. I didn't realize how complicated or expensive that was going to make things.

Having investigated the question of drainage for some time previously, I kept coming back to the problems of our climate. In Germany, as everyone still reminds me to this day, vines are planted on steep slopes and the water drains away naturally. In other wine-producing countries they don't get quite so much rain as we do and certainly get more heat which burns up the moisture naturally. If vine roots get waterlogged they just rot and die. So artificial drainage using six-inch pipes over all of the site was essential.

First we had to inspect all the fields: the lie of the land, the slopes, the gradients, which way the main drains would go, whether the ditches they would feed into could take the volume and a million other factors.

We walked all the fields and they took lots of measurements. I got back to the house at lunchtime. No cats.

The afternoon was taken up working out the costs. If we drained Hop Garden, how much would it cost? Were the slopes in Lodge Field too steep? Would we have to dig deeper trenches to get the correct flow? Would the ditches around Homestead and Pasture be able to take the outflow?

We had found an old map with the deeds of 1844 which had all the original names of the fields. I decided to give them back their names to keep the sense of history instead of using their Ordnance Survey numbers which sounded so impersonal. Hop Garden sounded better than 13474!

Hop Garden, we were delighted to learn, had obviously grown hops when it was owned over a hundred years ago by a family with the name of Kenward. They farmed the land for many years and employed many of the villagers. The hops were apparently sent to the sales in London but the surplus, we later discovered, was dried in an oast house, unfortunately no longer surviving, at the bottom of the garden. Beer was produced for local consumption in the pub next door and for employees at Harvest and Christmas. It became so successful that Mr Nelson Kenward set up shop three miles away in Heathfield town. He and his family and descendants are buried in the churchyard opposite, overlooking our vineyard. I often wonder what he would say.

Lodge Field got its name because there was an old barn or cattle lodge at the top corner which had been sold by the

Kenwards to the farm adjoining. Now it was being allowed to fall down and our attempts to buy it failed.

I never found out exactly why Homestead and Pasture got its name. I guessed it was because it was the closest to the house but I later found out that before 1844 it was called Horse Field, a very appropriate name now. Great Meadow must have been considered in its time a very 'great' field. Barley Gratton is where the barley was grown. The map also showed that Cross Farm owned most of the land locally and was the biggest and most important farm in the area, probably employing most people in the village.

By evening time the cats had still not appeared. Around nine o'clock I was going to go out to look for them but there was a knock on the front door. I had barely opened it when in stepped an elderly man in an old tweed suit and his Sunday best hat.

'Eels,' he said. 'Eels. Been farming this land for the previous owner. Assume you'll want me to continue.'

'Well . . . well,' I stuttered.

'Been no trouble up until now. Got on like a house on fire.'

'Well, in fact . . .'

'Helped them. Helps me.'

'Well, Mr er . . .'

'Eels. As in Eels,' he said. 'You'll have no problems.'

'Well actually, Mr Eels,' I said, 'no thank you. I really want to . . .'

'Ask anybody in the village. Been here for years.'

'But Mr Eels,' I spoke louder, 'I want to use the land myself. I want to plant a vineyard.'

He stopped dead.

'Vines?' he said. 'You want to plant vines? You mean grapes?'

'Yes,' I said.

'Here?' he laughed.

'Yes.' I was beginning to lose my patience again.

'So you don't want me to . . .?'

'No,' I said firmly, 'but thank you for the offer.'

I couldn't decide whether he was more stunned or bewildered. I opened the door for him.

'Good night,' he said, gruffly. He was not at all happy to lose thirty-six acres of free grazing!

'Good night,' I replied.

I went back to the kitchen.

'Still no cats,' I said. 'I think I'll go out and look for them.'

I walked all over the farm calling for them. I looked in the big barn and all the old farm buildings but couldn't see them. I was getting worried. I had heard of cats travelling back to their previous homes up to a hundred miles away.

The following morning I called them again.

'Something must have happened to them,' I said.

'Maybe Mr Eels has got them,' Peter laughed.

'I'll call the police. Maybe somebody has seen them.'

Just then I looked out of the window. There was a thick cloud of smoke coming up from the edge of one of the fields.

'Somebody's set fire to our hedges!' I cried.

'Mr Eels,' Peter suggested.

I grabbed my coat, leapt into my wellies and ran straight down there, sliding and skidding in the mud.

'What do you think you're doing?' I screamed as I reached the fire.

There were four men chopping down the trees and the hedges and piling the wood on the other side of the hedge on to their land, and the rubbish on the edge of my field where they had started a bonfire.

'Thought we'd clean it up for you,' said one of them, a man with fair hair. His face looked red more with guilt than work, I thought.

'Got to keep hedges in order,' said a taller man wearing a balaclava.

'But that's my hedge,' I cried. 'I didn't ask you to do it.'

'Good neighbours,' said the fair man.

'Helping out,' said the balaclava.

The other two kept quiet.

'But I don't want you to,' I said.

'It's only old wood.'

'Nothing to worry about.'

'But that's not old wood,' I shouted. 'That's ash. And that's the best for firewood so kindly return all my firewood and stop cutting my trees.'

They all looked at each other.

'Everybody knows you don't chop ash down and throw it on the bonfire. That's crazy. What do you take me for, a townie?' I continued furiously.

They looked at each other again.

'Well if you don't want us to . . .' said the fair-haired man.

'No I don't,' I snapped. 'This is my land. My hedge. My trees. I don't want you to do anything.'

'Well if that's how you feel,' said the younger one.

'Yes I do,' I said. 'So take all your saws and everything and get off my land. Thank you.'

They turned tail and went back through the gaps they had created in the hedge.

'And you can give me all my wood back as well,' I said, pointing to a neat pile of the best ash they had stacked on their side of the hedge.

The bleeders, I thought as I walked back across the fields to the house. They think that it's probably the first time you've lived in the country and they can do what they like. They don't give you a chance to move in before they begin.

I was still muttering to myself and calling down curses on everyone in sight when I got back to the house. I kicked my wellies off and went straight to the kitchen. There, sitting quietly by the cooker, were the cats: Eustace, Hilda and Squeaky on one side, Come-on on the other. All were licking their paws.

CHAPTER FOUR
A Bunch of Diddicoys

Sussex is a wonderful county. The adjoining county of Kent has a picture postcard prettiness. Surrey has lost lots of its character to the commuter and stockbroker takeover. But Sussex is still rural and largely unspoilt. Its beauty and tranquillity still surprise me, from the dark dense forests that just a few hundred years ago covered most of the land and the wide expanse of the gently undulating Downs to the dramatic clifftops and sea and the patchwork of fields with their hedgerows. It is still full of old farms, ancient buildings from barns to churches, families with good old Sussex names like Peasegood, Pelling, Cobbe and Morrey; traditions, superstitions, customs and even recipes. It has its farming community, its artists, its writers and its businessmen. It also has its fair share of eccentrics! Just forty-five miles from London yet it feels more like five hundred miles.

Cross Farm is in the village of Waldron. The name, I soon discovered when I started compiling a history of the house and village, derived from the word Walda, Anglo-Saxon for wooded place. Hundreds of years ago the whole area was woodland supplying timber for the iron industry. Scouring through the old deeds, visiting the public records office and chatting to locals, I soon found that it had a fascinating past with the usual stories of smugglers and ghosts.

From all accounts the village had not changed much through the centuries – the biggest events probably being the arrival of tarmac and electricity. The old school still stands, but is now a house, and the same fate befell the general store that supplied everything from farm implements to hair ribbons. The butcher's shop with its cattle in the surrounding fields is now the village shop. There used to be a glovemaker and a wheelwright but these had gone some time ago. One blunder by the planners was the conversion of the village forge into a car workshop which did not last long and the whole building was demolished to make way for a new house in the 1980s. The village pond by the church which was used by the forge was, regrettably, filled in in the 1930s.

There is even a Waldron 'ghost' although I haven't seen it. According to a newspaper of the time, on Monday, 19 January 1756 – about 9 a.m. to be precise – 'a great noise like thunder was heard in a well belonging to Rev Hamlin. On examination the water was found to be several feet higher than usual and in great ferment and agitation which subsided in about 15 minutes. Between 10 a.m. and 11 a.m. it returned and continued for half-an-hour which greatly alarmed the neighbourhood.' I had hoped that Waldron's ghost would be a bit more obvious and colourful but at least it's original!

The centre of the village now consists of the war memorial, the Star Inn, All Saints Church – and us. Three roads, each with a few houses either side, lead off from the war memorial: one towards Heathfield, another towards the village green and on out to Blackboys and the other past us and the churchyard through the sandstone rocks and on eventually to Horam.

The older houses are timber framed with outside walls of the old local red brick of a longer, smaller shape than the modern brick. They would have all been thatched originally but now are roofed with old clay peg tiles. The other houses, especially the large ones, are Victorian and the rest are comparatively modern. Our house, although built in 1622, was 'modernized' at the front in 1832 using local red bricks with glazed ends to give it a slightly checkered appearance.

In the church tower, which dates back to the twelfth century, is a peal of eight bells. Through the centuries the Waldron bellringers have obviously left their mark and one of their claims to fame is that in March 1890 the then group of eight parishioners rang the bells 'a full and complete Grandsire triples (5,040 changes)' in three hours and one minute.

The stone church, which stands slightly higher on a mound, has a picturesque lychgate made of oak with a moss-covered slate roof. The only decoration across the top of the gate is very appropriately the grapevine.

Just outside the church door is a great Saxon font hewn from a single block of local sandstone – probably from the rocks which were quarried to make a roadway as well as to supply the foundations for our eleventh-century tithe barn. The font had apparently been missing for years and one story is that Cromwell's men took it out of the church and rolled it down the hill. It ended up in the farmyard of Cross Farm and was used as a cattle trough. But that story does not account for the fact that we have to this day in the farm a very old font not unlike the one outside the church!

Although often described as a 'secretive village buried away in a maze of lanes', Waldron parish has produced two Lord Mayors of London. The first one was Sir William de Walderne in 1412 and the second Sir Thomas Offley of Possingworth in 1657 who left half of his huge estate to the poor.

In 1979, although there were still lots of woods and trees, Waldron and the surrounding area was very agricultural and mainly consisted of dairy farms. There were three pig farms, a few commercial orchards and lots of smaller farms with anything from turkeys and ducks to rare sheep and miniature ponies.

Our two farming neighbours, Mike Farrant and John Dew, were and still are dairy farmers and from our windows we could see cattle and sheep everywhere in the distance. Horses trotted by outside the house. Doves flew around the church tower. Chickens from the pub next door wandered up and down the lane. Life was slower, more relaxed. People had time to chat.

Soon after moving in I had gone to Heathfield by chance on market day. There were fruit and vegetables for sale, bric-à-brac and craft stalls. At the back there were big trailers off-loading cattle and sheep into pens which, fascinated, I stood watching for some time. I also met one of the old local farm workers.

'Don't like the noise. All the bustle. All that traffic,' he told me in his wonderful lilting Sussex burr. 'Never catch me going to the big city.'

'What! You mean you've never been to London?' I said in amazement. 'You've never been to the city?'

'No,' he said. 'I never been to Tunbridge Wells.'

It was then that I realized I was a million miles from Battersea. From buses and trains. From fighting for a seat on the underground. From queues and rushing and tearing about. This was the life for me.

In fact we were forty-five miles from London and fifteen miles from the coast. Our nearest town, Heathfield, was only three miles away but even that seemed much further. From a few old houses around a high street with less than twenty shops it has now quadrupled in size but it still to this day seems a long way away.

Soon after we arrived I was passing our old farm gate, which has now become a grander entrance, when an elderly lady in an old tweed coat, wellingtons and woolly hat came along the lane. I hadn't met many villagers so I stopped to introduce myself.

'Hello. Just moved in?' she said to me with a smile as she came up to the gate.

'Yes. Just moving in,' I said. 'Isn't it wonderful here? I was just thinking how lucky you are to have lived here all your life.'

'Oh, I haven't lived here all my life, although it feels like it!' she said laughing. 'Only moved in a couple of years ago.'

'Really!' I said in amazement. 'Where from?'

'Battersea,' she said.

Her name was Lydia. She explained that she and her husband, Edgar, now kept Welsh Black cattle and sheep on a farm down the lane and it was her job to unlock the church door each morning.

Our first real encounter with village life came, of course, in the pub. The Star Inn had a rather grubby picture of itself with a huge yellow star in the sky swaying outside the entrance on two chains from an upstairs window. We were literally in the process of moving in and Adrian had come to help us. After a day spent moving furniture we realized that we hadn't got a dinner and were very thirsty. We decided to walk next door to the pub, which had just opened. Inside it was very dark and the air smelt of wood, smoke, beer . . . and chickens? Unable to see, I tripped over something, setting off a frightening cacophony of noise and a flurry of wings. There must have been at least six chickens and a couple of ducks pecking at the floor which had a few crumbs here and there, as well as the odd crisp.

There were just two electric lights on, one over the tiny bar and the other over the well-worn and faded dart board on the wall. There was also a huge log fire that had not been cleared of its ashes for months which was casting an orange glow everywhere. It was very welcome because just then we realized that we were also very cold.

'I don't believe this,' said Adrian. 'This is straight out of the dark ages.'

'Doesn't anyone drink around here?' said Peter eyeing the empty room and the few bottles behind the counter. 'Not exactly what I was expecting.'

'It's fantastic,' I said. 'This is a *real* country pub.'

We stood there for several minutes. Adrian coughed. Still no one appeared.

'I could help myself,' he said, making as if to go behind the bar.

'You can if you like,' a woman's voice startled us. Verity, the publican, was walking in with a white and grey rabbit in her arms and a huge muscular dog following at her heels. 'Most people do if I'm not around.' She had a very theatrical accent – precise pronunciation and booming projection – coming from a woman about my age in a long skirt, T-shirt and cardigan, with short brown curly hair.

She switched on two more lights and we could see the stone floor, worn leather chairs and smoke-stained walls and ceiling.

'Hello, you're obviously our new neighbours. Welcome to Waldron.'

She put the rabbit on the bar and shook our hands. She gave the rabbit some crisps. The dog started smelling all around our legs. Adrian was getting nervous but the dog soon got bored and went back behind the bar where he crashed to the floor in a heap by Verity's feet.

'What is that?' Peter asked, quite relieved the dog had left him intact.

'That's Ben. He's a Rhodesian Ridgeback. The South African police use them. They can kill a man easily. But he's a love, aren't you, my Benny wenny.' She gave the dog a kiss on the top of his head.

'Have the first drink on me,' she said.

She peered at us closely and I thought we must all look very scruffy and dirty. 'Hope you don't mind us looking like this,' I apologized. 'We were going to wash and change but we're not really organized yet and besides we were all so thirsty and hungry. Do you do food?'

'No, it's not that. Golly,' she faltered, 'you must think I am very rude. Sorry. Well, I might as well tell you. You'll find out soon enough, I suppose.'

I thought: Oh no. Something bad is coming to spoil the dream. There's a wicked ghost in our bedroom; they're building an airport in Waldron. . . .

'You're not diddicoys,' she declared.

'No, we're not,' I said. 'What or who are diddicoys?'

She leant forward across the bar as she pulled the third pint. 'The rumour around the village is that the farm has been bought by a group of diddicoys. I couldn't care if you are but some villagers are getting quite worried. It's bad enough having the Londoners moving down here.'

'No, we're not diddicoys.' I repeated.

Practically in unison all three of us asked: 'What are diddicoys?'

'Gypsies.' She dismissed the question quickly having realized the rumours had no substance. 'The other silly rumour is that you're a bunch of eccentrics who are going to plant a vineyard.'

'That's half true,' I laughed, sitting on a bar stool in the corner. Peter and Adrian joined me. Certainly this was like no other pub we had ever been to but the warmth and the cheerfulness of Verity and the fire washed away the effect of the peeling paint, stained walls and grubby windows.

By now one or two men had drifted in. Some were obviously farm workers with various country smells and muddy wellies which Verity didn't seem to mind treading on her floor. Others were more smartly dressed. The pub had only one room but the wellies moved to one side and the black leather lace-ups went to the other. They were obviously all regulars, knew each other and had their favourite places in the tiny room. In turn, as they entered, they glanced in our direction and the farm workers nodded. We were only there for an hour but by the end of it we didn't feel quite so at home. The looks we got were not hostile but they certainly matched the weather outside. All except one. A ginger-haired man with tartan shirt and duffle coat had arrived to join a friend. As he walked up to the bar he waved at us and, after a quiet word from his friend and a few glances in our direction, laughed so loudly the rabbit woke up. He kept looking over at us and laughing. We were obviously being talked about.

'Odd lot,' said Adrian.

'Well, lots of what you call character,' said Peter. We decided to leave, having forgotten about food. As we reached the small door and had to bend slightly to get through, Verity rushed up with a tray and three dishes on it. The pastry was exploding over the sides of the dishes and there was steam everywhere.

'Thought you might like these. You can take them home. Bring the dishes back tomorrow. Hope you enjoy living here.'

It wasn't until weeks later – and after a few beers – that the red-haired man called Rufus, who looked more like a Canadian lumberjack than the turkey farmer he was, told us that we had caused quite a stir on our first visit to the pub.

'I thought it was hilarious,' he said still laughing. 'Verity was having kittens and she didn't have the heart to say anything but she was relieved when you took your pies home.'

He eventually explained that we had sat on the Wafflers' stools in the Wafflers' corner at the Wafflers' part of the bar. The Wafflers were a small group of businessmen who commuted to London but lived in the area and met once a week for a drink. To sit in their place was unheard of!

'They think they're special,' Rufus grinned, 'but you showed them. No one else has dared use their pitch.'

In future we respected the local tradition.

But there was not much time for socializing. My sense of urgency about the need to get the vineyard going was beginning to consume every waking minute of every day.

CHAPTER FIVE
The Housewarming Present

S oon after moving into Cross Farm I found myself wandering aimlessly over the fields with Mr Grant, a cheery middle-aged farmer-type from the soil department of the Ministry of Agriculture's local office, and his giant three-foot corkscrew.

'My auger.' He introduced it like a friend. 'I use it for soil samples. Wouldn't be without it. Couldn't do the job properly. It's twenty years old. They don't make them like this any more.'

He walked briskly down into Hop Garden field, swinging his auger like a walking stick.

'Aren't you the lady who was going to plant strawberries?'

'Yes.' I thought it better to keep the whole thing simple and not say much.

'And now it's vines?'

'Yes.'

He chuckled and looked straight ahead across the field. I was getting ready for another lecture on the impracticalities of growing vines. But all he said was: 'Well best get on with it, hadn't we?'

He screwed his giant corkscrew a couple of feet into the soil, screwed it back then tipped all the soil into a polythene bag. He did this about ten times then muttered, 'Not bad.'

He went into Lodge Field and did the same again in Great Meadow, Barley Gratton and Homestead and Pasture.

'Not bad,' he kept muttering.

'So you think the land is good for vines?' I asked him as we walked back to his Land-Rover. Behind it I noticed an old van and a large trailer belonging to some friends, George and Bettie.

'It's not as easy as that,' he said. 'I've got to have the samples sent to the laboratory and analysed.'

'How long will that take?' I asked as he clambered in alongside a springer spaniel who was sitting to attention on the driver's seat.

'About three weeks.'

'Three weeks. Why three weeks?' I said, dismayed. 'I need it as soon as possible.'

'But I thought you were going to plant vines in any case,' he smiled.

I turned to go back to the house to look for George and Bettie. They were a couple, much older than us, whom we got to know when George came to Oaklands with a garden contractor to clean out the pond there. They lived in an old observatory at the top of a hill in Surrey, and took in stray animals, including a cat from Greece which was always sick.

As I walked I was thinking about everything I had to do, including the preparation for the vineyard. All the old farm buildings had to be cleared out. Some of them were choked with old junk, others had stacks of old oak in them which I was certain I could use in the house. The big old tithe barn looked as though it would take a million years to clear and clean. Then there were the fields; I wanted to clean up the hedges and start clearing the ditches. They all had to be fenced, farm gates built, paths and roadways levelled. Not to mention the house. I still hadn't finished unpacking all the tea chests after the move. Rooms needed decorating. There were curtains to order and more lamps and other furniture to buy.

As I walked past the old farm buildings, I heard voices coming from the piggery. I looked inside. There, standing in the middle of one of the pens, were two donkeys.

'A housewarming present,' said George beaming.

'We knew you'd love them,' said Bettie beaming.

The donkeys he-hawed in support. The noise was shattering.

'But . . . But . . .' I stuttered. 'How do you look after them? I've never had a donkey before.'

'They're easy,' said George. 'Virtually look after themselves. You'll love them.'

'What's Peter going to say?' I had doubts.

'They'll help to keep the grass down,' said George reassuringly.

'So what do you call them?' I asked.

'Françoise and Hardy,' said Bettie.

'And which is which?'

'Françoise is the mother.'

'And Hardy is the daughter.'

'But how do I tell them apart?'

'Françoise is the one who's grey all over.'

'Hardy has the long brown hair on top of her head.'

'But why donkeys?' I pleaded.

'Well, they were going to the knacker's yard, and we rescued them. Then we realized we had nowhere to keep them and thought of you.'

'Thanks!'

'Must be going,' they cried as they clambered into their battered old van. 'Must get the trailer back before it gets dark.'

'Got to feed the cat,' said Bettie. 'And put on a new bandage.'

I looked at Françoise and Hardy. They were not exactly the prettiest donkeys I'd seen. Both were a dirty, dusty grey and both looked about six months pregnant. But they had big soppy eyes and noses like velvet. And they both licked my hands and coat.

'You've won,' I said as I stroked their quivering noses.

I went back to the house.

'We've got two donkeys,' I told Peter.

'You can have the donkeys,' he said, thinking I was joking, 'but I'll have a horse.'

★

Two weeks after Adrian helped us move in he, Ruth and their children left Wickford. For them the break was even greater. Their lives were very ordered in a very ordered world. Chubby, blonde and precocious, Alexis was just five and always wore clean and pretty dresses. Quiet and thoughtful Stuart was eight and always in clean trousers and shirts.

They arrived with one removal lorry when the snow had turned to slush and everywhere was so muddy that the lorry got stuck inside the farm entrance and dug itself deeper as the driver cursed louder and foolishly kept trying to move.

With cries from their parents of 'Now don't get dirty,' and 'Mind the traffic . . . I mean mind yourselves,' the children ran off to explore. In their excitement, Wickford and young friends left behind were already forgotten.

We had made and hung across the front door of the cottage a big banner with the words 'Welcome to Cross Farm . . . and to the good life' in huge red felt-tip letters. We helped Adrian and Ruth unpack so the very unhappy removal man and his mate could sort out the lorry. All the time we were talking excitedly of the future. Upstairs in their elected bedroom Adrian and Ruth looked across the fields.

'One day you will see nothing but vines,' I said.

'I tell you what I can see,' interrupted Ruth, 'and I hope it's a good omen.'

We all peered and could just make out a rainbow or at least part of a rainbow.

I got all excited: 'The end is in Lodge Field – that's where the crock of gold is! That's where our vineyard will be.'

They all laughed.

'Nonsense,' said Peter. 'That's where the overdraft starts!'

'Where are the children?' Ruth suddenly remembered them.

'You're in the country now,' said Peter, 'don't fuss. They'll be okay.'

He hardly had time to finish the sentence when suddenly there was a lot of very loud he-hawing and screaming.

'What's that?' Ruth exclaimed.

We could hear more squeals and shouting. Adrian and Ruth both ran from the room, colliding at the door shoulder to shoulder. They rushed down the unfamiliar stairway. Both fumbled at the front door almost in a state of panic.

'Oh my God,' cried Ruth.

'Oh hell,' shouted Adrian.

'Don't panic,' I called after them, 'they've found our surprise.'

Adrian and Ruth ran out of their garden towards the fields in the direction of all the noise, Peter and I following. Inside the piggery two pairs of large brown doleful eyes and two sets of very large yellow teeth greeted them. He-haws mingled with squeals of delight from the children.

'I'll show you round and tell you my plans,' I said to Adrian and Ruth after the removal van disappeared in a whirl of mud and much more cursing.

They looked at each other and mumbled something about getting more organized. But I insisted. First I took them to the far, far end of the farm.

'This is where I want to grow my Mullers,' I screamed into the wind with tears in my eyes. 'A nice gentle slope. Good hedge cover, plenty of protection.' I took a deep breath. 'Relatively little risk of frost. A good microclimate. They should do very well here.'

'What's Miller?' Ruth screamed back at me.

'Not Miller. Muller. Muller Thurgau,' I shouted. 'A German vine. A good commercial variety. Crops most years. Makes a nice fresh fruity wine.' Another deep breath. 'And also some Seyval. Seyval Blanc. A French vine. Good cropper. Good for blending. Also good on its own.'

'And the climate . . .?' Adrian shouted mockingly.

'Perfect.' I waved my arms across the field into the gale force winds. 'Perfect.'

We battled our way down into Hop Garden. 'Schönburger,' I screamed into the gale.

'Hamburger?' Stuart and Alexis giggled back.

'No, Schönburger,' I howled as the wind blew my hat off. 'Schönburger. Should make a wonderful exciting crisp wine. Perfect.' And as the hail came streaking down I went on, 'And Pinot. The classic champagne grape, Pinot Noir.'

I could see I was beginning to impress them all with my new-found knowledge.

'But do you have the climate?' Adrian asked as the heavens opened again.

'Of course,' I screamed. 'Most days.'

We battled on through the other fields. Adrian and Ruth kept wanting to go back to the house, dry out and make some tea. But I insisted we kept going.

'Once you're wet, you're wet,' I pointed out. 'You might as well carry on.'

We scrambled through the hedge into Great Meadow. 'Won't be able to do this for long,' I cried. 'Going to get everything fenced.'

In Great Meadow I explained as best I could that I wanted to plant Mullers as well as some other varieties. It was a big field, over eleven acres. I was sure it would be a good site for vines. Then we dragged ourselves up into Barley Gratton, the biggest field.

'Here as well,' I shouted.

But nobody seemed interested any more and Peter was mumbling something about horses. As the wind screamed even louder and the rain battered everything in sight we fought our way back towards the house.

'Before we go back, I want to show you something else,' I cried.

'But, but . . .' they all implored.

'Don't worry, it's all inside,' I said.

'But we've got to get there first,' Adrian muttered.

I took them to the smaller open barn, which was now piled high with rubbish.

'This will be my shop,' I said. 'Here I'll sell my wines, all the food we can produce. Everything will be natural. No chemicals.'

I could tell they didn't believe me.

'And now,' I said, 'the tithe barn.'

We clambered up the muddy slope outside and I wrestled with the door.

'This,' I said, finally wrenching it free, 'could be the winery – where we make the wines – but I also thought it's so beautiful we could make a wine museum or hold the occasional concert here. There's lots of scope.'

Again I could tell by the blank stares they didn't believe me.

'Is that all?' Adrian mocked, smiling at Peter who was shaking his head.

We went back to the donkeys in the piggery and I said, 'We could keep some pigs or other animals.'

'What!' exclaimed Ruth. They all looked at me.

'Well, we have all this land,' I started to explain. 'The vines will take some time to develop and I thought we could start up a farm. Be self-sufficient.' Adrian looked at Ruth. Ruth looked at Adrian. They both looked at Peter who shrugged his shoulders and said: 'I'd rather have a horse. But it does make some sense so long as you realise you've got to do all the work.'

The following weeks were hectic to say the least. Somehow you never realize how many goods and chattels you have until you move. But to add to the general disorder of moving in there was much to do outside if my plans were to charge ahead. Peter and Adrian went back to commuting to London, leaving Ruth and me to get down to the real hard work! School for the children had been painlessly sorted out.

What I had still to sort out was my grand scheme – and what

to do with all the other fields. What I didn't need was lots of surprise visitors, however well intentioned.

'Put them in the cowhouse,' I heard as I was opening the gate between the farmyard and paddock.

It was George and Bettie – again.

'They'll be happy there,' added Bettie.

'You mean the donkeys,' I said.

'No. The geese,' they said. 'We've brought you some geese.'

'Oh no!' I cried. 'Why didn't you . . .?'

'They'll go with the donkeys,' said Bettie. 'Keep them company.'

'Good guard dogs,' said George. 'The Romans always used them.'

I went into the cowhouse and was greeted by two enormous hissing geese. One immediately put his head down, stretched out his neck and made straight for my leg. He took a large lump of denim and a small lump of flesh, made his point and let go.

'The bloody thing bit me,' I yelled.

'He doesn't know you yet,' said George soothingly.

'But I don't want any geese,' I cried. 'I don't know what to do with them, especially if they go for me.'

'Nothing. They'll look after themselves,' said George.

'But what do they eat – apart from my leg?'

'They eat grass,' said Bettie triumphantly. 'They'll eat all this grass for you. Save you a lot of work.'

'But I've got so much to do,' I pleaded. 'I'm too busy trying to get my vineyard under way.'

'Don't worry, I'll come and help if you need it,' said George. 'The geese will not only be good guards but they will eat a lot of this grass down. You've got so much here.'

As we walked back into the cowhouse one of them came charging at me again like a bat out of hell, neck down, wings flapping and hissing like a thousand steam engines. I turned and fled, closing the old worn-out half door just in time for the goose to hit its beak on the back. One up to me.

'What sex are they and do they have names?' I asked.

'Husband and wife,' laughed Bettie, 'and they haven't got names yet.'

'Okay, then they will be George and Bettie,' I decided, getting my own back.

Later, when everyone was home, I decided I had better make a formal introduction. George was not the sort of animal to stumble upon unawares, I thought.

It didn't go too well. Alexis screamed, Stuart fell over in the mud, Ruth leapt in the air and Adrian yelled something I didn't quite understand. And Peter laughed.

'Don't worry,' I shouted. 'He's harmless really. Just a guard dog.'

'If this is your idea of a joke . . .' Ruth shouted as she clutched the children. The gander immediately took to Ruth. He looked at her, put his head down and went straight for her leg. She screamed so loud that the children started crying again. The bruise – a lovely shade of purple and yellow – lasted for weeks.

I turned to our new guard dog. 'You don't attack family, they live here. Only unwanted intruders.'

He hissed.

I tried to get him back into the cowhouse. But would he go? I tried coaxing him. I tried shouting at him. Once I even tried grabbing at his wings. But to no avail. 'Sod you,' I said. 'Stay out and get wet or maybe get eaten by the fox.'

However, George soon got his comeuppance, from an unexpected source. Three days after his arrival Mr Grant from ADAS, the Ministry of Agriculture Advisory Service, came back. As soon as he opened the farm gate George, who was busy eating the grass, went for him, head down, hissing for all his life was worth. He was a good guard goose!

In a flash Mr Grant stepped aside like a toreador, grabbed George by the neck, put one hand tight over his beak then with the other held both his wings tight together over his back.

'Don't. Don't,' I screamed. 'You'll hurt him.'

'You'll never be a farmer,' he laughed.

'I don't want to be a farmer, I want to be a vigneron.'

Mr Grant threw George over the top of the cowhouse door in a cloud of feathers. George hissed but very timidly.

'So what are you going to do with all this land when you start planting vines?'

I looked at him.

'Well, you've got to do something with it,' he said. 'You can't just leave it. One goose can't eat all that grass.'

'You mean the soil test shows this will be good for vines?' I asked. 'I knew it.'

'Well we didn't know much about vines,' he said, 'or to put it better – we don't know anything about vines. The soil is obviously good for soft fruit, strawberries for example, so I suppose it will be for vines. That's your decision.'

He handed me the test results.

The PH was between 6 and 6.2 and I knew it should be 6.5. We had a mixture of clay and sand and some parts of the land were more clay and others more sand. The farm actually sits on a bed of sandstone rock. Vines, I know now, are pretty tolerant of moist soils but too many people think that if you 'starve' a vine it will do better. That's just not true. The results showed the lime, phosphorus, potassium and magnesium content of the soil and after some discussion with Mr Grant and a few phone calls I decided that we needed to increase some of the levels before we started planting.

'But Mrs Biddlecombe,' Mr Grant said as he was leaving, 'you're not going to plant your vines all in one go.'

'No. Not all in one go,' I said.

'So . . . the rest of the land?'

'Well, I'll be a farmer as well,' I said.

Inside the cowhouse I could hear George preparing for battle.

★

Now that I knew the soil was suitable, the big question was which vines should I grow? The decision was vital.

I was about to embark on a very long-term venture without really knowing if it would be successful. I had no experience. My knowledge of vine varieties was next to nothing. Land husbandry was still a mystery. The effects of climate, fertilizers, and all the other millions of things connected with growing vines, including diseases, were joys yet to be discovered. And what about wine making? I had never made any. Not even a demijohn in the bathroom! It would have been sensible to have gone over to Germany or some other country with similar conditions and vast experience and spent a few years training. It would have been logical to have enrolled at one of the viticultural institutes there.

Every wine-producing country has colleges and universities to teach every aspect of the science of growing and making wine. Except England. In England, nothing of that kind was available. Let's face it, in 1979 England was not a wine-producing country of any importance. In any case, I didn't have the time. At the grand old age of thirty-six I reasoned that time was against me. I would have to learn the hard way. In fact I didn't stop to think about it much. If I had, things might have been a lot different now!

While I was conducting my rather haphazard experiment at Oaklands I had started to compile notes on how to establish a vineyard, including details of vine varieties. With the lack of written material – apart from very vague references in amateur gardening books – I was forced to rely heavily on other people's experiences and common sense. Then one day while we were living at Oaklands I had visited a nursery in Oxted, Surrey, to buy some bulbs and look at their shrubs. A rather dusty shelf with a few leaflets and books caught my eye, and one book in particular stood out. It was so dirty I could barely see the name but it read *Outdoor Grapes in Cold Climates*. It was only a quarter of an inch thick and measured about 3½ inches by 6 inches. I wiped the cover. The book had obviously sat there for years. It said 'Report No. 1 from the Viticultural Research Station, Oxted, Surrey by R. Barrington-Brock M.B.E., F.R.I.C., B.Sc., F.R.P.S. 1949' and the price '6/-'.

'Obviously popular,' I said to the girl behind the till. 'But how much is it?'

Blank faced, she looked at it. 'I dunno.'

'Could you find out?'

She gave me an odd look and disappeared without saying anything. By the time she got back with the middle-aged owner of the nursery I had practically read it.

Halfway down the preface I read, 'Suffice to say, however, that we are already certain that some lesser-known vine varieties will give us excellent results out-of-doors in Southern England.'

'Do you know,' the nurseryman said, rubbing a compost-covered hand across his face, 'I don't even remember when I got that. You're the first person in years to ask about it.'

'Does this research station still exist?' I asked getting quite excited. 'Is this man still around? How much is this? Are there any other books by him?'

He obviously wanted to get back to his potting. 'I really don't know. There's not a lot of interest in vines. How about . . . 50p?'

'Done!'

The discovery was a godsend.

As it happened, the book was a collector's item and having scanned second-hand bookshops and asked the antique and second-hand bookshop Southeran's in Sackville Street, off Piccadilly, near Peter's office, to look out for any other publications I began to start a collection. The books proved invaluable.

Even better, Mr Barrington-Brock was still alive, growing vines and an absolute mine of information and helpful advice. He was surprised I was able to get copies of his books. A large man with greying temples and glasses, he did not look his age which was well into his seventies. He was passionate about vines. His enthusiasm rubbed off and talking to him it was easy to get carried away. One thing he was certain of, England could produce wines equal to any in the world.

He started his Viticultural Research Station in 1946. Everything about his work was very scientific and mainly based on his experience and knowledge of the German and French wine regions. He had experimented with many different varieties and training systems and I remember he lectured me long and hard on choosing the right rootstocks and clones. There was much to learn but his enthusiasm spurred me on.

After several months I obtained his Report No. 2, *More Outdoor Grapes*; Report No. 3, *Progress with Vines and Wines* and three updated copies of Report No. 4, *Starting a Vineyard*. He reported on vine varieties, training methods, fertilizing, diseases and even wine-making experiments. He warned about the dreaded disease of Phylloxera and stressed the need to use only grafted vines on immune American rootstock. He dispelled several theories and introduced new ones. But all the way through the message was clear: in England, where the hours of sunshine could be considerably less than in other countries, grapes would eventually ripen even in a poor year. In a good year the results could equal northern France, Germany and other less hot wine countries.

I had also written to a few viticultural colleges and institutes in France and Germany. I suppose because I wrote the letters in English, the response wasn't good. I could imagine these old hands in France and Germany laughing. 'Madame thinks she can grow and make wine in England! Ha, ha!' But one institute, at Geisenheim in Germany, did reply. They sent me a list of vines for cold climates with explanations – in English!

'I prefer this way of choosing varieties,' said Peter every time we opened a bottle of wine.

Theory was one thing. What the varieties tasted like was another. What was the point of growing wine we didn't like?

Every time I read or heard about a vine variety that seemed a possibility, I tried to get wine made from it. Some varieties were easy. Muller Thurgau is grown all over the world and in later years I organized a tasting of forty-two different Muller Thurgaus from more than fifteen countries. But others were difficult if not impossible to find.

'If you can't sell it,' said Peter, 'at least we should like it.' He had the best job – and still does. We nicknamed him our official taster. But almost every Saturday evening Ruth, Adrian, Peter and I would sample a bottle or two of wine. I bought as many English wines as I could but it wasn't easy since I first had to find the vineyard and contact the owner.

'Yuk,' said Ruth.

'That's awful,' said Adrian.

'Let's give up,' said Peter.

Frequent comments way back in 1979.

But occasionally it was . . .

'This *is* nice,' from Ruth.

'That's more like it,' from Adrian.

And 'Not at all bad,' from Peter. That's his highest accolade.

From me it was always an enthusiastic, 'Ours will be better!'

It was obvious I would have to hedge my bets slightly. No point planting just one variety. Our climate is so unpredictable I would have to select some early ripeners and some later ones to spread the risks.

'It will also help when we come to pick and make the wine,' I said. 'We can stagger the picking.'

'But you've never made wine before. How do you know?' asked Ruth.

'I don't know. But it's obvious it will give me time. Anyway I don't have to think of the wine-making side of things yet,' I assured her.

In the end I decided on three main varieties – Muller Thurgau, a cross from the classic Riesling, which everyone else was growing with success. It appeared to be a heavy cropper though a bit prone to disease. But most of the bottles I tried had a lovely, fruity freshness and it was, after all, my very first taste of English wine – the one that sparked my interest in the first place.

I picked Reichensteiner because not many people were growing it and that seemed as good a reason as any in view of my decision to grow the most popular one. Reichensteiner ripened earlier and was also slightly disease prone. I only managed to taste five different bottles of it and I liked it.

The third main variety would have to be Seyval. Everyone raved about it.

'You can always rely on it,' I was told by one grower.

'Lots of fruit,' said another.

'Doesn't need much looking after,' said a third.

I tasted quite a few different Seyvals, although I could not understand why I couldn't buy a French version. After all, the variety was developed in France. That, one could argue, was a good reason for not growing it. But the wines I tasted were fresh and fruity, although a little acidic. But then there were so many other factors that went into the final taste: the soil, the microclimate, the wine making.

For good measure I chose three other varieties to try in smaller amounts. Ortega, although prone to wasp damage and one of the earliest varieties, seemed to produce a good taste; Kerner for vigour, and Schönburger. This last one was an even bigger gamble.

The Germans didn't grow it but oddly enough recommended it. And I couldn't find anyone in England growing it at the time. Now it's my favourite variety. Difficult to grow but producing lovely luscious pink-green grapes of marvellous quality. A joy to look at, press and drink.

'How about some red wine . . . I prefer red wine,' asked Adrian.

'Too risky with our climate. I've only tasted one English red and it was awful. No, let's keep it simple for now. Maybe later.'

There were red varieties available and one or two growers

had planted some as a result of the hot summer of 1976. If we had summers like that every year . . .

'Be warned,' I was told more than once. 'England is the poor relation. The French and Germans still laugh at us over there so they look after their own first. The English second. To some extent you'll get what you're given.'

But off went my order for vines in the summer of 1979 for delivery in April 1980. I had ordered a total of five thousand vines – five hundred more than I thought I needed for good measure.

'God, I hope you got it right,' said Ruth.

'Don't worry,' I said, secretly worrying if I had. Arithmetic and calculation are not my strong point.

As well as choosing the vines I also had to make the land ready for them. Mr Grant had given me the names of two drainage contractors who had already done much work for vineyards in Kent. One had already been to see me. I rang the other. The words 'I need drainage for a vineyard' did not produce the usual laugh, snigger or exclamation of surprise at the other end of the phone.

'So you know what I'm talking about!' I was delighted.

'Oh yes,' said a big, gruff, kind Kentish voice at the other end. 'You need intensive drains probably, judging by where you are. We'll come down and have a look.'

'What will it cost?' I asked gingerly.

'Probably an arm and a leg . . . and maybe a case of wine in a few years.'

There was still a long way to go but at least the treatment of the soil, the vines and the drainage were being sorted out. Yes, things were going quite well, I thought.

CHAPTER SIX
Gladys and Nora

I had not planned for donkeys or geese. I hadn't exactly planned for any other animals although the thought was always there.

But having decided to be self-sufficient I had to start somewhere. Most sensible people would start with the small, more manageable animals first, like a few chickens or ducks. Get the feel of things. Learn how to handle something small. Not me. I wanted cows. You can talk to a cow better than a chicken, I thought. Anyway, they just look better to me.

Of course in those days a cow was just a cow. But at least I was sensible enough to start with small ones.

'So how do I know which ones to buy?' I said, just out of curiosity.

'Look at their eyes, me dear. They should be bright and alert. No pus or anything.'

The man standing next to me must have been in his seventies. His clothes were old and worn. Underneath his coat he wore dungarees and black wellingtons and he carried an old walking stick. He was boss-eyed and had a roll-your-own cigarette in the corner of his mouth which looked as though it was stuck to his lower lip and had been there for weeks.

'And the size?'

'About average. They should have good bones. Clean lines.'

'Anything else?'

'No scours. Scours can cause you a lot of problems. It's the quickest way to lose them. It can kill in just a few days.'

'What's scours?' I asked.

He looked me squarely in the face to see if I was making fun. When he realized I wasn't he said, 'The shits.'

'So which ones would you buy?'

'The Herefords. They look good. Alert. You shouldn't have any problems, me dear.'

'Which are the Herefords,' I whispered, not wanting to show my ignorance.

He rolled his eyes to the sky and said pointing: 'The red and white ones.'

Which is how I became the proud owner of Gladys and Nora, my first two Hereford calves.

I had never been to a cattle market before. But bright and early one spring Friday morning out of curiosity I jumped in the Land-Rover and drove to the weekly calf market at Haywards Heath. I hadn't intended to buy. I just wanted to see what happened and learn a little.

Inside one of the long sheds were about twenty large pens. In each pen were ten to fifteen calves, each with a paper number glued roughly on its back. They were tiny, some the size of an Alsatian, others a little bigger. Some of them were poking their heads through the railings mooing for all they were worth. Others were standing listlessly in a corner staring at the wall. Most were milling around together pushing and butting each other. One or two were lying on the cold concrete, all skin and bone, shivering.

'Don't worry about them,' said my helpful old farmer. 'He'll have them.' He nodded towards a smartly dressed businessman with a waistcoat chatting to the auctioneer. 'He runs the abattoir. They'll be gone by this afternoon.'

I wanted to buy them all, to save them. I wanted to walk away but I also wanted to stay.

'So what do I do now?' I asked.

'Wait till the auctioneer calls out their numbers. Then bid.'

'How much?'

'See how the bidding goes.'

'But how do I know if it's a good price or not?'

'You'll soon find out, me dear.'

The auctioneer climbed on to a platform at the end of the calfhouse and we all gathered round – about thirty of us. All old farmers, and me. The businessman in the smart suit sat right at the front. The auctioneer, who looked the huntin', shootin', fishin' type, banged his gavel on the ledge.

'Lot-nummer-one-Two-nice-calves-What-am-I-bid-Twenty-the-pair-Twenty-five – Thirty – Thirty-five – Can't-go-wrong – Soon – put-on – plenty-of-weight – Forty – Forty – Lot-nummer-two-Friesian-Fifty – Done – Lot-nummer-three . . .' He was going so fast I couldn't understand him. I caught just the odd word.

'So how do I know when to bid?' I asked my adopted adviser, who was standing with his hands in his pockets.

Not a murmur. He was staring at the auctioneer.

Lots four, five and six went through in a split second. Then suddenly we'd jumped to Lot twelve. Then back again to Lots seven and thirteen together. Lot twenty-one was next. Then lot eleven.

'Why does he keep changing the order?' I whispered.

The farmer just kept staring at the auctioneer.

'Lot seventeen-eighteen-and-nineteen – taken-as-one – What-am-I-bid? – Lovely-group-of-Charolais-calves – couldn't-be-better-plenty-of-potential – Lot-twenty-two, twenty-five-and-twenty-seven-together-what-am-I-bid? Fifty – Fifty-five – Come-gentlemen – Sixty – Seventy.' Suddenly the auctioneer was pointing at my two calves. I looked at the farmer. He just continued staring at the auctioneer.

'Lot-eighty-eight and ninety-three – Two-nice-Hereford-Friesian-crosses . . .'

I looked at him again. He didn't move.

'Now-what-am-I-bid – Make-a-nice . . .'

I nudged him. Not a flicker.

'. . . pair – Plenty-of-growth – Who'll-start-me-off?
Now . . .'

I tapped him on the shoulder.

'Excuse me . . .' I whispered.

'What-about-you-sir? . . . Fifteen – Twenty – Anything-else?'

'Shall I bid?'

'Now-come-on-gentlemen – Who'll-give-me-twenty-five?'
the auctioneer galloped on.

'How much?' I continued, straining my ears to understand
this strange English.

'. . . five. Twenty-five – Thirty. Thirty. Thirty . . .'

'Now? Shall I bid now?' I nudged him.

'Sold,' shouted the auctioneer and slammed his hammer down
on the platform. 'Lots eighty-nine and ninety-five. Thirty?
Who'll-start-me-at . . .'

'That's not fair,' I said to the farmer. 'I was just going to bid
for them. I wanted them.'

'What do you mean, dearie?' he said at last turning to me. 'I
thought you wanted them.'

'I did,' I said. 'But I was asking you when I should bid and
you . . .'

'But you've got them,' he grinned. 'They're yours.'

'How? I didn't bid.'

'You must have done, least the auctioneer thought you did.
You can't get out of it now. Too late.'

The rest of the auction continued. But I left them to it and
went to make friends with my two little calves. They had soft,
soppy faces and such gentle eyes. They kept wanting to lick my
hand.

'Better go and pay for them, luv,' said one of the market men
who was cleaning out the pens ready for another sale.

I walked across the yard, queued up at the cash desk, paid my
cheque and collected my receipt like a proper farmer. Then I got
the Land-Rover and drove it up to the cattle shed. Everything
was deserted – apart from my two lovely little calves. Then it

suddenly hit me. How was I to get two calves out of a pen and into the back of a Land-Rover?

If I opened the gate they'd run away. Much as I loved them I didn't fancy the idea of running through Haywards Heath chasing two little calves. But if I got one out and not the other how did I get it to the Land-Rover? Then when I got it to the Land-Rover, how did I get it inside?

Just then the man who'd been cleaning out the pens came back, obviously waiting for me to move my calves.

'Having trouble, luv?' he grinned. 'Hang on.' He disappeared back out of the door.

I went up to the calves and gave them a stroke.

'Here you are, luv,' he said, returning with an armful of straw. 'Throw that down in the back of your Land-Rover. I'll put them in the back for you.'

I scattered the straw neatly in the Land-Rover. He then threw the gate wide open. Instead of making a quick escape to Haywards Heath, the two calves stood stock still, uncertain of their long legs. He bent down, put one arm under a calf's neck, the other under her belly and lifted her clean off the ground.

'Okay, luv, open the door,' he shouted. Then he threw the calf in the back.

'Careful,' I said. 'You'll hurt her.'

He grinned. 'First calves?'

I nodded and ran to close the door.

'Don't worry,' he said. 'She won't move.'

He went back and picked up the other calf the same way. This time he lowered her gently in the back.

'Do you know what to do now?' he asked.

'I'm going to get them home.'

'Then what?'

'Well . . .' I began.

'Get some sugar water,' he said. 'Give them a big drink soon as you get back. Let them calm down. Then give them some milk this evening. That's special milk – just for calves.'

'Sugar water?' I said. 'Where do I get sugar water from?'

'Glucose from the chemist,' he laughed and disappeared into the cattle house.

I drove slowly through Haywards Heath, stopping from time to time to try to get the calves to lie down. But they insisted on standing up and looking over my shoulder and every time they moved I was worried that they might break a leg. Then one tried to get on the seat next to me. I was driving along with one arm stretched out and waving at intervals to stop them joining me in the front. Then suddenly there was this warm, sickly, milky smell. 'Oh no,' I exclaimed, 'you couldn't wait.' It was probably all the excitement but I had to open my window, which was the signal for one of them to put her leg up as if to jump out. I stopped at a small chemist's shop, closed the window and ran in. There was an old lady at the counter.

'Sugar water,' I said. 'I need some sugar water. Glucose. Quickly please, I'm on a yellow line.'

'What kind?' she asked blankly.

'Dunno,' I said. 'I just want some sugar water for my two baby . . .'

'Well how old are they?' she said sharply.

'Dunno, a few days I guess.'

'You don't know?' she repeated, staring at me.

'Dunno,' I said. 'I've only just got them.'

'Just got them?'

'Yes. They're outside in the back of the Land-Rover. Quick, give me anything, please, quick. I don't want to get a ticket.'

She took a packet off the shelf and handed it to me. I grabbed it, thrust money into her hand, turned and ran out of the shop. As I reached the door I heard her saying, 'Just had twins. Doesn't know how old they are. And they're in the back of a Land-Rover!'

As I opened the door the aroma hit me. I didn't find it too unpleasant so I decided not to chance a fully opened window. The windows were soon steamed up and the journey back took at least twice as long as it should have with the other calf adding to the bouquet!

When I got back to the farm, the place was a hive of activity. Dennis had arrived. We met him when he worked as a young apprentice for the local builder at Oaklands. He'd worked for us ever since at weekends and odd times not only to earn extra money but because he simply enjoyed it. And he was now busy helping in the house. George had turned up to clean out the ponds. Piles of chestnut stakes had been delivered so we could start clearing out the ditches and fencing off the fields.

Two big drainage machines were parked by the paddock with mountains of coiled plastic pipes and even bigger mountains of pebbles ready to start laying drains in Lodge Field. Stuart and Alexis were feeding the donkeys. George the gander came up to me to say hello. After a good talking-to I had managed to cure him of his habbit of hissing at the hand that fed him. Bettie, the other goose, just sat in the corner of the paddock looking broody.

'Everybody, everybody,' I shouted as I pulled up in front of the cowhouse. 'Look at what I've got.' As I opened the door, both calves stood there with big brown eyes looking at us all.

'But you don't know anything about calves,' said Ruth.

'I prefer newts,' said George. 'They fetch ten pounds a time, especially the golden-crested ones.'

'I suppose now you'll want me to build a pen,' said Dennis with a wide grin.

'But don't you like them?' I said. 'Aren't they wonderful?'

Ruth began to stroke one on the head.

'They're lovely. What are you going to call them?' she asked.

'One after Peter's mother,' I said.

'And one after yours,' Dennis laughed.

'That's it,' I said. 'Let me introduce you to Gladys and Nora.'

Dennis went off to fix up a pen for them in the old stable.

'So how do you get them out of there?' Ruth said.

'Like this,' I replied smoothly, picking them up by putting

my arm under their bellies like a cradle and lowering them on to the ground one by one. 'Anybody knows that.'

They stood stock still as if terrified to move.

George, the gander, didn't like them much.

'And how are you going to get them in the cowhouse?' Ruth said.

'You need a halter,' said George.

'What's a . . .?' I began, then stopped myself quickly.

'With a halter they'll run alongside you just like a dog.'

'They're exhausted,' I said. 'I'll carry them.'

I bent down and picked up Gladys, my mother's namesake, in my arms.

'You bring Nora,' I shouted at Ruth. 'It's simple. You've got nothing to worry about.'

'What if he . . .?'

'He, you mean she, won't,' I said. 'She's done enough already.'

By now Dennis was rigging up a makeshift pen with a couple of old iron gates and some old wooden pallet boards. I threw the hay inside and levelled it out for them. I mixed up some glucose in warm water in two buckets and put them down on the floor.

'Go on then,' I said.

They just looked at the buckets.

'They've got to have a drink, the man at the market said. Perhaps they're tired. I'll try them later.'

I tied the handles of the buckets to the side of the pen, gave the calves a kiss each and left them in peace and quiet to recover from what must have been an ordeal.

Now I had to find out where I could get some proper calf food, hay and straw. Thank goodness for Yellow Pages.

Mum and Dad, who had both just retired, drove down from Battersea for the weekend to see what we were doing. They thought I was mad to give up my comfortable existence in London and then the luxury of Oaklands.

'All that mud,' Dad would moan.

'All that work,' Mum would complain.

'Come and see our new arrivals,' I said.

I led them out across the courtyard to the old stable. Both were wearing polished leather shoes and were picking their way gingerly through the mud.

Inside the cowhouse Gladys and Nora were curled up fast asleep.

'Aren't they lovely?' they whispered.

'What are you going to do with them?' Dad asked.

'What do you think?' I said.

'You're not going to eat them?' My mother looked at me in horror.

'I'm a farmer,' I said. 'I can't keep them as pets. But I'm not eating them yet, they've got to put plenty of meat on.'

'How do you feed them without a cow?' asked Dad.

'That's easy,' I said, assuming an air of authority and knowledge. 'I've got special calf milk that I have to make up with warm water. Give them a bucket and they just lap it up. I've gradually introduced them to calf nuts and hay and they've taken to it easily. There's nothing to it.'

At that moment Dennis came in.

'Has she told you what she's calling them?' he asked.

'Gladys and Nora.' I replied.

'And why?'

I heard the outside phone ringing and ran to pick it up. It was Peter's mother.

'I thought you'd forgotten me,' she said. 'I hadn't heard from you for so long.'

'Not at all. Not at all,' I said. 'I promise from now on I'll think of you every day . . .'

CHAPTER SEVEN
Fresh, Flowery, Refined – and English

I t was oh so genteel. And oh so English.

'Would you care to taste the wine?'

I was offered a glass of chilled white wine by a smiling middle-aged lady in a tiny print floral dress, straw hat with matching ribbon and beautifully painted pink fingernails. We were in the ancient barn of Charleston Manor, a beautiful stone manor house tucked away on the edge of Friston Forest in the Cuckmere valley of the South Downs.

'This sums it all up,' said Peter.

It was one of those really lovely English summer days. The air was clear and clean, the sky was blue, the sun was brilliant and warm, the grass a vibrant green and cultivated flowers mingling with flowering weeds were spilling over pathways, tubs and hanging baskets.

English wine, though still in its infancy, was showing off to the selected few. There was none of the razzamatazz and gaudiness of the average trade show, for this was not the average kind of trade.

I had come to learn what I could and, more importantly, to taste some wines. I remember the day well because it was also the day I was supposed to be preparing for my first Waldron village fête. The two events, while completely different, typified all that is uniquely English.

'Since you are new to the village, and although you're not WI or church, we thought you and your sister — or is it sister-in-law? — would like to get involved,' said Mrs Pugh, a well-spoken little woman in her sixties who had the air of someone who felt important in village affairs without being pompous. She lived in the former Victorian rectory which had been made grander by being re-named Waldron House. It is amazing how a name changes the status of a house. Every year she threw the house and garden open for the village fête.

Apparently she was worth a lot of money and all I remember of her husband was that he never spoke and was a hopeless driver, driving his car in the middle of the road totally oblivious to the chaos he left in his wake!

'We'd be delighted,' I volunteered feeling trapped. 'What do we have to do?'

'Well, the committee thought that you could help in the boutique — would you like that? Cakes, tombola, books and all the others have been allocated.'

'Fine, no problem.' I was thinking of old clothes, tatty jackets without matching trousers or tatty trousers without matching jackets, outdated limp dresses and misshapen cardigans — all smelling of mothballs or dampness.

'Perhaps you could come on Friday to help get it all ready and we'll brief you then. Tea and biscuits in the drawing room first at ten.'

When Ruth and I arrived at Waldron House, the committee were already pouring cups of tea.

'How nice of you to help,' said Mrs Pugh, assuming the manner of a grand hostess and immediately ushering us over to the tea trolley.

'Ladies,' she clapped her hands, 'in case you don't know, this is Mrs Biddlecombe, the new owner of Cross Farm and Mrs Robertson, her sister . . . or is it sister-in-law?'

'Sister-in-law,' I smiled.

'Yes, quite so. They have agreed to help us. Isn't that nice.'

There were nods and smiles all round and a few hellos. Most of the ladies were elderly and looked well-heeled. They were all dressed up in silk dresses or suits with a fair smattering of diamonds and pearls. And none of them looked as if they had ever done a hard day's work. Two in particular, who obviously thought they should be at a Buckingham Palace tea party instead, eyed Ruth and me up and down. We had turned up in not-so-new jeans and sweatshirts, assuming we would be lifting and carrying dusty cast-offs.

'Darling,' said Mrs Pugh without any affection, grabbing hold of a beige cashmere twinset and Jaeger skirt, 'will you look after Mrs Biddlecombe and her sister, show them what to do and all that?'

The beige cashmere was introduced as Lady Pinkley and we shook hands. 'It's all for a good cause,' she was saying.

'Which charity?' I asked.

I might have guessed.

'The retired gentlefolk,' she replied, 'Mind you, it's a lovely occasion, and we don't get any riff-raff to the fête . . . none of your Heathfield sort.'

I looked at Ruth and Ruth looked at me.

'. . . only very nice people. Our MP Geoffrey Johnson Smith, sometimes comes. He's a charmer.'

I felt like rubbing my nose with my sleeve and scratching myself but instead I said, 'Does it matter who comes, so long as they spend their money to help other people?' I smiled as sweetly as I could but Ruth nudged me sharply in the back.

The minder in cashmere shot me a severe look, narrowed her eyes and after a few seconds said: 'Yes, well, quite so. We had better make a start, I think.'

I looked at my watch. I wanted to get to the Wine Fair by lunchtime and at this rate it was going to be difficult. I was particularly conscious of the time because Peter had agreed to work from home that day so he could come with me, 'providing I can get back before five o'clock to call the office.'

'I don't want to be here too long,' I whispered to Ruth as we walked into a large downstairs room.

'Neither do I,' said Ruth, 'especially with her!'

The room had been cleared of most of its furniture and rails full of clothes were everywhere. There were two trestle tables piled high with clothes and lots of cardboard boxes with everything from handbags and jewellery to shoes, ties, gloves and hats.

'Get a load of this lot,' said Ruth, her mouth dropping wider and wider. 'This is jumble?!'

'I wouldn't mind some of this,' I said holding a long green silk evening dress up against me. 'There's nothing wrong with this . . . it doesn't even look as if it's been worn.'

Lady Pinkley overheard and said: 'We don't accept old clothes and you must remember some of our supporters are extremely wealthy people. I know for a fact that that dress you're holding has only been worn once.'

Our job was to help price the clothes and hang them in a logical order.

'Now price them, ladies,' she was giving us our instructions, 'bearing in mind it is for charity and the clothes are quality.' And off she went to finish her tea.

'This is going to take all day,' I said, 'I'll just have to go in two hours.'

'Look at this!' Ruth was now engrossed in having a quick sort-out for herself. 'Do you think they'll let me buy this?' she said, holding a pure Aran jacket with leather buttons against herself.

'Mrs Biddlecombe,' Mrs Pugh was calling from the doorway, 'you're wanted on the phone. You can take it in the drawing room.'

It was Peter: 'There's a man here to see you about corks.'

'I didn't know he was coming . . . I mean he didn't let me know.'

'He says he was passing.'

I ran across the lane back to the house.

'John Bird of Rank Brothers,' he said as he stretched out his hand smiling. He did not look the run of the mill door-to-door salesman, being dressed in a green-grey check tweed suit with green woven wool tie and a dull mustard-coloured waistcoat.

After thirteen years I can now spot a salesman ten briefcase lengths away. It is not so much their clothes, although generally they are pretty standard, it is more their look and the way they greet you. But I always spared a few minutes even if I really did not have the time. One day, I always reminded myself, I would be out selling myself. Still, it took me ages to get rid of Mr Bird.

I was on my way back to the vicarage when Peter opened his upstairs study window and leant out. 'Are we still going to this thing?'

'Yes, why?'

'I've seen an ad for a horse in *Friday-Ad* – it looks good.'

'Oh Peter, you promised! See you later, must dash.'

When I got back to Ruth she glared at me.

'Where have you been?'

'Corks. The cork man came. I couldn't not see him. How are we doing?'

There were still hundreds of garments to price and hang. And it was already 11.30. After hanging a bundle of clothes I found Lady Pinkley and made my apologies. She was not amused.

Within the hour Peter and I were off with the dogs in the Land-Rover.

'But I won't be able to drink much so I might as well go and see this horse,' he moaned.

There were only a dozen or more vineyards at the fair. All had a trestle table in front decorated with vine leaves, real or plastic, and most with their names either sketched out by hand on a sheet of board or professionally printed on a small banner.

Three vineyards were from Kent, one from Sussex, two from

Essex and the others came from Suffolk, Norfolk, the Isle of Wight, Hampshire and Somerset. Some had displays of photographs showing the development of their vineyards. A few were actually selling potted vines. There was an obvious lack of wine with just a few bottles here and there in buckets of water or in wine coolers. Most of the vineyards were small in size and either had only just started or had only one or two years' production behind them.

We accepted the glass from the floral Kent lady and it tasted like she looked. Fresh, flowery, refined – and English.

At each stand, some belonging to vineyards I had already been to, we chatted and sampled. Some of the wines were awful. Peter took one glass, smelt it, sipped and started choking.

I tried to laugh nonchalantly and said to the unfortunate man behind his table: 'Oh, he really likes it!' I glared at Peter and as we moved on I said with clenched teeth, 'Did you have to make it so obvious?'

'Well it was awful,' he whispered, 'I didn't mean to choke but it caught the back of my throat. I hope ours will be better than that! How much were they asking for it?'

We moved on round the beautiful long barn, sipping various wines from different counties and chatting to each producer in turn.

Peter interrogated them about the financial aspects.

'How much did it cost to set up? . . . How many staff do you employ? . . . How much money do you make?'

Gradually I edged away, pretending I was not with him since it soon became obvious that one or two did not like the direct approach. He did not look like a tax inspector but you never know, do you?

'Can you make a profit? . . . Do you live off the vineyard? . . . What's your mark-up?'

Halfway down the second lap I heard a loud voice say, 'Mind your own business.' I knew to whom it was referring and carried on tasting a Muller Thurgau blend from Essex.

As I was about to approach the last table Peter caught hold of my arm.

'You see,' he was triumphant, 'I bet I've managed to find out more than you. Most of these guys are either fruit farmers who are diversifying on a small scale or pretty well-off and don't know much about cost-effectiveness, financial planning or, for that manner, profit.'

'Well?' I said. 'You don't expect them to tell you all their finances, do you?'

'And I'll tell you something else, most of them haven't a clue about selling. One or two are switched on but the rest – well, they live in another world.'

'Shush,' I whispered as we reached the last table.

Behind it was a middle-aged man in a brown tweed jacket, checked shirt and woven brown tie.

He spoke with a deep, slow, deliberate voice and as soon as he began talking about vineyards, vines and wines I knew he had come late into the wine business. Some people say you can always tell a policeman, in the same way you can always pick out a solicitor, a salesman, a public relations man and so on. Each profession has its typical characters.

Mr Reeves was a former policeman who had been the bobbie in a village near to Oaklands. He was now running a vineyard in Lamberhurst, Kent, which he had started up several years earlier as part of the fruit farm he managed. His knowledge was, nonetheless, pretty wide, no doubt partly due to the fact that he had spent many years in Germany and was married to a charming German lady whom we met later when we struck up a friendship. He is retired now but still comes to see me. 'I knew you'd do well the first time I met you,' he says now.

Peter started his interrogation again. But this time instead of meeting hostility he got answers.

'Oh yes. It is certainly viable,' Mr Reeves said, 'and if you start with four acres that is big enough to make you some money but small enough to keep under control without too much cost.'

As the conversation got deeper and deeper into finances Mr Reeves' patient, step-by-step explanations of every aspect of establishing a vineyard reassured Peter.

'Look,' he said in his policeman-like way, 'buy the minimum of equipment in the first year and don't put your posts and wires in. Ideally they should go in at the beginning but there is no need. That can wait. Spread your costs. The same as you should spread your risks by selecting, say, three main varieties, an early ripener, a mid-season ripener and a late one.

'You'll hear all sorts of figures being bandied about but you'll have to accept a set-up cost of three thousand to four thousand pounds to the acre. On top of that is your labour, which if it is you will be free. Allow for a small tractor and mower and in the third year, if possible, a tractor-mounted sprayer.

'If you can produce wine in year three that's fine but it won't be much. In any event you will have your wine-making costs. We can make the wine for you or you may choose to make it yourself. You will then have your labelling costs as well as promotion expenses. Halfway into year four you can sell but you will not see a full return for at least six to seven years.'

He carried on, making his various points with a biro and notepad as he spoke: 'That is just basics, allowing for nothing to go wrong and without any allowances for how you are going to sell – wholesale, your own shop and so on.'

Nowadays, I am often asked to advise people who want to plant vineyards and we have even set up an Advisory Service – a far cry from the early days. There is one question I always ask right at the beginning: 'Do you have plenty of money and a friendly bank manager?'

Mr Reeves gave us a glass of wine each and it certainly tasted good.

'How did you get into this?' I asked. That was when he told me he'd been a policeman.

'Yes. Loved the job but I had to retire. But you know grapes have been grown in England for a long time. And when you think about it, if they can grow them in northern Germany and France, where the weather is not much different, why shouldn't we grow grapes here? Look at a map of Europe and look at the latitude line from southern England across to Europe, that tells you all you need to know.'

He went on: 'And the grapes will always ripen so you will always get something.'

'Well, they have bad years in Bordeaux,' said Peter, 'and they just charge more for the good years' wine to make up for it.'

'That's right,' Mr Reeves was getting out some photos. 'You only need two good years in five, with the others being either mediocre or even poor, and you should get by. Have three good years in five and you'll do well.'

He showed us pictures of the vineyard at different stages and offered to help us if we needed his advice. After over an hour chatting with him we left the dark barn and walked into the warm, bright sunshine feeling very cheerful and confident.

Outside there was some horticultural equipment including two mini-tractors ideal for vineyard work, and some small sprayers. Colin Manwaring of Heath Engineering was at the fair to chat about fungicides and herbicides.

'Our main business is with fruit farmers, orchards, hop farms and the like,' he explained, 'but we see a future for vineyards. The idea is beginning to catch on. Where is yours?' He handed Peter his business card.

'Oh we've only just started,' I said.

'We're in Waldron, near Heathfield,' said Peter.

'I'll come and see you then, to look round, see how we can help,' Mr Manwaring offered.

As Peter tucked into some free samples of English cheese I moved on to a more interesting stand. 'Vineyard Supplies' had lots of small items of equipment from secateurs to hand presses.

'Hello.' The man on the stall was rearranging his small but extensive display which used up every square inch of his allotted space. 'I'm Tom Searle.'

'Hi. Gay Biddlecombe.'

'Got a vineyard?'

'Just starting.'

'Well, here's our list of products.'

He carried on rearranging things while I looked at his list and his display.

'A lot of my stuff is for the amateur wine maker but we're beginning to supply small vineyards with the odd specialist piece of equipment,' he said.

'Do you have a refractometer?' I asked.

'I've just the job for you,' he said, picking up a small blue and brown case.

I took out the gadget which I had seen only once before at a vineyard I had visited. It is for testing the sugar level in grapes which is measured in degrees Oechsle or °Oe. As wine growing and making in England is similar to that in Germany we have used many of their techniques and terminology and this applies to the specific gravity scale in grape juice.

If grapes fail to reach at least 55° to 60° Oechsle they will produce poor wine. If it is less than 50°Oe you are either a poor grower, growing the wrong variety or you had bad luck with the weather. Normally grapes in England should produce a gravity of around 65° to 75°Oe but in good years it can be anything up to 95°Oe. But that's in good years! The natural sugars determine the alcohol content and therefore the 'body' of the wine.

Nowadays I can tell simply by tasting the grape when it's ready for picking, although with a well-equipped laboratory we never pick until we know the exact sugar and acidity levels. But when Tom showed me the refractometer I did not have enough experience and certainly did not have a winery laboratory. So I gulped at the 'special' price of eighty-five pounds but decided it would be worth it. Just before our harvests, even now, I use it by taking a grape, splitting it and rubbing some juice on the prism. When closed the gadget can be held up to the light and on a tiny screen a blue level shows the degree Oechsle or sugar content.

Tom came closer. 'What do you think of the wine here?'

'Very good,' I said, 'one or two I didn't like but on the whole . . .'

'I drink red myself. Now Italian reds you can't beat.'

'Well, that's a different ball game,' I said. 'No one here is trying to compete with that, but English wine is for a different market anyway.'

'Do you like red wine?' he asked.

'Yes, I like all wine if it's well made and has plenty of flavour.'

'Well, keep it quiet,' he said, 'but I import some Italian red wines at good prices. I've got a lovely Brunello di Montalcino – interested?'

We left with a mixed case of English wines, an armful of brochures, a carrier bag full of cheeses, my refractometer and a case of Brunello.

'That was another fine mess you got me into,' said Ruth imitating Laurel and Hardy.

Peter had dropped me off on his way to look at the horse advertised in the local advertising free magazine called *Friday-Ad*.

'Well, what happened?' I asked.

'I've been there all afternoon hanging clothes!'

We got on with our evening chores. After only half an hour Peter was back.

'How was it?' I asked.

'It was nothing like the advertisement. A bit like a cart-horse. I want a seventeen-hand hunter. Something that moves.'

'We can't afford it.' It was my turn to think of the money. I was thinking more of what Mr Reeves had been saying.

The following morning was Waldron's big day. We could hear the loudspeakers being tested and the brass band rehearsing.

Ruth and I had to be on duty by eleven to get the clothes out in the garden by a side door. At noon there would be a grand opening ceremony by someone none of us had heard of – but we were assured by Lady Pinkley that his brother's wife had met the Queen!

We did not hear the opening because someone had forgotten to turn on all the speakers but it didn't matter. By 12.30 lots of people were milling around in warm sunshine to the jolly tune of 'Sussex by the Sea'. The gardens were quite small, given the size of the house, but from its neatly cut lawn, surrounded on two sides by a half-hearted rock garden, there was a glorious view of the South Downs.

Our first customer was Mrs Bates. She lived in the village and was married to the Canon. As he was very old and doddery, she frequently had to help him. Mrs Bates was always smartly dressed but wore a lot of make-up. She must have been in her seventies and looked like a younger sister of Barbara Cartland and the Queen Mother. She always wore a hat and carried a handbag.

'How nice to see you both,' she said in her slow deep plummy voice, 'it is so kind of you to help. Now what can I buy to get things going?'

'Come on, sir, it's all for a good cause,' I called to the man hovering just far enough away, he thought, not to be accosted and forced to put his hand in his pocket.

He hesitated. I'd got him, and I wasn't going to let go.

'This tie would go well with that jacket. It's pure silk – you'd pay ten pounds or more for it in the shop and we only want two pounds for it! Tell you what, how about two ties for two pounds – one free? Come on.'

I got my two pounds.

'Oh madam, we've got just the jacket to contrast with that dress you're wearing. Try it on, it is Hardy Amies . . . top couture . . . and it's only fifteen pounds. Go on, it doesn't cost to try.'

She was feeling the cloth and looking at the label. I had her.

'Look, here's a mirror. I'll hold your shopping. Just see what I mean . . . the colour really suits you . . . there . . . a perfect fit.'

I then changed tactics.

'Tell you what,' I whispered, 'give me eight pounds. It's worth every penny and we do need the money for the old folk.'

I got my eight pounds and another happy customer moved on.

'Gay, I don't know how you do it,' Ruth was laughing, 'you've found your vocation. You should be down Petticoat Lane.'

She added: 'But I don't think you're too popular. You're getting lots of dirty looks from madam over there.' She nodded in the direction of Lady Pinkley and some of the ladies who were watching us, deep in conversation.

I waved cheerily.

'Come on, sir,' I called to a neighbour I recognized who, arm in arm with his wife, was casually strolling past, 'why not buy your daughter something for her wardrobe?'

'Ha, ha,' Jeremy mocked, 'nice try, Gay.'

'Come on then, look at these lovely clothes . . . every one's a bargain.'

Jeremy had picked up a hat and placed it on Sue's head.

We all laughed.

'No, it doesn't suit you at all. It's too frumpish. God, the things some people wear! Now, try this.'

She stopped laughing.

'That was *my* hat. I gave it to the committee.' She was not amused!

'That's what I mean. You're too young looking for that hat,' I smiled.

And so did Jeremy.

Lady Pinkley's black patent leather shoes were picking their way across the lawn towards us.

'Oh, you've done it now,' said Ruth bowing her head and nudging me.

'Oh hello,' I said, 'we've raised nearly a hundred pounds in half an hour. Not bad, is it? How have you done on coats?'

She stopped fussing, rearranging some of the folded clothes on the table between us.

'Oh, we haven't counted yet – it's too early.' She went back to her side of the garden boutique.

The brass band was playing. Balloons were everywhere. Most of the village was there as well as lots of outsiders. A loudspeaker kept announcing the sack race, the raffle, the tombola or the second-hand bookstall.

'Don't forget the cake and jam stall, everyone.'

Mrs Pugh came over to ask if we needed help.

'No, we can manage, thanks.'

'Well done,' she said. She leant over the jumpers, 'One or two of the ladies think your tactics are not quite . . .'

'Do they want to sell this lot or don't they?' I grunted.

'Quite right,' she said hastily, 'carry on.'

CHAPTER EIGHT
My First Tractor

The morning began at seven. The drainage men arrived and wanted to double check the details.

I looked at the layout again. We were going to run the main pipe across the middle of Lodge Field. Other pipes would then feed into it, herringbone fashion. The main pipe would then feed into the ditch at the bottom of the field. Then the water would be carried off to the big ditch at the edge of Barley Gratton and away, eventually ending in a small river. The levels and falls had to be just right.

The drainage machine itself looked like a giant yellow combine harvester on tracks. As it crawled along it dug up a trench about twelve inches wide for the pipes. A dumper emptied the pebbles as a base for the pipes and the second giant machine led the coiled pipes along the trenches. It looked like an enormous snake burrowing into the ground.

Once the pipes were down more pebbles had to be laid on top to allow the rain to filter through. Judging by the lorry loads of pebbles that kept arriving the south coastline was obviously sinking!

The foreman clambered into the huge trench maker, pressed the button and immediately it began digging the main trench like a knife cutting through butter. The other machines then coughed and gasped and choked and moved up behind him. All because, I kept thinking, the vines mustn't get their feet wet.

I got back to the house and Keith Harvey was waiting for

me. He was going with me to collect some hay. I jumped up into his battered old Land-Rover and we were off. We had met him in the pub and got chatting to him. He was an agricultural contractor who seemed to do anything and everything a farmer did not have time to do himself. In his mid-thirties, he was a short, wiry man with a Sussex accent. He was going to clear some ditches for me and trim back the hedge around Lodge Field. He was also going to pull out the dying trees in the garden that were blocking a lovely view of all the land. His wife made the steak and kidney pies for Verity and delivered them daily from their home about four miles away.

'So how much do you need?' he asked me as we shot down the lane, past Lydia's farm and along by a local convent.

'No idea,' I said.

'How many calves have you got?'

'Two.'

'Two?' He was obviously surprised.

'Yes. But I'll probably get more.'

'More? You'll have to if you're going to keep all that land under control.'

'How many?'

'How much land have you got?'

'What, for cattle?'

Suddenly he braked sharply. 'Damn. I think I hit him,' he said and pulled up by the side of the wood. 'Rabbits,' he mumbled. 'Too many of the damned things.' He jumped out, walked back and picked up a rabbit lying in the middle of the road. In a second he'd broken its neck and thrown it in the hedge.

I was a bit taken aback. I'd never seen anyone do that before.

'What did you do that for?' I asked as he climbed back into the Land-Rover and we pulled away. 'The poor thing.' I felt a bit sick.

'Put it out of its agony,' he mumbled. 'So how much land have you got?'

'What, do you mean now? About forty acres. But I want to plant vines on them.'

'When? This year?'

'I wish I could.'

'Next year? Year after?'

'Probably.'

'So you've got to do something with the land now. You can't just leave it. You've got to look after it.'

'So what do you suggest?'

'Well, forty acres I would say – let it all down to hay now. You won't get a good harvest but you'll get something. Then in the summer you'll need about twenty to thirty bullocks. They'll keep it down for you.'

'So I don't have to do anything till then. Oh good. Because . . .'

'Not if you want to spend a lot of money.'

'What do you mean?'

'Sure you can wait till next summer. Then go to market, buy yourself some bullocks and you'll be all right. But it'll cost you.'

'How much?'

'Twenty to thirty bullocks, about four to six thousand pounds.'

'That's the last thing I want to do!'

'You'd get your money back, of course. And more. Providing you looked after them. Providing nothing happened to them.'

'So what do you suggest?'

'I'd start buying calves now. Four, five, six at a time. Get used to them. Get familiar with them. Then some more. Then some more. By the time you've finished hay-making you'll be able to put them out to grass. Won't cost you so much.'

'Sounds sensible to me.'

We swung into a farmyard surrounded by broken-down old barns. There were tractors and old farm machinery of every description all over the place. I was about to jump out when what looked like four massive white wolves hurled themselves against the Land-Rover.

'Forgot to tell you,' said Keith. 'They're as gentle as anything really.'

The farmer then appeared and called off the dogs which he said were a kind of white Alsatian.

'Hay. You want some hay, lady? How much?' he said. I looked at Keith.

'About twenty bales now. We'll come back for the rest.' He pointed to one of the barns and Keith backed his Land-Rover and trailer up to the pile of hay.

'Okay. I'll give you a hand,' I said, throwing the bale nearest to me on the trailer.

'No. No,' he said, shaking his head. 'First check the hay.'

'Check the hay?' I said, puzzled by what he meant. 'How do you check hay?'

'Smell it.'

'Smell it?'

'Sure. Smell it. If it's sweet, it's perfect. If it's dry and dusty don't touch it.'

I was learning more and more every day.

'If you like it, the calves will like it,' he laughed.

I started smelling the different bales and he was right. Some smelt fresh, like new-mown grass. I could have eaten them myself. A few smelt damp and flat. One bale I picked up near the edge of the stack had white dust all inside.

'Probably harvested when it was still wet. That's what causes farmer's lung,' said Keith. 'I know some old farmers who have a big problem breathing and cough all the time like heavy smokers. That's why you'll see some of us wearing masks or a damp handkerchief over our faces when we handle the hay.'

As soon as we had finished loading the best hay we could find, I went up to the farmer.

'How much do I owe you?' I said.

'Don't worry, luv,' he said. 'Pay me next time.'

On the way back to the farm, I told Keith. 'Wasn't that nice of him?' I said.

'Not at all,' he laughed. 'His way of making sure you go back to him again.'

As soon as I got back there was everything to be sorted out. The drainage men said they had slightly under-estimated the amount of pebbles needed to backfill the trenches.

'Okay if we go ahead?' they said.

George gave me a present of two big fat chickens. 'Company for the geese,' he said.

'But you shouldn't,' I said. 'You've already done . . .'

'I thought I'd clear some more of those waterlilies out of the ponds,' he said. 'I was thinking they could do with some more room.'

'Sure. Sure. If you say so.'

Tommy had turned up with Foxy, his dog, to help with the fencing. Tommy and his dog, a fox-coloured mongrel, were inseparable and lived alone together in a wooden shed hidden among some trees in a small woodland at the other side of the village. I had this idea that he was some kind of hermit preferring just his own and his dog's company. He was always scruffy and to some he must have looked a down-and-out, so in reality he probably lived in the shed because he couldn't afford anything else. It belonged to a woman he did odd jobs for but who lived elsewhere. I never asked many questions. Anyway he just turned up one day with Foxy and asked for gardening work.

The garden was a mess with a old septic tank in the middle as well as a telegraph pole and too many overgrown trees. I had very little time to spend on it so I just mowed the lawn or did a bit of weeding in the evenings. But I had plans for the garden. Besides, I felt a little sorry for this scruffy young man and his faithful equally scruffy little dog who would not take his eyes off his master for one second other than to chase and fetch a stick or ball he had thrown. When Tommy was good, he was very good. He'd practically tear away at the hedges with his bare hands and put up fencing posts like lightning. At other times, he'd sit on the grass and fall asleep. Today was a very good day.

'You'll never finish that field today,' I said to him.

'Reckon I might,' he said, hammering in another post.

I called Ruth. 'Okay. Let's go,' I said.

'Where?'

'To Robertsbridge,' I said. 'To buy a tractor.'

To most people Robertsbridge is famous as the home of Malcolm Muggeridge. At least in our part of Sussex. To me, it's where I bought my first tractor.

We drove through Heathfield, into the picturesque tree-lined village of Burwash and past Bateman's, Rudyard Kipling's old home and now owned by the National Trust, and on to Robertsbridge. Just past the railway station I turned into the agricultural engineer's. There was farm equipment everywhere. Ploughs and hoes, I recognized. But there were so many other items I could only guess at what they were used for.

'I've come for the tractor,' I said to the manager in his office. 'A Massey. Massey 35X. You've kept it back for me.'

He was an old man with that wonderful Sussex burr. He had on an old brown coat covered with grease and an old brown trilby pulled down over his eyes. There was a chewed pencil behind his ear and he was carrying a clipboard and a spanner.

We followed him into one of the big sheds.

'All tractors,' he said. 'But there's only one old Massey. Best little tractor they made. Go on for years it will. If you look after it.'

I nodded. 'That's what they say.'

'I remember the first old Massey that came into Robertsbridge. On Major Dennis's farm. Probably still got it, they have.'

'So how long will this one last?' I asked him.

'Probably just as long. If you look after it.'

The reason I had searched for this particular tractor was that it was narrower than most other models so it would get down between the rows of vines which would be planted six foot six inches apart. It would do other farm work too, like hay-making.

'A good all-rounder, ideal to begin with,' Mr Reeves had advised, 'but not easy to get hold of nowadays.'

Which was why I was keen to see it.

We walked past several tractors, all shiny and new and all of them huge with glass cabs. Then we walked up to what was the tiniest and certainly the oldest tractor in the shed. He patted it on the bonnet. All the others were painted in the bright colour of their manufacturers – red, green, orange. The one I was looking at had patches of a very worn and dull red paint mingled with rust and looked dowdy by comparison. My heart sank.

'Wonderful old machine,' he said. 'Don't make them like it any more.'

'You're right,' I said. 'You're right,' wishing I could afford a new one.

He looked at me, straight in the eye.

'You're going to take it out and see what you think?'

'Sure,' I said and jumped up into the seat. It was the first time I'd sat on a tractor in my life.

'Okay, turn it over,' he shouted. 'Take it outside and put it through its paces.'

I looked at it. It was completely unlike any car I'd ever seen, not even anything like the Land-Rover. I could see a key and some levers on the steering wheel. Either side of the big engine were two pedals. I pushed my foot down on one of the pedals and turned the key. Suddenly there was a terrifying screech.

'No. No. No. Don't do that.' The manager practically leapt out of his old brown coat.

'Sorry,' I mumbled. 'Hand must have slipped.'

'Press this pedal down, pull this lever, turn the key,' the manager said. 'Put her into first and release this brake pedal.'

I did exactly what he told me to do. The tractor shot

backwards and stalled. Another six inches and I'd have been out
of the back of the shed. After several attempts I took it for a spin
in the yard. It felt great. The elderly salesman showed me how
to operate the hydraulics and was about to start selling me a
trailer for the back.

'Do you want to have a go?' I asked Ruth, forgetting she
didn't know how to drive a car let alone a tractor. That had to
change.

'How much?' I asked.

'Well, it's a bargain,' the manager said.

'Yes. How much?' I repeated.

'£1,750,' he said.

'How much are these new ones?'

'£20,000. £30,000.'

'I'll give you £1,200 for it,' I ventured.

'Well . . . you might come back to buy another one day, so
how about £1,500?'

'Okay, I'll have the Massey.' After all, I thought, it was better
to have something with character. 'Can you deliver it? Is next
Tuesday all right?'

I went back to the office, signed all the papers and left as
quickly as possible before I had time to regret what I'd done.

As I turned into the High Street, past the wood which takes
you up to Malcolm Muggeridge's house on the Downs, Ruth
said, 'You've just bought a tractor and you don't know how to
use it – where the diesel goes, oil and all that.'

'I know. But I'll soon learn. It's sure to have a handbook,' I
said, over optimistically as it turned out. 'And how about you?
You've got to get mobile and eventually drive the tractor.'

'Oh no,' she said.

'Oh yes,' I replied.

We got back to the farm as the church bells started ringing.
Wednesday evening is bell practice in Waldron.

George was loading the last of the waterlilies into his Land-
Rover.

'I won't be in tomorrow,' he said. 'I've got to go and look at this lake.'

Tommy needed more wire netting for the fencing. And the drainage men wanted me to have a look at what they had done so far.

Lodge Field looked a mess. Before it had been a gentle, sloping field surrounded by high hedges. It had been covered with beautiful, smooth green grass with occasional patches of wild flowers. Now it had a ghastly heaped clay scar across the middle. Running off it were other, smaller scars. Piles of shingle waited at the side. Deep, heavy track marks were everywhere. Sitting in the middle were the two enormous yellow drainage machines gloating at the havoc they had created.

'Looks a mess to me,' I said. 'But I assume everything is in the . . .'

'Of course,' they said.

'Of course.'

'Trouble is we need more shingle,' they said. 'For the trenches. Using up more than we thought.'

'Not again,' I said. 'Why couldn't you get it right the first time?'

'Just two more loads and we'll be finished.'

'Okay. You did say it would cost an arm and a leg but at this rate I probably won't be able to afford the wine!'

'Next Wednesday,' they said. 'If that's all right.'

'Of course,' I said resignedly.

'Is this yours?' Ruth asked, putting an empty carton of yogurt on my desk. 'I found it by the wire netting.'

It was about 7.30 in the morning. I'd just got back to the house after feeding the calves. Gladys, as always, was no problem. As soon as I put the bucket of milk in front of her she lapped it up straight away. Nora was suddenly becoming difficult. Sometimes, like Gladys, she lapped it up in one go. At other times, like today, she kept playing with it. She'd put her nose in the milk, take a sip then try and knock the bucket out of the pen. I put my finger in her mouth, let her suck it, then gradually bent her head down in the bucket. First she'd suck up some of the milk. Then when she realized what she was doing she'd stop, throw her head all over the place and start attacking the bucket again. What should have taken maybe five minutes, today took about half an hour. Nevertheless, I thought calf rearing seemed easy. Later I was to discover that I had been lucky with my first two.

The donkeys luckily were not a problem. They grabbed their carrots and nuts and seemed eternally grateful for anything they got. George the gander was getting more and more friendly. On some days he even followed me around like a dog. Bettie was getting more broody.

I looked up from my pile of wine books at Ruth.

'I know,' I said. 'I put it there to remind me to look up Kerner again.'

'Kerner?' she said obviously puzzled.

'I wanted to check if we should plant any.'

'But I thought you had decided,' Ruth said.

'I have but I just read that this is a fairly new variety and is a good cropper.'

The problem was that I hadn't seen it growing anywhere or tasted any wine.

Fred Parsons, an old man of about eighty who ran a small vineyard I had discovered in Horam belonging to the cider company, Merrydown, said on my first visit: 'There's no point having fancy varieties if you don't get a crop. If you're going to do it commercially, you must be commercial.'

Nonsense, others said. If you're going to grow vines in England you've got to grow something different, something exciting. There's no point just copying the Germans only not doing it as well.

'If you want to experiment, experiment. But do it on a small scale. So if it goes wrong it won't be a disaster. If you do it on a big scale it could set you back years,' I remembered old Fred telling me.

'So what's your favourite variety?' I asked him once while I was trying to make up my mind.

'Strawberry vines,' he said.

I'd never heard of them before.

'Are they commercial?' I asked.

'No, of course not,' he smiled. 'They aren't for wine either. I just like them. They taste delicious.' He gave me a cutting which to this day bears lots of delicious strawberry-flavoured grapes.

I jumped into the Land-Rover with Keith who was taking me to buy some straw. Dennis was just arriving with decorating equipment and pots of paint. I wanted him to help redecorate the library, the old music room, which was the largest room in the house and which now housed all our books, for my parents' ruby wedding. I wanted to give them a surprise party and it was the perfect setting.

As we pulled away from the farm the postman was coming down the lane. I jammed on the brakes and grabbed the post. There was a letter from the solicitor. Maybe the Finance Corporation had discovered I hadn't planted any strawberries after all.

'Problems?' said Keith.

'Hope not,' I said nervously.

I tore the envelope open. There was a short letter from the solicitor – 'I thought you might like these.' He had sent me all the original deeds for the farm going back to 1704. They were beautifully written by hand in large black swirls on parchment. The early ones had wax seals and ribbons. At last I could begin to compile my history of the farm and village. There was a big map showing all the fields with all the original names.

One deed I spotted showed a map of the farm which in those

days stretched for several miles, almost as far as the eye could see. And it was owned and run by a woman, an Irish spinster by the name of Rosalie Frances Turner, who sold it in 1872.

'Super,' I cried. 'Just what I wanted. I'll frame them and hang them up in the lounge.'

'So what about the straw?' said Keith anxiously. 'Are we still going?'

Straw? Of course, the straw! I pushed all the deeds and the maps into the pocket on the door of the Land-Rover and spun off towards Burwash.

Buying straw was not as interesting as buying hay. We drove past Bateman's again, admiring the view across the Weald on one side and over to the South Downs on the other.

'Glorious Sussex by the Sea,' I said.

'The sea? That's fifteen miles away!' Keith said looking puzzled.

I turned into a tiny lane just off the main road. We bounced along a narrow track that gradually petered out into nothing.

'Where now?' I said to Keith.

'Behind the hedge.'

Behind the hedge was a tiny cottage and an enormous barn stacked to bursting with straw.

'Best straw in Sussex,' said Keith.

The farmer, a tiny, wizened little old man, turned out to be a straw trader. He bought and sold straw for a living. Sometimes he would buy straw straight off the fields, at other times from store. But whatever he bought had to be the best quality.

'He's got lorries going all over the country,' said Keith. 'He's worth a fortune.'

I only wanted about twenty bales but you'd have thought I was buying twenty lorry loads. He insisted that we inspect every stack. He even cut open some bales for us to inspect inside. To me it was straw. A marvellous deep golden colour – like a beautiful old Sauterne – but it was still straw.

'If you go to him once he makes certain you'll go back again and again for the rest of your life,' Keith said as we bounced back along the narrow track.

'So how long have you been going to him?' I asked.

'All my life,' he smiled. 'My father too.'

PN 752

CHAPTER NINE
How to be Self-sufficient

I soon learnt that if you wanted anything – well, almost anything – in life you rushed to the village shop on Friday morning to collect a *Friday-Ad*. This was – and still is – a magazine printed on newspaper with nothing but advertisements from its front cover through sometimes forty to fifty pages to the back cover.

Everyone, it seemed, who had something to sell – or who was looking to buy something in particular – advertised in it. From houses to garden sheds, antiques to junk, bicycles to cars, musical instruments to farm equipment and animals of every description. I even saw an advertisement in it once for a stuffed elephant's foot trophy! If you were really desperate and wanted to get the best offers you went into Heathfield or Uckfield where its advertising offices were and collected a copy on Thursday evening. Copies were left outside in stands or on an old chair outside big shops and village shops all over the area. Even if you were not looking for anything you could find something you never knew you wanted.

I used to imagine that come Friday evening the roads in the area would be extra busy, not with Londoners escaping into the country but with *Friday-Ad* readers tearing about to be first at the bargains.

I spent many a Friday evening or Saturday morning viewing a potential purchase and had already acquired lots of useful bits and pieces including an old chicken house, feed bins, an assortment of garden tools, a six-foot rubber plant and a lovely old oak coffer for the house.

Apart from the two chickens that George gave me I wanted some more youngsters to bring on and a cockerel. A farm isn't a farm without a handsome cockerel strutting around and cock-a-doodle-doing all over the place. And I wanted some ducklings and turkey chicks.

When I answered the advertisement the woman at the other end said she was taking messages for her neighbour who didn't have a phone.

'Just turn up,' she said. 'Joan doesn't go anywhere except across the field to me so she'll be there. But I'll tell her you're coming. I'll hang my pink knickers on the line – that's my signal!'

The directions had been clear and I knew I was to end up on a dirt track to Home Farm somewhere between Heathfield and Dallington. I turned off the main road, down a lane which had a garage on the corner. At the bottom of the hill I was to take the lane on the left. By the farm gate and telegraph pole I was to turn into another lane and five hundred yards further take the dirt track where a rusty old milk churn stood and a plank of wood with Home Farm painted in rough white letters on it. But the dirt track seemed to go on for miles. Was this still Sussex? Finally it stopped at a small turn-of-the-century house whose windows and front door were wide open. Next to the house were several small barns and ramshackle outbuildings. The view was tremendous, looking across the Weald, but the whole farm was a chaotic mess. There was a tractor, even older than mine, surrounded by chickens which were wandering all around the yard, across what would have been a front garden, and in and out of most of the buildings.

A Jersey cow looked up from a small paddock and beyond that were lots of chicken houses about to fall down. On the other side of the house was a very muddy pond around which ducks, of different colours but mainly white, and over a dozen geese were preening and cleaning themselves. There were plastic feed dishes of every shape and size all over the place.

As I walked towards the open door a collie ran out barking and snapping at my feet. After a few minutes he lost interest and ran round the back of the house.

'Anyone here?' I called.

No reply.

'Hello, hello . . . anyone here?'

As I turned to follow the dog a huge pig waddled up the path pushing me to one side and went straight into the house. Had I wandered into a time warp?

Behind the house I found a huge pile of manure and chickens rummaging about all over it.

'Hello . . . hello . . .'

I was about to give up when I heard a voice from one of the barns.

'Coming . . . just wait a bit?'

I walked towards the barn and peered in. On the floor were hundreds of small chickens. Not little yellow chicks but older ones with their adult feathers coming through.

'Is that the lady who wants some pullets?' said the woman, who seemed to appear from nowhere. She was about my age, very slim, with her brown hair tied back in a pigtail. Without make-up, her face had a red, well washed, ruddy look, with broken veins caused by the wind. She wore a pair of torn jeans and an old plain white T-shirt over which she had a navy blue smock.

She told me that she and her husband had bought the house two years earlier to get away from it all. The house was going cheap and she wanted to be self-sufficient.

'Just like me,' I said eagerly.

She explained that she reared chickens and ducks to make some extra money. She milked her own cow, produced her own pork, lamb and poultry, and grew all her own vegetables. I was beginning to feel envious.

'Come in and have some tea,' she said.

As we went into the house my envy faded rapidly. There were rabbit hutches everywhere and the stench was unbelievable. Chickens were all over the place, even on the kitchen table.

She clapped her hands and most of them strutted off.

She moved a pan of water that had been standing on the table to the Aga.

'I don't think I've got the time,' I said, 'I really must get back.'

She laughed. 'It won't take long on this.' She had thankfully misunderstood my sudden need to leave. 'We don't have electricity here. We're supposed to be getting it but we have to pay something towards it and we can't afford it. Anyway who wants it?'

'I know you don't have a phone,' I ventured. 'Do you have water?'

'From the well, yes,' she said.

'Main drainage?'

'God, no,' she jeered. 'Wouldn't want any of it really. This is what being self-sufficient is all about, isn't it?'

I could see her point. But it wasn't quite what I had in mind.

'It really is very kind of you but . . .'

'No trouble. Now, tell me about your place. What are you producing?'

I didn't watch while she made the tea and I declined the sugar which a chicken had just pecked at.

'Milk?' she pointed to a bucket.

'Er, thanks. I like my tea as it comes.'

I had to ask; 'How do you keep food fresh without a fridge or freezer?'

'I don't,' she declared. 'I pick it as we need it. Anything else goes to the chickens or the pig.'

'What about the milk?'

'The same.'

'What about meat then, you said you produce your own.'

'Well we don't eat much meat, can't afford to. We sell most

of it. But Lillie – the woman you telephoned – she lets me keep some in her freezer. We're great friends. She's just across the way but so much closer to the mains supplies.'

I was beginning to feel that my idea of self-sufficiency included rather more emphasis on order and hygiene as I looked around the mess and confusion. Paint was peeling off the walls and woodwork, thick grey cobwebs hung from corner to corner. Above the Aga, which had been set in an old fireplace, there was a mantelshelf. On it were various photos including one of two children looking very conspicuous by their smartness.

'Yours?' I asked with disbelief in my voice as well as obviously on my face.

'Yes,' she laughed. 'They're both at boarding school. We have to make some sacrifices but we think it's worth it.'

I hope they do, I couldn't help thinking.

I ended up buying twenty sixteen-week-old pullets at two pounds each. Half were the heavy red-coloured breed Rhode Island Reds, and the other half Light Sussex, which are white with black rings around their necks and black markings on the tips of their tail and wings. Both are traditional breeds which live well outdoors free range. They lay plenty of eggs, go broody, hatch their eggs and rear their young. Buying at this age meant they would begin to produce eggs within a few weeks of settling into their new home.

When she got them out for me and started crowding them into a cardboard box I noticed parts of their beaks were missing.

'Umm . . .' I ventured. 'Could I have ones without broken beaks?'

'Don't worry,' she laughed. 'I always trim their beaks to stop them feather pecking or becoming cannibals later. It's routine.'

'How do you do it?' I asked.

'When they're a day old,' she went on. 'But you do have to know what you're doing. Remove too little and it will grow again. Too much and the bird won't be able to feed properly. It's only about a third of the beak.'

[100]

I had set my heart on a fine-looking cockerel and she selected a young bird and put him in another box. He was later to be called Maurice after my dad, because he was always busy and looked very smart.

'What about turkeys?' Joan asked.

'Well I did want to buy some but I'm not sure,' I hesitated.

She led me to another building which was open along one side with wire netting enclosing over forty birds. I mentioned that I had read that you shouldn't keep turkeys with chickens.

'Oh that's Blackhead,' Joan said.

I laughed.

'It's fatal,' she said, 'but that's if you mix them with the chickens without treating their water.'

'Sounds complicated,' I said. 'I think I'll leave it for now.'

'Tell you what,' she said, 'you can have these two bronze turkeys. I've got so many and they're rather nice to look at. Better than the common white ones.'

'Thanks a lot,' I said. 'I'll bring you a bottle of our wine when we start producing it.'

She asked me all about the vineyard and every time I made to leave she kept showing me more things or asking more questions. She was obviously lonely in her self-sufficient primitive hide-away.

After two and a half hours I finally left, promising to come back if I needed any more poultry.

'When do we start collecting eggs,' Ruth asked as soon as I got back. 'I like a nice fresh egg, don't you?'

'Peter and I don't eat eggs,' I said. 'All that cholesterol.'

'So what the devil did you buy chickens for?'

'Oh . . . a farm's not a farm without chickens.'

'And what are we going to call those ugly things?' Ruth pointed to the turkeys, with their loose purple skin swaying all down their necks. 'Christmas Day and Easter?'

★

'Hello gorgeous . . . how about slipping behind the counter with me?'

Not many farmers get that kind of offer. But then it was true what Stan said as he puckered his lips: 'There aren't that many farmers wearing lipstick nowadays.'

There was always a cheery greeting from Stan. He was the short, chubby, dark-haired and red-faced man in khaki overalls behind the counter at the local agricultural supplies store.

My first of many frequent visits was to get the milk substitute for my new calves, Gladys and Nora.

When I lived and worked in London I used to love wandering around the jewellery department or perfumery at Selfridges, discovering the latest designs and smells. But that was nothing like the fascinating shelves at SCATS (which stands for Southern Counties Agricultural Trading Society). You could learn a lot by just rummaging amongst the boxes and reading the labels on various containers. There were all kinds of weird and wonderful gadgets hanging on the walls or standing on the floor.

On my first visit I hadn't a clue what I wanted.

'Just tell me what you want,' laughed Stan, 'and I'll give it to you. I tell that to all the ladies. Just come and get me . . . Would you like me to come home with you and show you what to do (giggle, giggle)? You could fence me in any time you want (nudge, nudge) . . . I'm saucy but lovable.'

He was a mine of information and was always giving me advice – 'for a kiss!'

They had everything I needed in the store which was about seven miles away through some lovely countryside with panoramic views across the Weald. Inside was equipment of every size for every farm animal, from bottles and teats for lambs to weighing crates for bullocks. Syringes, needles, disbudding irons, tattoo tongs, chicken feeders, all sorts. Outside were tractors, gates, feeding troughs and everything to equip a modern farm or smallholding. They even had clothes – milking coats, drenching overalls, dairy aprons. Altogether far more interesting than Selfridges.

'What are these?' I asked one day, picking up a lethal-looking tool like giant tweezers.

'Cutting toenails, darling.' There was a roar of laughter from Stan and his companion behind the counter.

'Whose toenails?' I must have appeared thick.

'Give us a kiss and I'll show you, you naughty girl. But it will hurt.' More laughter.

'Oh go on. What's it for?'

'It's a burdizzo.'

'What's that?'

'Oh – it doesn't half hurt, doesn't it, boys,' turning to his assistant who was now falling about laughing.

Laugh. Laugh.

'Well, it looks lethal.'

'It is.' Howls of laughter.

'Oh come on, Stan.' I looked and sounded stupid but I still wanted to know.

'Any time, love. It turns calves into bullocks.'

'How?' More howls of laughter.

'You grab hold of their testicles . . . oh . . .' he then raised his voice to a screech, 'and chop!'

I was to discover a less gruesome way of castrating calves later, on a calf-rearing course.

I still wanted to grow all my own vegetables. At Oaklands I had grown everything: potatoes, runner beans, carrots, parsnips, salad vegetables, cabbages and even peppers, aubergines and artichokes. I had a big fruit cage. I grew strawberries, blackcurrants, gooseberries, redcurrants and blueberries.

Now I wanted to do the same at Cross Farm but on a bigger scale. I had already sectioned off part of Hop Garden. I'd started turning over the soil with a hired rotovator and Ruth and I had planted potatoes, cabbage, Brussels, swede, parsnips, beans, peas and salad vegetables. I wanted to be totally self-sufficient.

I liked the idea of being in control of as much of my life as possible. Of growing the food I wanted without the use of chemicals. Many think people who insist on organic methods, who are vegetarian and who care about the natural things are cranks wearing sacking and going around bare-footed. But when you think about it everyone grew and ate organically years ago. I was becoming increasingly aware of nature and a more 'natural' way of living.

As we were sowing some seeds one day Debbie came by on Bobby, her little thirteen-two pony. At first I had thought she lived at the old vicarage opposite because I'd seen her come out of there a number of times. But she'd told me she only stabled Bobby there. She lived down the lane at Foxhunt Green.

She was twenty years old but looked younger especially when she wore no make-up. Short, fair and very slim, she was quite shy until you started talking about horses. She lived with her parents and her father had worked for Mike Farrant, the dairy farmer, but now worked for one of the local pig farmers. He kept a few sheep himself and later not only Debbie but also her father would work for us.

'Do you want some manure?' she asked.

'Yes please. We don't make enough yet,' I laughed.

Just then Keith turned up with his trailer loaded with my straw.

'Can you help me unload it, ladies?' he asked. 'Or is George about nicking your newts?'

I was puzzled. 'How do you mean?'

'A fortune. He's making a fortune from your pond.'

'Oh never, he's a friend.'

'Well, you saw him when he was here.'

'Yeah.'

'The way he kept picking up all those newts and putting them in his pocket. He makes ten pounds a time selling those. How many do you think he picked up a day?'

'What, here?'

'Of course . . .'

Ruth came up from the vegetable garden.

'Have you heard this?' I said.

'And all that rubbish he said he kept taking out of the pond,' Keith continued. 'He sold it all off to landscape gardeners. You get a lot of money for waterlilies.'

'And all the time . . .' I said. I was shocked and annoyed that I had been so naïve.

'How come he's making money?' said Ruth.

'First the usual trick. He goes in, cleans out the pond or lake. For a fee, of course. He takes all the newts and waterlilies, sells them off . . .'

'. . . at a nice profit,' I said.

'Then with the big ponds or lakes, he says he'll stock them with fish at his own expense. Then he'll charge people for fishing there and split the profits.'

'So how does he pay for that?'

'He doesn't. He gets the fish from other people's ponds when he clears them out. All part of the job. He leaves them there for a while to breed, then he goes back, puts up an old garden shed by the side of the lake . . .'

'. . . which he gets from a rubbish dump,' I interjected.

'. . . gets an old age pensioner to sit there all day,' Keith went on.

'. . . because he's cheap . . .' It was all becoming clear.

'. . . and charges everybody five pounds for a day's fishing.'

'Some catch fish. Some don't,' said Ruth.

'Which is always the same with fishing,' I said.

'He tells the owner he only sold a few tickets, pays the old age pensioner and pockets the rest.'

'No tax. No VAT,' I said.

'But because the fishing's not been a success he then offers to clean out the pond for them free the following year.'

'I'm in the wrong business,' I said.

We reached the house.

'I just want to check my order for the fertilizers,' I said to Ruth. 'You make the coffee.'

I turned to go up to the office. A sudden scream shook the foundations.

Ruth came out of the kitchen carrying a tea plate. On it was the chewed-up remains of a squirrel. Without a head.

'This, I suppose,' she said, shaking the plate at me, 'is to remind you which fertilizers to order.'

CHAPTER TEN
The Vines – and Elsa – Arrive

The arrival of the vines was quite an occasion – the real beginning of my grand scheme. It was April 1980, our second year at Cross Farm. Having ordered over five thousand I was expecting an articulated lorry filled to the soft top.

The lorry was certainly huge. As it came to a halt outside our gate it practically filled the lane. It was an articulated lorry but with two enormous trailers with the German name of the transporters written large all over them. One or two of the villagers had come out to watch. Nothing so big had entered Waldron before!

A large, plump, plain-faced man in jeans, checked shirt and leather jacket jumped out of the cab clutching a large sheet of white paper.

'Gross varm?' he said slowly, pointing to the address on the delivery docket.

'Yes, that's us,' I said, excited by the long-awaited arrival.

He looked at the gate without a smile and motioned with his hand that he had to drive in.

He started speaking quickly in German and although I recognized, or thought I recognized, the odd word, I just kept saying, 'Ich sprechen nicht Deutsch.' But I caught on not by what he said but by his actions – he was worried about getting through the gate. He kept shaking his head and muttering, 'Mein Gott.'

I beckoned to him to follow me. I showed him where I wanted him to offload the vines. I started gesticulating as much as him and Ruth just stood there laughing.

Our German friend, however, did not see the funny side of it.

'Fancy sending a bloody driver who can't speak bloody English,' I said to Ruth.

'Bitte?' I think he got my meaning so I smiled and mimed that Ruth and I would help him unload from the road if needs be. But he wouldn't have it. Mumbling away he got into his cab and slowly drove up to the middle of the village. There was no way he could turn into our gateway from the direction he was facing because, being on a slight slope, the road did not give him enough swing. Now the village has only a small triangular green with a war memorial in the middle. On one side is the pub, on the other a house and the other a high wall. Within inches of all of them he turned the lorry and backed down towards our gate, with anxious villagers looking on.

'God,' I cried, 'he's not going to reverse in here.'

'Oh yes he is,' said Ruth.

'I hope these Germans are as good drivers as everyone says they are,' I yelled. 'Mind the barn . . . mind the gatepost . . . mind . . .'

At a snail's pace and to the loud sound of airbrakes, he edged down the road, manoeuvring his gigantic vehicle gradually round into the gateway with less than an inch to spare on either side. Twenty minutes after he started he was safely inside and parked without touching one blade of grass along the green verge.

Ruth clapped him as he jumped out of the cab with a very red face and bands of sweat across his forehead.

There was strap after strap to unfasten and then he pulled back the side of the second trailer to reveal his precious cargo.

'Doesn't look a lot,' I said to Ruth as we started to help him unload them.

'I wouldn't say that,' said Ruth. 'You wait till we start planting them.'

The lorry was loaded with all kinds of equipment including two stainless steel wine tanks.

'It won't be long before you're back with some of these for me,' I said to the plump man, who barely smiled but obviously didn't understand me.

'Ja, hier ist . . .'

'Going to show the Germans how to make wine,' I laughed.

'Ssh, Gay,' said Ruth nudging me, 'you'll start an international incident.' She smiled at the driver who was lifting out the vines in bundles wrapped in sealed black polythene bags.

'Ja . . . vine. German vine ist sehr gut, ja.'

Never mind.

The vines were bundled together in groups of twenty-five or fifty and tied with a metal ring to which a metal label was attached with the varietal name, rootstock, etc. They looked like thick straight twigs with thinner shoots at one end and lots of string-like roots at the other.

The driver, like all delivery men, just wanted to unload quickly and go. I counted the bundles. Yes, I'd got five thousand vines. I signed his slip and, after consulting a map, he eased his way out slowly, muttering in German about wine.

It was mild for the time of year and our first job was to get the roots, which were still damp, in tubs of water. I had bought a load of old plastic dustbins.

'They mustn't dry out,' I kept telling Ruth. 'And we must keep them in the dark.'

'Oh, like all of us, you mean.'

Keith borrowed a dung spreader for the manure we were to spread in Lodge Field. The limestone had to be spread separately by the suppliers who had bigger machines that would not clog up with the chalky substance.

Every gardener knows the value to his plants of lime applications on the soil and vines, which prefer a slightly acid soil, are no exception. It not only lightens a heavy clay and therefore helps with the drainage, but it encourages a stronger root system and enables the roots to absorb essential nutrients. When it was spread the whole lot had to be ploughed in.

This process had to be completed at least two weeks before planting was to start in May. Apart from getting stuck twice and breaking down three times Keith kept going so we could begin on time.

'But we'll never be able to work on this,' I said looking at endless huge lumps of soil.

'I'll have to rotovate it down for you several times,' he said.

'I'll need it fairly flat.'

'Well then, I'll rake it over – which is going to cost you more. Gor, these vines are good business.'

That weekend would be spent preparing the vines for planting. Mum and Dad were due to come down and Peter and Adrian had been told to be prepared.

'Why can't we just plant them,' asked Ruth, 'like anything else?'

'We've got to trim the roots to stimulate fresh growth and make it easier to plant them,' I said, 'and prune last year's growth to two buds, then dip the tops in this special vine wax to preserve them. We'll have to use a couple of old saucepans to melt the wax.'

'What, all five thousand of them!' exclaimed Ruth. 'You always leave the good news to last.'

Peter and Adrian weren't all that keen either, since it looked as if the job would take the whole weekend.

'I know,' I said. 'With Mum and Dad coming down we'll all muck in and have a picnic as well. It will be fun.'

I had planned to take two weeks for planting, starting on the following Saturday. The weather forecast was good. Peter decided to work from home in the early morning and evenings and Adrian had taken his spring holiday. Dennis agreed to help as did Tommy when he was able – or rather, when he felt like it.

Everything was organized. The five thousand six-foot bamboo canes had arrived, together with fifty giant bales of peat from the local horticultural wholesaler.

I bought two new spades and forks, four trowels, secateurs and masses of jute string. I hired a large spray tank for the back of the tractor – a brain-wave, I proudly thought. We would have to water the roots when we planted to help start them off and I couldn't figure a way of transporting all the water along the rows to each vine until Mr Reeves, the ex-policeman and vine grower I had met at a wine fair, suggested the tank with a spray gun at the end of a hose.

The weather forecast was fine which was a mixed blessing. Although vines didn't like wet feet they also didn't like dry conditions for planting as there was a danger that the roots would dry out before they had a chance to spread and start growing. But we needed to plant in fairly dry conditions because it would be quicker. No point digging a hole that would fill just as quickly with rain.

The big worry was how we would begin to plant the vineyard. You can't just start digging holes, you have to have a system. Wherever you see a vineyard the vines are planted in straight rows an equal distance apart. I knew the theory. It wasn't just to look neat.

Imagine when the vines are old with lots of foliage and grapes on them, I was told more than once. You've got to drive a tractor down the vines, spray the vines and harvest them. So if they are equally spaced it is easier. And if the grapes are more or less the same distance from the ground, it's not only easier for spraying but also for harvesting.

I knew the theory. But actually doing it was another story. I tried plotting it on paper and lost my temper.

I measured the field and made a scale drawing. I then pencilled in my rows – six feet apart – and measured every three foot six inches between vines. But by the time I had finished my scale drawing I had two thousand vines over! Something was wrong.

Having decided to plant the vines three foot six inches apart and the rows six feet six inches apart I got two pieces of wood measuring exactly those distances. Then I joined them together at right angles. It should work. Shouldn't it? Anyway all was ready, or more or less ready, for the big day.

'Okay. Altogether now,' I said. 'You hold the vine like this. Then snip, snip, you cut the shoots off the top like this, leaving two to three buds. Then snip, snip, you trim the roots like this . . .'

'But there's hardly any left,' Ruth exclaimed.

'I know,' I said. 'Because of the way we're planting them. If we're going to plant them all by digging separate holes, putting the vine in, spreading the roots out neatly on the soil, covering them with peat then filling the hole in with soil, we have to cut them by half or we'll be digging holes two feet wide and four feet deep!'

'I suppose so.'

'So you cut the roots like this. Then dip the top of the vines into the saucepan of wax. Okay?'

We were all in the big tithe barn surrounded by the vines and every plastic dustbin, bucket, drum, feeding trough and metal bath I could find filled with water. The pan of wax was on an old camping fire. After several attempts it wasn't long before we had a system going.

It was cold, bitterly cold, but sunny. This was good for the vines as it meant we could prune them and store them in water without any risk of them starting to grow. Being dark, the tithe barn was ideal for storing them since the lack of light would delay budding. But it was bad for us. We all sat in the barn slowly freezing to death.

Snip. Snip. One hundred and eighty-four. The new secateurs I'd bought seemed to be getting stiffer.

Snip. Snip . . .

'My feet are cold,' said Mum.

'A nice drop of brandy would go far,' hinted Dad.

'You bet,' chorused Peter and Adrian.

'How about a cup of hot chocolate, Ruth?' I said. 'That will get us warm.'

Snip. Snip.

'Rather have brandy,' moaned Dad.

'Hear, hear.'

Snip. Snip. Snip. Snip.

'This is lovely hot chocolate,' Peter said when he sipped from one of the mugs Ruth brought back.

'I knew you'd like it,' winked Ruth.

Snip. Snip.

'Wait a minute, it's got brandy in,' I said sternly. 'We can't afford to get tiddly.'

Snip. Snip.

'Yes, sergeant major,' Adrian muttered.

'I wouldn't say that, Adrian,' Peter said. 'She's more like Sergeant Dhargenou.' To which everyone laughed, although I couldn't see any likeness between myself and that somewhat dictatorial character from *Beau Geste*.

Snip. Snip.

'Time you learnt to drive the tractor, Ruth.'

'Me?' exclaimed Ruth in horror. 'You know I can't even drive a car.'

'But what happens if we've just got to use the tractor and you're the only one around?'

'Well, I'll wait until somebody comes who can drive it.'

'But that might not be practical.'

'It'll have to be,' she said sternly. 'I tell you, I'm not going to drive that tractor.'

'Back to the vines. We've had a good break.'

'Yes, Sergeant Dhargenou.'

Snip. Snip.

'How are we going to plant?' asked Peter as we were snipping away.

'I've got it all worked out.'

'I bet you have.'

Snip. Snip.

I explained the theory.

'Who's going to mark out the runs and positioning of the vines?' Peter asked.

'You are.'

'Well, will the tractor go down between the rows?'

'Of course. But we will need a smaller tractor later on when the vines are bigger. But that's going to cost a lot more. I'll probably have to buy a new one that's specially adapted for vineyards.'

'Not more expense!'

'No point spoiling a ship for a halfpence of tar.'

Snip. Snip.

Snip. Snip.

'That's it,' I declared.

'I don't think I can use my hand any more,' said Ruth.

'I've got blisters,' Adrian moaned.

'Just wait till next weekend,' said Peter. 'We've got to dig holes for this lot. Every single one!'

The arrival of the vines coincided with another, equally important arrival. I'd always wanted a golden retriever, having happy memories of holidays in South Shields visiting an 'auntie' who had two goldens, Lady and Lassie. 'Auntie' Laura wasn't really an aunt. She was the sister of my Uncle Bob who was married to my real Auntie. I always liked going to see Laura. To me she appeared rich because not only did she have a lovely house but she also had a huge garden and her two goldens.

I always remember one particular New Year's Eve, which northerners celebrate more than us in the south. I was about ten years old, and left the grown-ups in Laura's lounge getting merrier and merrier and joined the dogs underneath the large kitchen table. The three of us saw in the New Year together sharing a turkey sandwich. I promised myself that one day I'd have a golden all of my own.

On moving to Cross Farm I contacted the Golden Retriever Rescue Society and its organizer, Brenda Lowe, who lived at Brenchley. After Cross Farm and I had been vetted and declared suitable it was just a question of waiting for the right dog.

Mrs Lowe, who was also a well-known breeder of goldens, rang me up one morning as we were getting everything ready for planting. I'd taken all five thousand bamboo canes down to the vineyard by tractor and that took several trips. The canes had arrived in large bundles which were too heavy for Ruth and me to pick up so I had to split the bundles. We were now putting tubs of vines all round the edge of the field so we wouldn't have to keep walking backwards and forwards to get them. The idea was that while we were not so mechanized the amount of legwork should be reduced to save time.

'You carry on,' I said to Ruth. 'I'll get the phone.'

I ran all the way back to the house.

'If you're still . . .' Mrs Lowe began.

'Of course I am,' I said immediately.

'. . . and if you've got the time?'

'Of course, of course. No problem.'

I crossed my fingers and tried to forget the five thousand vines we had to plant.

'Well,' she said very slowly, weighing every word like a Tory Party lady chairman introducing the guest speaker at their monthly luncheon. 'I've just been to see this really lovely retriever, Camrose actually. Really, really lovely. Good pedigree. The family are breaking up. A broken home and all that. And I'm very worried about the dog. Very.'

Not a word about the family, I thought.

'She's being left on her own day after day. Never goes out.

The woman can't bear to be in the house. Awful thing, broken homes – for the dogs. A frightful mess. Wondered if you . . .?'

'Of course. Of course. Smashing. No problem,' I said. I didn't dare tell her we were desperately trying to get ready for planting.

'That's if you have the time. Of course, you do realize that a dog – especially a rescue dog – needs time spent with it.'

I ran down to the field and told everyone I had to go out. 'I won't be long.'

'But Gay . . .'

The Land-Rover took ages to start. And, of course, it just wouldn't go into gear. I banged the red lever on the floor. I pushed the yellow lever backwards and forwards. Finally I got it to go. As I got to the big farm gate, Ruth came running up.

'The tractor,' she puffed. 'It's stopped working.'

'I haven't got time,' I cried. 'Call the man at Robertsbridge. Get him to sort it out. I won't be long.'

'You can't leave us to do all the planting!' She was annoyed.

'I know . . . but it is important. I promise I won't be long.'

And I roared away.

As soon as I saw Elsa I knew she was the dog for me. She was the most beautiful thing I'd ever seen – bright and alert with lovely eyes and the most marvellous mobile eyebrows. And so pleased to see me.

I found her cooped up in a tiny room in a house in Edenbridge in Kent, near to where I used to live. The garden was about the size of a pocket handkerchief.

'A bitch?' I said to her owner, a rather tearful, fragile woman who did nothing but smoke, drink coffee and cry into a tiny soggy tissue.

'You can say that again. Running off with my husband,' she cried.

Elsa started licking my hand.

'Likes her freedom does she?' I said.

'My God, she does.' The woman wept into another tissue.

'After running off with my husband, she was off with his brother the following week.'

Elsa looked at me. I looked at her.

'She'll have the time of her life . . .' I began.

'And with all the money I helped him to make,' she wailed into her destroyed tissue.

'I'll talk to Mrs Lowe,' I said.

'Talk to whoever you like,' she wailed. 'It won't do any good.' I patted Elsa on the head and whispered into her ear, 'Don't worry. I'll take you away from all this.'

Elsa looked pleadingly at me and frowned. 'Don't worry,' I reassured her, 'it won't be long now.'

As soon as I got back to the farm I called Mrs Lowe.

'I'll take her,' I said. 'She's a treasure. When can I have her?'

She promised to check and come back to me.

Then I asked about progress in the vineyard and found nothing had been done.

'Oh no, Ruth,' I said, 'I thought I told you to call the guy at Robertsbridge and sort it out.'

'I did,' she said.

'So . . .'

'He said "Bleedin' tractor" and slammed the phone down.'

'He did what?' I yelled.

I went marching into the office, picked up the phone and called him straight away.

'Now calm down, Mrs Biddlecombe,' he said obviously trying to soft-soap me. 'Calm down. If you let me get a word in . . .'

'You don't have to keep swearing at people,' I said angrily. 'There's no need for it.'

'But I didn't . . .'

'Oh yes you did.' I wasn't going to let him get away with that. 'I've just got back and Ruth said you said "bleedin' tractor" and slammed the . . .'

'But that's not . . .'

'So you deny it?'

'Deny what?'

'That you swore at her. That you . . .'

'But that's not swearing. That's . . .'

'Well if that's not swearing I don't know what is,' I said.

'Mrs Biddlecombe,' he said, his slow voice gradually increasing in volume. 'Mrs Biddlecombe . . .'

'There's no need to . . .'

'. . . if you will just listen for a moment . . .'

'. . . to adopt that tone of . . .'

'I-did-not-swear,' he bawled down the phone at me.

'Well. If that's your attitude,' I said, 'you can transfer me to your . . .'

'I-said-bleed-the-tractor. Bleed-the-tractor.'

I stopped dead.

'Bleed-the-tractor. That's not swearing. You've got to bleed-the-tractor then you'll have no problems.'

'Oh yes,' I said quietly. 'Of course. Thank you very much.'

I meekly put down the phone.

'Ruth,' I shouted out of the office and across the courtyard. She came up to the farm gate. 'Ruth, you're bleedin' stupid. He didn't say, "Bleedin' tractor". He said, "Bleed the tractor". Bleed the tractor. Not bleedin' tractor. Bleed the tractor, that's what you've bleedin' well got to do.' And we both laughed.

Finding out how to bleed the tractor, however, took a phone call to Geoff Burgess. But we did it. Geoff is the son of a local farmer, Roland, who set up a small workshop on his dad's farm repairing tractors and cars. He got used to our frantic phone calls for help every time something went wrong with the tractor, or any other machine for that matter!

The following Saturday morning we were ready to start planting. Ruth and I had everything we needed at the ready. We'd also put bundles of canes at strategic points around the edge of the vineyard, next to the tubs of vines.

'Okay. Let's go,' I cried.

'Right, what do we do, Sergeant Dhargenou?' asked Adrian.

'Dennis, you organize the tractor and water tank. Peter, start measuring. Adrian, start digging. Ruth, you and I will plant. Dad, you'd better help Dennis and Mum had better help us.' I dished out the jobs.

But by lunchtime we still hadn't started planting. It took ages to decide where to begin. Peter had to measure all round the headland leaving enough space for the tractor to come out of each row and turn into another. If the field had been a perfect square it would have helped!

Then, having decided where the first vine in the first row was going to go, Adrian, Peter and Dennis began digging. Ruth and Mum, on their knees, placed the vines in the holes. Dad squirted some water. I threw in some peat and holding the vine straight piled the soil back into the hole. Simple.

'This is going to take ages,' said Mum.

'Good job it's sunny and dry,' said Ruth.

Over an hour later we had planted the first row. My knees and back were already telling me I wasn't as fit as I thought I was. I stood up to look at our handywork.

'Oh no!' I yelled. 'I don't believe it!'

'What's the matter?'

'Just look.'

'What?'

'Well, just look at that first row. Can't you see?'

'Looks okay to me.'

'And me.'

'They'll all have to come out!'

'What!'

'Why?'

'Stand here,' I suggested. 'Just take a look at the way the row goes.'

Eventually they realized. We had started off all right but the other end of the row was about six feet further away from the hedge than the start.

'So what?' said Adrian.

'I can see what she's getting at,' said Dennis. 'If you follow that line, the problem will increase all the way up and you'll end up with an odd shape.'

'More precisely,' I said, 'we'll lose valuable planting space and the rows won't be north to south.'

'I told you the best thing to do was to use string but you wouldn't listen,' said Peter. 'You never . . .'

'Let's break for lunch,' said Ruth to pacify. 'We'll make a fresh start afterwards.'

The following morning we actually began planting. We had taken out the first row. All the rows had been measured out at exactly six feet six inches apart. There were canes everywhere: canes marking the beginning of each row, canes marking the end of each row, and hundreds of canes in between where vines were to go at three-foot-six-inch intervals.

Peter had used miles of string to get a straight line along the row north to south as well as east to west. Using the wooden marker posts with the string was obviously going to work.

'Okay, let's go,' I said again. 'We're already a day late. We've got a lot to do.'

This time the men took it in turns to dig and Peter kept double checking the distances. But there was something I had forgotten in the rush to get started.

'An official photograph!'

'What?'

'I've got to take an official photograph of the start of this vineyard. For the family history book if nothing else. Everybody . . .'

Despite the moans I think everyone felt a sense of occasion.

'Mum, you dig the first one in . . . like the Queen Mother planting a tree.'

Click.

'Now one of me . . .'

Click. 'Now one of all of you . . .' Click.

'Let's get on with this,' Adrian moaned, tripping over the string for the fourth time.

We moved along to the next vine. Dig. Insert. Squirt. Handful of peat. Fill in. Stamp down. Another vine was in, safe and sound.

'We'll soon have this finished,' I chortled, 'if we can keep up this pace.'

Dig. Insert. Squirt. Peat. Fill. Stamp. Another vine was planted.

'Not that difficult once you get going,' Ruth muttered.

'Once you get going,' Adrian mumbled.

An hour later we'd finished the first row. We all stood back to admire it. Everyone looked warily at me.

'Are you happy now?'

'Yes!'

'I don't believe it, fellers,' said Peter. 'We've actually got it right.'

'But this is going to take ages,' Adrian muttered. 'Sixty or more vines in one row. We've got over sixty rows . . .'

'And some rows are longer than others,' Ruth pointed out.

'It's going to take us at least 120, 150, maybe 200 hours . . .'

'That's not including the measuring up,' Peter said.

'We'll just have to go faster,' I said.

Chorus: 'Yes, Sergeant Dhargenou!'

By the third row Adrian was complaining of his back. Ruth was on her knees. Peter was mumbling something about the office.

'I need a bath,' Ruth grunted.

'My back. My back,' Adrian wailed. 'Somebody will have to help me up.'

Dig. Insert. Squirt . . .

We worked from 8 a.m. to 6 p.m. that first day. By nine o'clock the following morning we were all in the vineyard again, Peter still marking out the rows.

'Can't you do it quicker?' I said. 'This is going to take ages.'

'My back,' Adrian wailed.

'I'm getting some knee pads,' Ruth added as they both collapsed on the ground before tackling row five.

I switched the tractor on and pushed it into gear. We had decided to swop jobs to give us all a change.

But it was still dig, insert, squirt, handful of peat, fill, stamp.

The worst part about the planting – apart from the aches and pains – was the jokes. The battle between Peter, Adrian and Dennis to see who could tell the funniest jokes didn't stop. But it helped to make us work faster.

Dig. Insert. Squirt . . .

But after three days we were in a regular routine and going at a good pace. Ruth and I would see to the animals before joining the others. The weather stayed fine and Mum brought the picnic down each lunchtime to save our aching legs.

'You're all mad,' she said every time as the days passed. 'How did I ever have a daughter who'd end up like this?'

'Stop. Stop,' I shouted. 'Stop everything. Elsa's coming today. I've just remembered.'

It was day four and I had arranged for Elsa to arrive mid-morning. I ran up to the house as fast as my aching legs would carry me. There was nobody there. I was dreading Elsa's owner changing her mind about giving her to me. I rang Mrs Lowe. No reply. I left a note pinned to the gate for her to hoot her horn three times when she arrived.

By the time I got back to the vineyard Peter had finished marking out all the rows.

We were up to Row 18. But we were getting quicker.

In the middle of the afternoon we heard the signal – three hoots.

'Quick, everyone,' I yelled. 'Let's break. Come up and meet Elsa.'

Everyone was eager to down tools. Any relief was welcome. A little yellow car was parked in the courtyard, and in the boot was Elsa, wagging her tail.

'Sorry I'm late.' It was the owner looking a little bit more cheerful. 'I asked Mrs Lowe if I could come and see Elsa's new home. Hope you don't mind.'

Elsa leapt out of the boot in one go. She stood still for a second. She looked at me and wagged her tail. She then took in the house, the farm buildings, the old tithe barn and all the fields in an instant. Then she went absolutely bananas. She ran to me, to the house, to the barn, across the courtyard and back to me again. She then turned and ran to the house, to the cowhouse, into the paddock and back to me. Hardly pausing for breath she turned and bounded up to George and Bettie, to the chickens, to Come-on who was lounging quietly on a wall. Then she ran round and round in circles.

'She's lovely,' said Mum.

'Oh, she's gorgeous,' said Ruth.

'She's obviously happy to be here,' said the woman climbing back into the car. 'It's one less thing for me to worry about.'

'Don't worry,' I shouted out to her as she drove away. 'We will look after her.'

She was two years old. Her coat was long, curly, silky and the colour of pale sand. Her tail was wagging non-stop. And on her face she had the biggest smile I've ever seen on any dog. She made us all laugh.

I took her into the house where she ran everywhere. It was as if she was discovering her freedom for the first time. Outside I took her into all the buildings and introduced her to all the animals.

We then walked and leapt and bounded down to the top of the fields. As soon as she saw them she stopped dead, almost skidding in her tracks. She looked from left to right. Once, twice, three times. She blinked as if she couldn't believe the world could be so big. Or that it could all belong to her. Then she literally threw herself headlong into the first field and ran, and ran, and ran. She looked as though she was going to run for ever. George the goose came to stare at the spectacle. Françoise and Hardy ambled out to take a look. The calves stopped munching. Nobody had ever seen anything like it.

I called her and she came to me immediately. We went into the house and had lunch together. I gave her the biggest bowl of milk she'd ever seen in her life. I took her to her new basket. I took off her old collar and put on a brand new red one which I had bought in anticipation. She was home.

After that the planting was easy. Every morning we started at eight o'clock. The rows seemed to lay themselves out across the field. The water pump worked like a dream. Dig. Insert. Squirt. Peat. Fill. Stamp. Everything went like clockwork. And all the time Elsa raced around the field, rolled in the mud and the dust, clambered on to the tractor, sniffed the vines and then raced off round the fields again. She was having the time of her life.

It was still taking us on average one day to do about three to four rows. Some rows were longer than others because of the shape of the field. It was still back-breaking work. But as Elsa leapt and ran and charged all round the field, frequently coming to me for a cuddle, it didn't seem so hard.

She obviously loved water, as most retrievers do. When Dennis squirted her with the water gun she loved it. She barked at him to do it again and again. Then she rolled on the rotovated soil covering herself from head to tail.

By the end of the day her lovely pale sandy coat was clogged with darker sandy soil. We had to hose her clean and she loved that too.

Dig. Insert. Squirt . . .

We took different jobs in turn. One morning I'd drive the tractor, then in the afternoon I'd be crawling along the ground, putting the vines into the holes, spreading their roots. The next day it would be Ruth's turn. Sometimes Peter would be digging the holes. Other days it would be Adrian or Dennis. But whatever we did, we all agreed Peter was the only one to check the measurements.

We discussed everything under the sun. Wine. Farming. Elsa. Why the gear box in the Land-Rover was playing up. Why I needed a van of my own. How to bleed a tractor.

Now and then I would have to go back to the house to make a phone call. But Peter was always running backwards and forwards. He was telling his clients he was out of the office travelling — travelling up and down the rows of a vineyard. They thought he was joking.

Finally, twenty-three days after we'd started, we'd finished. I was given the honour of planting the last vine. Our first vineyard was ready. Far from being impressive, it looked somehow insignificant. The soil had been virtually parched yellow by the sun. Across this yellow dust were rows of tiny twigs with the green wax binding the graft together just peeping above the surface. We had to plant the vines about two inches from the graft where the new shoots would appear. This meant we were planting about eighteen inches deep, digging a hole wide enough to spread the roots at the bottom.

As I planted the last vine, we all collapsed in a heap around the tractor.

Peter had had the foresight to bring down a bottle of chilled English wine and since the day was warm we enjoyed it all the more.

'Oh my back,' Adrian kept moaning. 'Never again!'

'A bath. A bath. I'm going to be in a bath for a month,' Ruth wailed.

'But we haven't finished,' I said.

'Well, we know you and Ruth have got to look after them . . .' said Adrian.

'But we haven't quite finished *this* job,' I said as lightheartedly as I could.

Everybody looked up at me. There was dead silence.

'The plastic,' I continued. 'Now we've got to cover every single row, every vine with plastic sheeting to stop them being choked with weeds and keep some moisture in the soil while they are young.'

Silence. Absolute silence.

'But don't worry,' I continued hastily. 'We can do it with the tractor. I've arranged everything. It will only take a few days – maybe just a weekend.'

The problem of weeds had worried me. I didn't want to spray. A few days before we'd started I had chatted to a local strawberry grower and asked what he did about weeds.

'Black polythene,' he'd said. 'Expensive but by God does it save on the work.'

One or two vineyard owners had used it and Bob Westphal and his son David swore by it.

'Oh well in that case . . .' Adrian and Ruth began to mock.

'Except that we've got to follow on behind and make a hole in the plastic so that the vine pops through the middle.'

'You mean every vine?' Ruth asked.

'Come on – let's go,' I said. 'The sooner we start, the sooner we'll get it done.'

I leapt on the tractor. Elsa leapt on the transport box behind. She was still ready for action. She was the only dog for me.

CHAPTER ELEVEN
The Answer Lies in the Soil!

'Hello, I'm from the *Kent and Sussex Courier*,' the fresh-faced young man with blond curly hair said. 'I hear you're planting a vineyard?'

'Don't tell me my fame is spreading before I've even produced any wine,' I laughed.

He had driven up in a little white van with the name of his paper written in blue and black on both sides.

Looking at him I felt an old hand. I saw immediately through his eagerness, the new notepad he held authoritatively and the poised pen, that he was a cub reporter, new at the game, sent out on an easy story.

'How did you get to hear of the vineyard?' I asked.

'We have our sources,' he said very seriously.

I tried not to laugh.

'Okay, what would you like to know?'

He opened his notepad and poised his Bic biro: 'Why are you planting a vineyard in Sussex?'

Now being a bit of a cynic I thought there were two ways of answering that question but my good side got the better of me and, I said to myself, you were a cub reporter once. Except in my days in London I was sent out to find a rat-infested bomb site and whip up a petition by local residents.

So off I went telling this *Courier* cub all my dreams, theories and plans for the vineyard. As I talked I got faster and faster and I don't think he got much of it down.

'But can we grow grapes in England? . . . Will you be competing against the French? . . . How old are you? . . . When will you have your first wine?'

He was studying his notepad as if wondering what else to ask but couldn't think of a suitable question.

Then with renewed enthusiasm he asked: 'What did you do when you lived in London?'

'Oh I had a very important job. A very difficult job,' I said.

'What was that?'

'I was a journalist. Well actually I still am,' I smiled as he went red. 'Once a journalist always a journalist, eh?'

'Oh yes . . . yes. You mean you wrote for newspapers?'

'I did just what you're doing, then moved on to the nationals and freelanced for some magazines too.'

'Oh smashing! That's what I'd like to do.'

He then started asking me questions about London newspaper work.

'You never know,' I laughed, 'you might end up planting a vineyard.'

He was very serious. 'Oh no, I don't think so.'

Back to the interview with 'Someone told me once that the Romans grew vines here. Is that true?'

It was about this time that I met Hugh Barty-King, a professional social and industrial historian who was also a writer. He had written a history of English wine which I had bought just before we bought Cross Farm. It was a fascinating account of how vines were first introduced by the Romans, and how through the ages there had always been vines grown here.

I was more interested in later developments like the famous vineyard at Castle Coch in South Wales, planted by Lord Bute and Andrew Pettigrew, his head gardener, in 1875. Apparently Pettigrew and his boss spent much time in France visiting vineyards and talking to proprietors. They certainly researched their project more than I did!

Castle Coch's vineyard was, according to Hugh Barty-King's

book, 'greeted with jeers' in *Punch* magazine. The book adds, 'It predicted in 1875 that if ever wine was produced from Glamorgan it would take four men to drink it: The victim, two others to hold him down and a fourth to force the wine down his throat.'

The interesting thing is that while there are now over three-hundred vineyards in England and Wales, *Punch* no longer exists!

Barty-King lives at Ticehurst, less than ten miles away, and I first met him on a typical English summer's day. He was tall and very thin, with lots of white hair and dressed as though he had just walked out of a first-class Caribbean hotel. He talked extremely fast but was a mine of information, having visited most of the vineyards that were already established. He was gathering and preparing information for a further book following on from his history and he wanted to include us. Nowadays when I have groups visiting us for conducted tours I always touch on the history – thanks to Hugh.

Few people realize, for instance, that England has owned the French vineyards more than once in its history. That's a nice point to rub in when we have French visitors who can be quite snooty about English wine. In fact if it wasn't for the English through the centuries the wine world would not be what it is today. We've grown wine. Made wine. Been the most important wine traders in the world as well as large consumers of wines like port and sherry. Our English glassmakers were even responsible for the special bottle that made champagne possible. We certainly have done our bit!

We now have an exhibition on the history of English wine in the winery for visitors to read and now and again I have long discussions with an historian or wine lover about a particular point or issue, especially which Roman Emperor introduced the vines to England!

'Unfortunately,' I tell my tours, 'we have no evidence of vines being planted on this site but certainly the Romans planted vines in Sussex.' I point out that our village church has a lychgate decorated with grapes and vine leaves and that we are surrounded by places called 'Vines Cross' or similar, so I like to think that we really are carrying on a local tradition.

No one seems to know exactly what the early wines tasted like. Apparently the English were storing their wine in wooden barrels and serving it from bottles while the Greeks, who had over a thousand years' more experience, were still using earthenware containers. In the sixth century, someone called Murchertach, son of Erc, drowned in a barrel of wine. It would appear to be his one claim to fame!

By 731, according to the Venerable Bede in his *Ecclesiastical History of the English People*, 'apart from fruit trees, horses and sheep, vines grew in many places' and the Anglo-Saxons called October the 'Wynth Moneth'. It still is . . .

King Alfred the Great was truly great! He drew up laws not only on planting and keeping vines but on the compensation a vineyard owner should be paid if anyone damaged his crop.

And vines were not just found here in the south. As Christianity spread and more wine was needed for religious ceremonies, vines were planted as far north as Scotland.

The Domesday Book could be seen as a drinking man's guide to the eleventh century! There were over forty vineyards in the south then but although Cross Farm is included there is no mention of vines.

Later, when our vineyard was well established, we were commissioned by the Lord Chancellor's office to produce the official English wine to celebrate the book's nine hundredth anniversary and because we were mentioned in the book we became known as the Domesday Vineyard. But that's another story.

The Saxons popularized wine and in those days both red and white wine were produced, but it was the Norman conquerors who set about improving on quality, introducing French viticulture and wine-making techniques.

By the twelfth century vineyards were everywhere, including

Windsor Castle. Richard II 'made money by them', and Richard III, we are told, paid his vineyard manager 6d a day.

Shakespeare – dear Shakespeare – who was born, and died, on St George's Day, frequently wrote about vines, grapes and wine. But he failed to tell us about the giant vine of North Allerton, Yorkshire, which in 1585 covered 127 square yards and was then a hundred years old.

Most people have heard of the famous Hampton Court vine, a Black Hamburg, which I now grow only for show in our vineyard restaurant. This vine grew to 110 feet in length and 30 feet wide and produced between 2,000 and 3,000 bunches of grapes, each weighing on average a pound! This was to be matched only by the vine at Valentines in Essex which covered 147 square yards and produced 2,000 bunches.

Books began to appear about growing vines in England and over the years I have amassed a collection, although most of them are not of practical use for modern growing. Still, John Rose, a gardener to Charles II, wrote *The English Vineyard* in the seventeenth century, preferring 'poor soil stony without much iron, instead of rich, fat land'. He criticizes vine growers who blame their soil and the climate for their failures instead of their own carelessness and shortcomings, which just about proves that times don't change much!

One book was a sell-out. William Hughes' *The Complete Vineyard: or, an excellent way for the planting of vines according to the German and French manner and long practiced in England* of 1665 was reprinted within five years.

As early as 1677 wine makers were being told to add sugar to the must, the grapejuice before it ferments, to increase the strength of the wine and in 1767 a W. Edmonds published a book for English vineyards who wanted to make 'wine of grapes equal to that of France'. He was also a great advocate of English white wine.

This thriving industry was dealt a blow though, in 1786, when a certain shrewd killjoy called Peter le Brocq managed to obtain a patent for growing vines and immediately threatened to sue anybody who used his method without paying royalties. This made people think twice.

But you obviously can't keep a good wine grower down and by 1862 more and more people had become interested again. I like the view of Thomas George Shaw, a Scottish wine merchant who at that time said, 'In wine-tasting and wine-talk there is an enormous amount of humbug.' There still is, Mr Shaw!

The first harvest at Castle Coch was in 1881 – despite *Punch* – and they sold the whole of their production to a single wine merchant for five shillings a bottle. Unfortunately, the vineyard disappeared during the First World War but I have to this day a blown-up copy of a photograph Hugh Barty-King lent me of some of the vineyard workers with their precious harvest. Looking at the photograph now, and having known some of the more recent pioneers such as the late Jack Ward at the now famous Merrydown Cider Company, I really do feel proud that I am carving my small niche in this fascinating history.

I had given the young reporter my full spiel and he had been scribbling away. He seemed more than happy with the interview.

'I've got reams and reams,' he said, just as eagerly as he had introduced himself over an hour and a half earlier.

As he left he said: 'They may want to send a photographer – will that be okay?'

'Yes, of course,' I said, brushing my hand through my hair.

'You have my lad,' the tall, skinny, long-haired woman of about forty was crying. She was almost hysterical.

'I beg your pardon.' I was taken very much by surprise but held out my hand to try and stop the woman rushing past me.

'You have my lad,' she repeated. 'He's my baby. Where is he? Where *is* he!?'

Tears were rolling down her face leaving white trails in her make-up. She was dressed in overtight jeans, a floral blouse which did not leave much to the imagination and high-heeled leather boots.

'Now calm down,' I shouted, 'or I'll have to ask you to leave.'

She immediately stopped and looked me up and down.

'I do not have *your* lad or anyone else's and if you would explain I may be able to help,' I said more calmly.

There was a distant neighing by our new arrival.

'That's my lad,' she called, 'you have got him. I knew it. You liar!'

'How dare you! Now look here . . .'

She rushed past me down to the pole barn where we had made a large pen for Peter's new horse.

The donkeys started to he-haw adding to the noise. And the geese, who had been a little late, I thought, started hissing but were not sure who or what they should be hissing at.

Peter, who was totally oblivious to anything but his new friend whom he was stroking and talking to, looked up.

'He's mine. He's my lad.' The woman collapsed crying on a bale of hay Peter was about to split for his new, sleek, bay thoroughbred gelding who had arrived only twenty minutes earlier.

Peter looked at me: 'What's all this about?'

'I don't know,' I said, 'but she is obviously in a bad way.'

She was still crying and saying all kinds of things about her lad, her husband and her friend. An odd eternal triangle, I thought.

I went over to Peter and whispered: 'I hope we're not going to be in trouble. I told you horse dealers are not to be trusted. There's something fishy going on.'

Peter had seen an advertisement in *Friday-Ad* for a sixteen-hand thoroughbred and since it was only four miles away decided to take a look. This time I went with him since this was more the size I wanted to share. As soon as Peter saw him it was love at first sight! His name was Dittons Lad and he certainly was handsome. He was being offered at £750 by a horse dealer called Sam Beeney. Mr Beeney lived on the main A22 London to Eastbourne road in a tiny house with a few stables and paddocks.

'Put him through his paces,' he said. 'He's perfect in every way. Okay in traffic, good to shoe. A real gent.'

Peter took him for a ride while I chatted to Mr Beeney, who avoided answering my questions about where Dittons Lad had come from.

'I don't have any papers for him,' he said, 'you take him as you find him. But I've dealt with horses all my life and this is a good 'un. He's cheap because I don't have papers and I don't want to keep him long. I don't keep any horse long. Fast turnover and plenty of satisfied customers. No, I can't say fairer than that.'

I began to get suspicious. But just then Peter returned, flushed with excitement and activity.

'He's beautiful,' he called. 'You should have seen him go, Gay. And on the road he's perfect. Didn't turn a hair when lorry after lorry went whizzing past.' He laughed and bent over to stroke the horse's neck. 'He's obviously a goer and seems to love it. Lovely smooth canter and smashing trot. Does exactly what you tell him. And he's got lovely ears . . . look at his ears, he's listening to everything I say.'

'So you like him,' I smiled.

'Yes, I'll have him,' Peter said. He was never one for negotiation.

'Peter, don't you think . . .'

'He's just right, just what I want.'

'But, Peter, we ought to get him vetted first, and,' I dropped my voice, 'and perhaps talk about the price, you know . . .' I was trying to signal with my eyes. But Peter was blind to all but Dittons Lad.

So it was arranged that Mr Beeney would deliver the horse in four days' time, on the Wednesday.

[135]

'Of course the £750 is cash,' he said to Peter.

'But, Mr Beeney,' I began to protest, 'you didn't say that at the beginning. If you want cash you should lower the price.'

Mr Beeney looked at Peter: 'Well, the price is a good one. You know that.'

'Yes, yes,' said Peter who by now was not prepared to let anything stand in the way of his having Dittons Lad.

'Call yourself a businessman,' I said as we were leaving. And to Mr Beeney I said: 'Okay, cash, but I want a receipt.'

'Doesn't trust me,' he smiled at Peter, 'does she, gov'nor?'

Peter arranged to work at home on the Wednesday of Dittons Lad's arrival. I spent the morning working in the vineyard and as soon as I heard the Land-Rover and horse box drive in I rushed up to the farm gate with Elsa, whose amazing sense of smell told her something interesting was about to happen.

Ditton's Lad, or Laddie as Peter was now calling him, was already out of the box, head held high, ears twitching and eyes alert, looking at and listening to everything in his new home. He called out to see if there was another horse and the donkeys replied. The two old girls were excited at having such a handsome male companion. Even Elsa barked a welcome.

As soon as we paid the cash and I was given a small handwritten, barely legible receipt, Mr Beeney was off.

'I hope this is all okay,' I said. 'I don't like cash deals and no proper receipt.'

But Peter was already leading Laddie around, showing him his new home and offering him Polos, apples and carrots and talking to him as though he was a new baby. There was also no tack with the horse so I suggested Peter put him in the pen with some hay and water and then telephone the local saddlery to come and try some saddles, bridles and all the other expensive gear he would need.

And this was when the crying Sue Brown came in.

'Now I've seen where he is I am happy.' She was back in control and smiling. 'I'm sorry about the outburst. Very sorry.'

She was obviously very nervous and highly strung but explained that she and her husband had separated. That did not seem to upset her at all. But the fact that she and Laddie had separated did upset her and now and again she cried as she continued her story.

'He's such a love,' she said. 'I'll have him back if you'll let me when I can get some money.'

'Well, let's hear the rest of the story first,' I said.

'I couldn't keep him you see. I've got no money at the moment and until the divorce comes through I won't be able to touch the house and things. I gave him to a friend who said she would try and sell him for me. I did agree. But I wish I hadn't now.'

'But if you did agree he could be sold . . .' I said.

'I know, but she didn't tell me. She just sold him to Sam Beeney. A dealer of all people. She only told me on Monday and Mr Beeney wouldn't talk to me. So I've kept a watch on his place since Monday afternoon. I didn't want him sold for dog meat or to a bad home.'

'I don't believe it,' I said. 'You've actually been spying on him.'

'Well it was my Lad,' she said. 'When I saw him leave this morning I pleaded with him not to sell Lad and to give him back to me. I followed him but then lost him, the bastard. Then someone said they saw a horse box come in here.'

She cried again: 'I'm sorry. I'm just so upset. She had no right to sell him.'

'Look,' I said, 'we bought him in good faith and my husband already dotes on him. Let me show you round.' I told her of our plans to build proper stables and showed her the fields Laddie would have.

'It's a lovely place. He *is* lucky, and I can see you'll be good to him.'

With promises that we would not sell Laddie and that she could come and visit him as often as she liked she left.

We still have Laddie and he will be with us until he dies. He and Peter are the greatest of friends and although now he's getting on a bit, he still loves to go out with Peter up on the Downs or through the woods. And he's still a gentleman.

Pickles arrived soon after. Horses are herd animals and I never believe in keeping animals without a companion. And besides I wanted my own horse.

Pickles suits his name. He seems to like getting in a pickle or at least creating one. Peter calls him a cart-horse and as a result Pickles does not like Peter and takes every opportunity to bite him. But handsome he certainly is, with his Welsh breeding and high-stepping hackney style. He and Laddie are great pals and are growing old gracefully together.

The horses are a great help in the vineyard too.

Manure is the best feed for the vineyard and it is amazing how much you get from just a few animals. When we had the cattle we had mountains of it but nowadays we rely mainly on the horses. We spread it regularly but not once the grapes are really formed. I learnt that lesson very early on.

Adrian and I had gone on a one-day pruning session at a vineyard near Haywards Heath in West Sussex. It had been organized by the local Agricultural Training Board of the Ministry of Agriculture who also wanted to know more themselves about this new approach to land use.

There were only eight people on the one-day course and two of them were local Ministry men. Being English we started late and with coffee and biscuits then the owners, a middle-aged couple who ran an apple orchard as their main earner, marched us down to their two-acre vineyard. They had already had one harvest and we were promised a glass of their wine with our ploughman's lunch which was included in the ten pounds a head fee.

As we got into the vineyard our wellingtons were already covered in thick clay but since the course was about pruning and not soil management nothing was said about it. We had to climb over fencing which was fixed to the last post in each row of vines.

'Surely you don't have to climb over the fence at the ends of each row?' I asked.

'Yes, we thought it was better to plant as many vines as we could instead of leaving a big headland,' said the man.

'But what about spreading this manure,' I said, pointing to the ground which had a thick layer of matter on it. 'What about the mowing and all the other work? Doesn't the fence get in the way?' I persisted, not seeing the logic in his reply.

'We just step over it or lift things over it,' he said in a matter-of-fact way.

'Crazy,' whispered Adrian, 'a masochist!'

We were shown vines that had just been planted, vines that were three years old and coming up to their first cropping year and vines that were five years old. With a sharp pair of secateurs the owners began explaining their pruning principles.

'Right,' the man said, 'you are all going to have a go. Let's all work in these two rows of three-year-old vines. Remember we don't want to keep more than twenty buds.'

We all began a bit cautiously. My first vine looked so weak I decided to reduce it to four buds.

'Oh,' said the owner, obviously annoyed, 'we could have taken fruit from that this year. I did tell you it was a three-year-old vine.'

'I know,' I said, 'but with all due respect this vine is too weak. If you cropped from it this year surely you could run the risk of poor quality grapes and weakening the vine so much it could die. Isn't it better to give it another year to develop so that next year it will be a lot healthier?'

The look was the kind you give to a know-all who actually does make a valid point which you are not going to admit to.

'Yes, well, would you check with me in future?'

'Of course.'

At lunchtime we broke to have our taste of their wine. They explained proudly that this was their first wine, a Muller Thurgau and Seyval blend. With great respect and a sense of occasion everyone smelt the wine and admired its appearance.

As Adrian and I smelt it I could see his nose wrinkle and his eyes met mine. As one of the other pruners asked about the vinification Adrian whispered: 'What's that smell?'

'It has an interesting nose,' I said, 'very earthy . . . not typical Muller . . . what is it?'

I got that look again. It was obvious the owners were beginning to look upon me as a troublemaker and were not sure whether to ignore me or answer me intelligently.

'Oh, I wouldn't say that,' said a retired accountant, 'I rather like it.'

'Yes, well done,' said a large lady from Maidstone looking first at me with a frown and then smiling at the owners.

I had the distinct impression that I was being put in my place. As we tasted it the polite comments spilled over themselves.

'Oh, it's jolly good . . . I like it.'

'A lovely, well, garden . . . English garden bouquet and a fruity . . . yes . . . fruity taste.'

'It has a certain something. Very distinctive.'

The taste was certainly distinctive. I could not quite place it but it was awful. I kept sipping and anxious eyes kept flashing in my direction. Aware that I should not make enemies in my own industry I said: 'Yes, very interesting . . .' There was a slight sigh of relief.

'But,' the owner's back straightened as I went on, 'may I ask a few questions?'

'Fire away,' he said with a stiff smile, 'but I think we had better be quick. We have to eat lunch and get back for more pruning.'

'What did you spray these grapes with? And when did you last spray?'

'Oh . . .' he laughed with relief, 'no problems. We stopped

spraying two months before harvest and we only used wettable sulphur twice during the year. We don't believe in spraying. In fact we are going over to totally organic methods. Organic fertilizer and organic sprays.' He beamed.

'Ah!' I thought aloud then checked myself. That was it. I realized what the smell and the taste was.

'What kind of organic matter?' I asked.

'Oh, horse muck, cow or pig manure, whatever we can get,' said the wife cheerily as she passed pieces of French stick around on paper plates.

I looked at Adrian. He looked puzzled.

'And when do you spread it?' I could see they were beginning to tire of my questions and the others wanted to get started on their lunch.

'Oh . . . all the year round,' the wife said as she went back into the kitchen.

'Yes,' her husband laughed, 'vines need feeding, the same as we do.'

Everyone else laughed politely and began tucking into a large slice of Cheddar cheese and a bowl of home-made chutney.

'But surely . . .' But I decided not to pursue the matter and just vowed that my manuring would not take place once the grapes had formed.

When you hear 'wine experts' say a wine's taste depends to some extent on the soil they are not thinking of horse manure!

A few days after my interview the phone rang.

'Can I come and take a photograph this afternoon for the *Courier*? We'd like a picture of you in your vineyard.'

'Yes, fine,' I said, mentally re-scheduling the next few hours. Photographers never seem to give much of a warning. On went the heated rollers.

He was an elderly man with glasses and carried a large square silver metal box held by a thick strap which was pulling his jacket half off at the right shoulder. He had a very bored look on his face and a 'let's get this over with as quickly as possible' voice.

'Right, where do you want to take the photo? The vineyard is over there,' I said.

'Have I got to walk all the way over there?' he moaned. 'It's miles away.'

He obviously had not been having a good day. He begrudgingly trudged back to his car, donned his boots and walked down the field with me to the vineyard.

'Now, where shall we have you?' he was muttering as he got his camera out.

'I'll tell you what,' I said, 'I'll bend down and be inspecting the vine with a pair of secateurs in my hand . . . okay . . . like this . . . yes?'

He took a dozen shots.

'I can't give you a glass of our wine, I'm afraid,' I said, 'because I haven't made any yet but in a few years' time . . .'

He grunted and left.

In his book Hugh Barty-King concludes that any aspiring English vigneron who plants his first vineyard 'will do so in the knowledge that he is following in the footsteps of those who, having proved the irrelevance of "unsuitable" climate and soil and discounted the superiority of foreign vintages, have built up a tradition of English wine – the pace-setters of the English Viticultural Revival, which, in 1978, is only just beginning to gather momentum.'

And my momentum had just started gathering. My first bit of publicity was about to break on the world.

The following Friday morning, there it was in black and white. A half column of text and a photograph of me grinning at the camera. The caption read: 'Fifty-six-year-old Mrs Anne Smith with her prize-winning cake'!

CHAPTER TWELVE
How to Milk a Cow

While I'd been waiting for the vines to arrive I had followed Keith Harvey's advice and gradually built up my herd of cattle. Gladys and Nora were now sturdy young heifers and what used to be a gentle nudge and a nuzzle from them left me covered in bruises. Once I had been able to lift them into the back of the Land-Rover but now I couldn't even get them to budge if they didn't want to.

I'd bought more calves at the market, mainly week-old bull calves. At Haywards Heath I was now a regular with the best of them and if I was not exactly bidding by raising my eyebrows or pulling my ear, I reckoned I could at least tell a good calf from a bad one as well as the rest. I was also buying calves at Hailsham, the other market in the area.

I converted the old stable in the courtyard into a full-scale calfhouse. I bought special calf pens and fitted them all round the walls. Each pen was open halfway up at the front so that the calves could get their heads through freely. In front of the hole was a bracket to take their feed buckets. Each pen was big enough to take two calves while they were still young and I liked this idea because they would keep each other warm and also it would stop them feeling lonely. By now I had twenty calves.

*

'Sorry I'm late,' said the vet as she leapt out of her little red car outside the calfhouse. 'Been at the hospital all night.'

She grabbed her big leather bag and old brown overall.

'Sorry,' I said as we went into the calves. 'Family problems?'

'No, I work there,' she said. 'Three nights a week. It helps to pay for my holidays.'

I opened the gate to little Shandy's pen. He had scours pretty badly and hadn't drunk any milk for three days. I had tried glucose again and again with the bucket but it was no good. I left it to see if he would drink it by himself. After all, he might not have liked the idea of sucking my fingers and having his head plunged into a bucket. Still no luck. He was obviously getting weaker and weaker. His ribs were showing and he was shivering.

The vet, who was a bright, tiny wiry girl in her twenties, knelt down beside him.

'Soon have you right as rain,' she said, rubbing his ears.

She broke open a box of syringes.

'Shandy,' she said. 'Nice name for a calf. Better than Buttercup.'

'It was Peter's idea,' I explained. 'He said we should call all our calves after a drink so whenever you came to look at one we would all have the drink it was named after.'

'Have you taken its temperature?'

'No – I didn't know how to.'

'Here,' she handed me a thermometer.

I was about to take its temperature when she said: 'Oh no! Not like that. Up its . . .'

'Of course,' I said. I mumbled something about taking a calf-rearing course.

'Good idea,' she said.

After a few minutes she pulled the thermometer out and wiped all the muck off.

'It's 102.5.'

'What should it be?'

'101.5. He'll need to be kept warmer than this,' she began.

'Give him a jacket or something warm to wear and fix a heat lamp over him. He'll need some vitamins and antibiotics. Do you know how to give injections?'

'No.' I felt stupid and helpless.

'Well, you ought to,' she said. 'Still it makes more money for me.'

She got two bottles out of her car and after filling the syringe and making sure no air was trapped, handed it to me.

'I've never given any injections to anything before,' I said.

'Look, it's simple,' she said. 'Thump the side of his neck like this.' Thump. Thump. 'Then plunge the needle straight in.'

The needle was over an inch long. What if I hit the wrong place? What if I hurt him? What if it broke . . .?

'Look, it's easy,' she said, and banged the needle into the side of Shandy's neck again. 'Now you try it.' She handed it to me.

'Go on. His skin's as tough as leather. Come on,' she urged.

I grabbed the syringe, clenched my teeth and jabbed. I felt the needle hit – well, hit leather, then go through. I pushed the syringe.

'There,' she said, scrambling up and getting all her things together. 'That wasn't bad, was it?'

I felt better.

'That should do it, but call me in two days if there's no improvement. Oh yes, and take this.'

She handed me a large plastic bottle with a bright turquoise mixture inside.

'It's our special cocktail,' she laughed. 'It will help dry him up as well as feed him. Keep him off milk for two days and gradually introduce it again in weaker mixtures.'

As we walked back to her car she was telling me about her hospital work.

'We had an old man in last night who'd had a heart attack. The doctor who was on just couldn't give him the injection. Kept looking at him.' She threw her bag and coat into the boot. 'I grabbed the syringe from him, jabbed it in him myself and gave him the shot. I saved his life but I shouldn't have done it though. I'll probably get fired.'

'Fired?' I exclaimed. 'Why?'

'Part-timers are not supposed to give injections.'

'Yes. But that's stupid. Didn't you tell them you were a vet?'

'Tell them I'm a vet! The old man would probably have had another heart attack,' she laughed, climbing into her car. 'How would you feel going into hospital and being treated by a vet?' She switched the engine on. 'I'll have the shandy next time,' she shouted as she roared out of the farm gate.

I went back to the calfhouse and had another look at little Shandy. He was still lying down in the pen. I rigged up a lamp for him and cut up one of my old jumpers, pushed it over him and pulled his legs through the holes I had made. He was resting his head on his front legs like a dog. He still looked miserable but he was now flapping his ears. Maybe the injection was beginning to work. I gave him some more straw and tucked him in. I then started feeding all the other calves. I mixed the milk and tested it to see if it was the right temperature. All down one side of the calfhouse there were no problems. All the calves lapped it up like mad. A couple got so excited they managed to lift the buckets out of their holders and fling them across the stable. One or two were problems. One calf, Bacardi, a tiny Hereford cross, would only sup if I kept my fingers in his mouth. As soon as I took them out he stopped. Pernod, a lovely off-white Charolais, was worse. He would take only two or three sups then stop altogether. If I put my fingers into his mouth a hundred times and then gently pushed his head into the milk he still refused to drink any more. He just would not drink. But somehow, unlike poor little Shandy, he was as tough as an ox. I kept thinking I must learn more. I'll have to take that course in calf rearing.

*

Mike Farrant, the dairy farmer across the ridge from our fields, whose land bounded most of ours and whose house was the only one we could see clearly on the horizon, occasionally sold me a calf or two. He still farms there today.

He is a tall thin man who always carries what looks like the world's entire problems on his shoulders.

'Hi, Mike,' I would say extra cheerfully. He'd look up from whatever he was doing with doleful eyes, a meek smile and a frown at the same time.

'How's things?' Always a dangerous question but it came out before I realized.

'Oh, well, I don't know . . . it's bad, very bad,' he'd begin.

He certainly did have problems. His father had rented the farm called Burnt Oak on a three-generation lease so Mike had felt safe in the knowledge that his two sons, Martin and Stephen, would follow him in farming. Then suddenly about two years after we moved to the area the owners somehow broke the lease, found a small let-out clause, and told him he would have to buy the farm or get out.

Mike only knew farming so there seemed to be no option. He borrowed the money and has probably been in debt ever since. His sons help him now. Stephen is tall, ginger-haired and obviously a born farmer. Martin goes to all the wild parties, dyes his blond hair all colours of the rainbow and likes fast cars.

Mike set up a free range chicken farm with his wife Doreen to make more money and that brought him even more worries. Everything in life was sent to worry Mike. But no matter how down he was or how busy on the farm, he and his sons were always ready to offer help. Farmers help farmers no matter how busy they are because one day they will want help themselves.

I added to Mike's worries. When we planted the vineyard I called in to see him.

'How's things?'

I got a defeated look.

'Oh,' he groaned, 'I got a cow gone down with mastitis, another with milk fever, one of the milking units has conked out, the fox has had some of the chickens, Martin had to be rushed to hospital after a crash last night, the roof of the old barn is about to cave in, one of the tyres on the tractor has got a puncture and I'm having trouble with the couple who've just moved in over the road.'

Where do I start, I thought.

'How's Martin, is he okay?'

'God, I don't know, Gay,' he said, 'but they said he should be okay. Probably be in plasters for months.'

'What's the problem with the new neighbours?'

'Damn townies,' he groaned. 'They came into the country because they like the country. And what do they do?'

He was shaking his head and looking even more pained.

'Well, what have they done?'

'They've complained, would you believe, about the smell.'

He threw back his hands in the air in desperation.

'What smell?' I asked.

'Exactly.' He tried a smile but it didn't work.

'There's no smell,' I said, trying to give him a boost.

'They don't like the smell of the silage. Now I ask you, what do they expect in the country?'

Mike had a huge silage pit by the road, near the big sheds where he wintered his cattle. Now silage does have a smell, it's true, which I had only discovered at this stage in my life. Silage, for those who are not initiated, is fresh new grass cut early in the season and either put in a huge pit or piled high then made airtight by sheets of polythene and weighted down, usually by old tractor and car tyres. It 'cooks' or ferments as the grass heats up and ends up looking like thick matted wet brown hay. But it is highly nutritious and cows love it. It has quite an aroma but it's a sweet smell, not at all repugnant.

'Oh ignore them,' I suggested cheerfully, 'if that's all they have to think about why should you be so worried?'

'They've complained to the Council,' he groaned even more.

'Don't worry,' I laughed. 'I'll support you. Us countryfolk should stick together. You're a farm. What do they expect you to smell like, a perfumery? Essence of Dung? Eau de Silage?'

He managed a half smile.

'You're doing the right thing,' he said.

'What do you mean?'

'Not going into farming.'

'Well, it's about that I want to have a word with you.' I tried to sound as light-hearted as I could but his face darkened.

'Don't worry,' I reassured him. 'It's just that it's about the vineyard. You know it's planted in the field next to yours . . . I mean . . . I don't know how much you know about vines . . . they're quite hardy really but . . . well I have to be a bit careful you see . . .'

I had rehearsed this conversation several times. How do you tell a farmer who has lived and worked on his farm all his life that if he uses sprays of any kind on his land that will damage the vines, you can sue him! Especially a man like Mike.

'Oh! Is that why you're here?' he said.

'Well . . . I need to check . . .'

'You don't have to worry.' Mike's face brightened a little as though my message was not to tell him that the end of the world was nigh. 'You're worried about any herbicides I'll be spraying, aren't you?'

'Well, yes.' I was frankly surprised he had thought about it.

'Don't worry,' he assured me even more cheerfully. 'If I use anything I'll come and check with you first. But I've already been in touch with the Farmers' Union to see what information they have.'

'Oh, that's very decent of you.' I was so relieved.

'Well, I brought it up at our last meeting,' he said. He was one of the local officials which was another of the burdens he carried. 'One of our members, who shall remain nameless but who farms near your land . . .'

'Oh, I've met him . . .'

'Well, he said he was here before you so you'll have to fit in with him and not he with you. I don't think that's quite the attitude. After all we're all neighbours and you've got to earn a living off the land the same as we have.'

'Quite right,' I cheered. 'But does he realize that if he damaged my vines with any spray I could take him to court?' There, I had said it.

'Probably not but don't worry,' he actually laughed, seeing the funny side of that remark. 'I'll try and make sure he toes the line.'

'Thanks, Mike.' I started to walk towards the road. 'That's a great help. You've made my day. And if you need any back-up over the Perfume de Burnt Oak let me know.'

He laughed and his frown lifted.

All this had come about as a result of a meeting I had attended of the WDVA – the Weald and Downland Vineyards Association – a daft name, I thought, because apart from people living there no one else knew where the Weald or the Downland was!

I had joined to meet other growers and had struck up a friendship with one or two members. The meetings were not exactly riveting but now and again there would be a guest speaker who would talk on a subject mildly relevant. At the last meeting we were handed a leaflet about herbicides and fungicides issued by the Ministry of Ariculture.

One member stood up, slightly the worse for too many tastings, and said: 'I live next door to a farmer who last year used a highly toxic spray that killed some of my vines and ruined the others for that whole year – by the way I have four acres. Is there anything I can do?'

Several people shouted out things like 'Shoot him!' and 'Typical!' and 'Shame!' and 'Let's get him!'

The chairman said: 'Well, yes. You can sue him for the damage and the loss of the crop.'

One member stood up: 'Have you taken issue with him over this?'

The slurred voice behind the beard said: 'Well, it's difficult . . . he's my father-in-law.'

Debbie was working for us now and was a great help. She helped with everything. She'd been riding since she was a little girl. Her first pony she'd bought with her own pocket money. As her father kept sheep and worked on a farm, she knew a little about animals.

'My dad says if you've got feeding problems with calves you should get a cow,' she said as she started helping me clean up the calf pens. 'Calves always go to a cow. Especially a friendly old mother cow who likes calves.'

'We could try it,' I said.

'It would be good for the calves,' she said.

'I'll think about it,' I said, although the last thing I had time to do was think.

Once we had planted the vines, everything seemed to happen incredibly fast. One day the vineyard was a dusty, yellow field covered in neat lines of black plastic. The next day it was covered with the fastest growing grass and weeds in the world. The little vines which, when we planted them, were barely two inches high had sprouted and the new growth was suddenly over two foot high and waving gently in the wind.

Now a part of every day was spent trying to keep on top of the grass and the weeds which were still growing like wildfire. I had taken the plunge and bought a brand new 'mini' tractor just for the vineyard and with it a mower. It was a bright orange Kubota costing over five thousand pounds but it was worth it. After the bigger Massey it was a joy to drive. This time I had a full demonstration by the rep. And this time I had a proper manual – all 216 pages of it, most of which I couldn't understand.

The new mower meant I could charge down between the vines and keep the grass down. But along by the plastic sheeting it was difficult. The grass was either growing in great big thick tufts or it was spreading from one side to the other practically hiding the plastic from view altogether.

'Spray weedkillers.' That's what everybody kept telling me. 'It's the only way.' But I didn't want to risk the vines. It could set them back. If I used a contact weedkiller there was the risk that some would splash on to the vine leaves. If I used a residual weedkiller there could be some damage to the roots. And in any case I wanted to avoid as many chemicals as I could – for safety's sake and for the environment.

The only alternative was a brushcutter. I would need a heavy duty one, not the sort that most gardeners use for trimming the edge of the lawn but one that would tackle even the thickest growth.

Ruth and I tried it the first day we hired it. Harnessed to each of us in turn it sped through the weeds. But there was a problem. Rip. Rip. As we got close to the polythene it just cut it to ribbons.

'It's no good,' I said.

'It's noisy too,' said Ruth.

We both looked at each other.

'It's a hands and knees job, isn't it?' said Ruth.

In the calfhouse the vet was giving Pina Colada a hefty jab.

'Scours, again,' she mumbled. 'This is costing you a fortune, the number of times I've been here.'

'I'm not going to let him die, you know,' I said firmly.

'Most farmers would let it die,' she said. 'It just isn't worth the money. I think you know what to do now,' she went on. 'I've got to go to the abattoir. They've got problems with the chickens. They're slaughtered all right but after that some get an infection and some don't. I don't understand it.' She threw her bag in the back of her car, leapt in and drove off. 'Of course you could get a cow,' she shouted out of the window.

I went back to the vineyard. As I got to the gate I could see Ruth across the field on her hands and knees.

And there was still the vegetable garden to weed.

'Why don't you spray?' Debbie asked.

'Can't,' I said. 'Sprays damage the vegetables. What's the point of growing fresh vegetables if they're going to be covered in chemicals?'

'Yes. But weeds . . .'

'Oh it's no problem,' I said, dropping down on my knees. 'You can easily weed by hand. A bit of hard work never hurt anybody.'

By the time I was ready to give the calves their evening meal I reckon I must have spent over three hours on my knees. I felt like a Spanish peasant visiting Lourdes. My knees were red, my legs ached, my muscles had locked, I could hardly move. Debbie lifted me to my feet.

'Well. What do you think?' I said.

We both looked at the vegetable garden. There was the tiniest corner of civilization. The rest was still covered by tropical rain forest. How I fed the calves that night I can't remember.

'Must have another look at Pina Colada,' I mumbled at Peter after we had had dinner that evening. I left him going upstairs to his office and went out into the chilly night. The next thing I remember is waking up just after midnight sitting on a bale of straw alongside Pina Colada's pen.

'Where're we going?' asked Ruth.

'It's a surprise. But it will make life easier.'

'Oh yeah.'

That morning Debbie had come in with the *Friday-Ad*.

'Advertisement here for a cow,' she said. 'I just thought . . .'

'House-cow needs good home. Good milker. Calves well.' I read.

The farm was between Haywards Heath and Newick and it would take only half an hour to get there.

'Ruth,' I called, 'want a trip out?'

'Anything but weeding,' she replied.

We jumped in my new little Mini-van. Well, new to me. It looked about fifty years old and was falling apart but it was easier to drive than the old Land-Rover. And not so expensive to run. Elsa leapt in the back.

Crystal was a dream. She was dark brown for a Jersey with those big droopy eyes, big wet nose and a wonderful deep moo. She seemed friendly and manageable. Nowhere near as big as a Friesian, she was about the same size as our donkeys – maybe a little bigger. Which meant we shouldn't have problems controlling her, I thought.

The farm she was on near Haywards Heath was pulling out of the dairy business, so they were selling most of their milkers. I'd never bought a cow before but she seemed nice and friendly so I agreed to take her for £275.

'She's used to the milking machine,' said the dairyman, stroking her and obviously very fond of her, 'although the boss advertised her as a house-cow.'

'We haven't got a machine,' I said. 'We're going back to the natural way.'

'Gor. I remember my old mum milking by hand every morning. She taught me when I was six,' he smiled. 'Those were the days. Farming's all different now. She could strip out a cow in less than ten minutes.'

'Could you just show us?' Ruth said.

Within seconds he had a mug of milk.

'Go on,' he said, 'best milk you can get . . . the natural way. None of this 'ere treated stuff.'

Ruth hesitated. 'It is safe?'

'Don't be daft, Ruth,' I said, grabbing hold of the mug and taking a drink, 'what do you think they did years ago?'

'I know but is it clean?'

'Gor. It's straight from the udder, girl. Can't get more natural than that.'

As we drove off the dairyman was saying: 'I'll be sorry to see her go, won't I, old girl?' Wiping what looked like a tear from his eye.

'Don't worry, she's going to a good home,' I shouted.

The following five days before she could be delivered we spent wrestling with the grass cutter in the vineyard, trying to control the weeds in the vegetable garden and tying the vines to the canes to help them grow straight. Not to mention feeding the donkeys, geese, chickens, looking after the calves and nursing Pina Colada.

The old piggery had two natural partitions and we had already used it for the geese, the donkeys and the calves. But the geese now had an old green-painted garden shed to go in at night, the donkeys had a rough shelter near the vegetable garden and the calves had the old stable which was temporarily called the calfhouse. So the old piggery, which had not seen a pig for years, became the cowhouse. To this day it is called the cowhouse. You can imagine visitors who ask for our restaurant being a little surprised when they are told: 'Go through the cowhouse.'

We gave it a good clean out for Crystal's arrival, removing all the old straw and manure through the tiny ancient door just wide enough for a small wheelbarrow.

'I hope we can get her in.' It suddenly occurred to me that we might have problems.

We disinfected the floor and walls, put fresh straw down and got ready a feed bucket and a water bucket. I realized that the building was not completely suitable because it didn't have a gully for all the liquid waste and there was no water supply apart from a stand-pipe outside. Another job to be done!

Crystal arrived in a cattle truck all by herself. She seemed to be very snooty about us at first. She stood in the back of the truck surveying us, trying to make up her mind whether to stay or not. She then ambled down the ramp with a full udder swaying beneath her and thought a long time about joining us. Once she was on dry land again we tried to lead her into the cowhouse. No luck. She wouldn't budge.

'Get a stick,' said the delivery man. 'That'll move her.'

'No,' I shouted. 'Leave her alone. It's all new to her. She's getting used to us.'

At which she presented us with our first batch of cow dung. Ruth and I patted her on the head.

'Well you can't leave her there,' he said.

'We'll get her in, don't worry,' I said.

'You'll have to,' he laughed. 'Otherwise you'll have to milk her there.'

I looked at Ruth. Ruth looked at me.

'Well you're going to have to milk her soon, aren't you?' he said slowly. 'Look at her udder, she's bursting!'

We looked at each other again.

'Well you can't let the calves take everything, can you?' he continued. 'I mean, you'll never know how much they've taken. And what if you've got a calf who won't come for its milk?'

'I know. I know,' I said. 'I'm not daft.'

Ruth looked at me.

'Just trying to help, lady,' he said and jumped into his lorry and drove off.

Eventually Crystal managed to put one foot in front of the other and swayed and stuttered her way to the cowhouse like an elderly granny on her first day at the old people's home. As she approached the entrance she stopped again. Her stomach was so big she looked wider than the door.

'We'll have to push her in,' I said.

'But what if we can't get her out once she's in?' Ruth asked.

'We'll worry about that when it happens.' A favourite reply of mine.

We got behind her and were about to push her through when she repeated the performance – all down the front of my jacket!

'We're certainly going to have lots of manure for the vines,' Ruth laughed.

'Push,' I called.

And with one go she was in. We put her in her new pen and I closed the gate.

'Well, I don't know how to do it,' Ruth said.

'Of course you do, it's easy,' I said, removing my jacket.

'You do it then. You've got to squeeze and pull,' said Ruth, 'or is it pull and squeeze?'

'You have a go.'

We got a clean bucket and decided we should milk her outside the pen on the concrete floor. As we opened the gate again she charged out, had a good sniff everywhere and then, after about ten minutes, leant across her gate to grab a mouthful of hay.

Just as Ruth got her hands underneath and the bucket in place Crystal did what we dreaded. It splattered over the concrete floor and some went in the bucket.

'Oh shit,' I laughed.

'Precisely,' said Ruth.

I started to squeeze one teat. Squirt.

'Hey,' I cried, 'look at that!'

Another squeeze. Nothing.

'Squeeze and pull,' said Ruth.

An hour later, taking it in turns, we had about an inch at the bottom of the bucket.

For the next hour we must have followed Crystal round and round the pen. As soon as she stopped I would grab a bucket, push it under her and pull. Then she'd be off again. And again. And again. And again. We tried putting a halter on her and tying her to the gate but the halter seemed to be made of elastic. If she didn't pull backwards and forwards, she swayed sideways. Once, when she jammed me hard up against the gate, I thought I was going to be squashed to death.

Eventually, more out of exhaustion I think than boredom, she actually stood still for about thirty seconds. In that time I managed to get at least three eggcups of milk out of her, which for my twelfth attempt I thought wasn't bad. I mixed the splash of milk with some warm water and gave it to Pina Colada. His ears twitched a little more. Maybe this was the answer.

Within a week we were experts. Ruth was milking away as if she had done it all her life. Sometimes she got two gallons out of Crystal in the mornings, sometimes more. In the evening it was usually about a gallon.

Crystal soon settled into her new home and I think she liked all the attention she was getting from Ruth and me as well as the children. I had read in my self-sufficiency book about feeding her and we gave her the cow nuts recommended by Stan at SCATS. But she liked anything and everything. She loved bread and even Polo mints!

I remember the first day we put her out on grass shortly after she arrived. She tossed her head about and jumped around with her udder swaying so frantically it looked as though it would drop off! She was like a young calf full of the joys of living.

Pina Colada had recovered and was bursting with energy. His pen in the calfhouse was now too small. Instead we built a pen for him alongside Crystal who regarded him as her very own, licking him when she could. Crystal was the answer to his prayers as well as ours.

One morning we had finished milking and were going down the vineyard to tackle the grass again. There was a screech of brakes in the lane. As I ran to the gate, the vet came in.

'Just passing,' she said. 'Just left the abattoir. I thought I'd look in and see how Pina Colada was doing.'

'Fantastic,' Ruth said. 'No problems. He's getting his milk now. Three times a day.'

'You got a cow then?'

'Sure. Crystal. She's lovely.'

'I thought it would do the trick.'

We took her into the cowhouse to meet Crystal.

'Now about Pina Colada,' I said.

'Sorry,' she said. 'Later. Got to go. Got a calving to do now.'

I walked up the lane with her to her car.

'The abattoir,' I said. 'Did you ever find out what was causing the problem?'

'You'll never believe it,' she said climbing into her car. 'The man who did all the killing – a big fat man, about twenty stone who's so big he has to wear two aprons to go round him – well, he was killing the chickens and gutting them. Then, to relieve the boredom I suppose, he would put love letters inside the chickens to the women at the end of the line who did all the packing. Most of the time they saw them and took them out. But, of course, they missed some and that caused the infection!'

CHAPTER THIRTEEN
Sancerrely Yours

'Don't be Pouilly-Fuissé,' I began.
Silence.
'But if it's raining you will probably have your Macon.'
Silence.
'Be Sancerre at all times.'
Silence.

It was dreadful. It was awful. It was more than dreadfully awful. I just wanted to be anywhere but at the Hailsham Rotary Club Annual Dinner where the only beverage seemed to be . . . beer!

'I read about you in the *Courier*,' said the secretary from his office in Hailsham High Street, referring to the article about the vineyard that had recently appeared.

'Oh. I hope you enjoyed the piece,' I replied politely, feeling a bit like a celebrity.

'It's just that we are looking for a guest speaker for our annual do. The person we wanted and booked can't come now. We're desperate.'

Well, it wasn't exactly the kind of invitation a celebrity would get and it could have been put a little better but what the hell. It was my first request to give an after-dinner speech.

'We'll give you a free dinner,' said the coaxing voice, 'and you never know, you might sell some of your wine.'

'I'm not producing any wine yet,' I said.

'That doesn't matter. Please say yes . . . it would save me a lot of bother.'

The secretary was obviously well versed in all the social graces and I thought things had to get better, so against my better judgement, I decided to do it. Anything for a laugh. And it would be good practice for the future!

'Won't you be nervous?' Ruth asked.

'Well, I've only got to chat away for fifteen minutes and I could start promoting our wine. I know we haven't got any but one day . . .'

When Peter got home that evening I didn't tell him I was going to do it. Instead I asked: 'Do you think I should agree to give an after-dinner talk to Hailsham Rotary?'

Without any hesitation came the expected reply. 'Of course, it'll be good practice . . . pave the way for the future. They might all be customers one day.'

'Well you're coming too,' I declared.

'Oh . . . do I . . .?'

'Yes! I'm not doing it by myself. In any case we're invited to dinner.'

'What do they want you to talk on and for how long?' Peter asked over our dinner that evening.

'Wine, English wine. Anything so long as it's about wine,' I said.

'It will have to be funny,' said the expert.

Both of us had been guests and sometimes organizers of various functions which required speakers, particularly after Peter set up his management consultancy business. I remember one seminar ending with a dinner at which the chairman of the company, which was one of Peter's clients, made a speech. Peter had suggested politely that the speech should be short and amusing since everyone had done nothing but listen to serious lectures all day. Peter wrote a brilliant and funny speech for him. But instead he spoke for over half an hour on the history of the company, his family and politics. Guests were falling asleep, making excuses to leave or just shuffling about looking at their watches.

'Tell you what,' Peter said. 'I'll write it for you. It will be fun writing one about wine.'

'Oh would you?' I was pleased – one less job to worry about. I could hear his brain going full steam ahead.

I was to give the talk on the Saturday evening in two weeks' time so there was plenty of time to practise and learn it by heart. I wanted to appear professional and not have my head buried in notes. I had been to some Rotary dinners in London as a cub reporter and the ones I had attended had been pretty good do's.

By now our morning and evening chores were getting more and more. But despite the fact that we did not eat many eggs it was a joy to gather them in the mornings and Ruth and I took it in turns to clean out the chicken house. Maurice was doing his job too. Every morning without fail he would cock-a-doodle-do again and again. We were at least sounding like a farm!

In the meantime there was also my calf course to think about. I had to be up bright and early to get all my chores done, walk the dog and be off by 8.30 a.m. It was organized by the Agricultural Training Board and I had to be at Yew Tree Farm, fifteen miles away, by 9 a.m. sharp, equipped with wellingtons, waterproofs, notepad, pen and a packed lunch.

When I arrived on the first morning, dead on 9 a.m., there was no one about.

'Hello, anyone there?' I called as I walked around the farm-yard. I could hear cattle across a large concrete yard that was spotlessly clean. I walked in the general direction of the noise and soon found myself in a large cattle shed with lots of Friesian cows obviously waiting to go out to pasture.

'Hello. Anyone there?'

Again, no reply.

I couldn't get past the cattle so I came out to see a young lad coming towards me.

'Am I at the right place for the calf course?' I asked.

'I suppose so,' he said. 'I'm on it too.'

'Where is everyone?' I said. 'I was told to be here at nine. It's already ten past.'

After half an hour two other young men of about eighteen arrived and I was beginning to feel out of place. Then a large red-faced man turned up from the direction of the house some way away.

'Hello, I'm Stan. This is my farm. You lot here for the calf course?' he said.

'Yes. I was told to get here at nine,' I said.

'Ah, well, Mr Baker is going to be a little late – about ten o'clock he says – so why don't you wait in that shed over there and I'll be back in a minute.'

'What a way to run a course!' I half mumbled to myself and the others who didn't seem to mind at all. They were on a day off from the farms where they were training.

Shortly afterwards a young girl in her teens arrived and, thank goodness, a few minutes later a man of at least fifty.

At about ten past ten Mr Baker arrived with an armful of literature, a large briefcase and a red face.

'So sorry to keep you. My name is John. I suppose you've had a chance to look round,' and without waiting for an answer said, 'Good.'

We all had to introduce ourselves and say why we were doing the course and in turn we were each issued with a clear plastic folder with a blue flap on which the words 'Training Recommendations' were printed. Inside were twenty blue leaflets, each headed 'ATB – Calf Rearing' and each with a suitable drawing in the middle relevant to the sub-headings like 'Mixing Milk Substitute', 'Training a Calf to Drink and Bottle Feeding', 'Castrating Calves' and even 'Disposing of a Dead Calf'.

My annoyance at having been kept waiting, or rather at having had to rush my chores and Elsa's morning walk, gradually faded as I began to feel confident that it really was going to be worthwhile after all.

The older man in our group, called Dick, was about to set up his own smallholding and the girl had been sent by her father who ran a farm near Brighton.

Mr Baker, or John as he insisted we call him, gave an introduction and explained what we would be doing all day.

'We've got a lot to cram in so don't let's waste time eh?' No one said a word.

The day was crammed with instruction. My earlier misgivings were unfounded. Both John and Stan, who we were reminded had given up a day's work to act as fellow instructor, took us through from buying calves, what to look for, making pens, feeding, weighing and ear-tagging before lunch. But since I had more or less mastered these skills already I was looking forward to the afternoon session.

'How many calves does your father have?' John asked the seventeen-year-old girl who looked more like fifteen and was called Anne.

'Two hundred,' she said.

'And you three?' he looked at the boys.

'About eighty,' said one.

'Fifty,' said another.

'About the same,' said the third.

I was feeling a bit sheepish.

'What about you, Dick? How many calves do you want to rear?'

'Well,' Dick obviously felt the same as I did, 'I only want to start with a few . . . see how I get on, you know . . . maybe a dozen.'

'And Gay?'

'I started with two,' I said with utter confidence, 'and now I have twenty.'

'Right. That's fine, everyone, a real mixture.'

We munched away at our packed lunches and Dick started asking me about my calves.

'Aren't you the lady with the vineyard?' John interrupted.

'Yes,' I beamed, 'how did you know?'

'Can't remember . . . oh yes, didn't I read about you in the local paper?'

The rest of the lunch break was devoted to questions from the group about the vineyard. It obviously made a welcome change from calves.

'Right, let's move on,' said John. 'We've got lots to do. This afternoon we're dealing with sickness and in particular scours.'

By 4.30 I had grilled both John and Stan on the various problems I had encountered. No one else seemed to ask questions or perhaps they didn't have a chance.

'Right, tomorrow it's castrating and de-horning. Be here at nine sharp . . . don't be late!' and off John roared in his red Mini.

'How about . . . don't get S-c-h-lossed . . . or don't R-io-j-a the boat!' Peter said as soon as he got into the house that evening. He had been writing my talk in the train.

'Yes, that's fine,' I said. 'I'm doing castration tomorrow . . . I don't fancy that.'

'Ugh,' said Peter, 'what's for dinner? Veal?'

'Definitely not!' I said, 'although I suspect one of them on that course works for a veal producer.'

'Don't tell me you gave them a lecture against veal production,' Peter laughed as he went upstairs to change.

The following morning everyone was at Yew Tree Farm by ten past nine, including John.

'De-horning first,' he said, 'then castration.'

'Sometimes pays to do it at the same time,' laughed Stan, 'then the poor little beggars don't know which end to think about!'

'According to the law an anaesthetic must be used . . .'

I had left de-horning and castrating to our vet but I thought I had better learn.

'. . . and it should be done under one month old.'

A calf was waiting in a pen for the demonstration which was to be done by Stan. He jumped in the pen and pushed the calf into a corner with the calf's head between his legs.

'Can I have a volunteer please?' he asked.

No one volunteered.

'Come on, Gay,' he said, 'let's show the men!' I was relieved in a way. At least someone else would be picked as the castration volunteer.

I got into the pen.

'Right, you hold the calf's head to one side . . . watch, everyone . . . to the right and make sure his back end doesn't swing round. Now we'll do the right horn bud first. Gay get the scissors and clip the hair over the bud . . . a bit more . . . just a bit more down towards the eye . . . watching, everyone, how I am holding the calf by the ear? . . . you should be able to do this without any help.'

He pointed to where I thought he was going to put the No. 18 three-quarter-inch needle with the anaesthetic cartridge.

'Now, Gay, inject the anaesthetic just below the ridge of bone midway between the horn bud and the eye.'

'Shouldn't you do this? I've done injections before but not this one near the eye,' I kind of pleaded.

'Come along,' urged Stan, 'you're here to learn.'

'Before injecting the needle, coat the area with the skin antiseptic on the cotton wool. That's right. Good. Now I'll hold the head firm. Just insert the needle here, at right angles to the ridge . . .'

The calf's eye was looking back in my direction. And all the other eyes in the room were on me.

Don't be daft, I thought. Get on with it. With a deep breath, I gently inserted the needle.

'Now inject half of the anaesthetic . . . that's it. Good. Now we'll do the other side. Come on, Dick, you have a go.'

John had switched on the de-horning iron. 'We're using electric ones but often you'll find the calor gas ones are used simply because of lack of electricity.'

I had already seen the calor gas one used and I thought that the sound of the hissing and the flame must be a bit unsettling for a calf.

'Now, Gay again.' Stan was persistent. 'The end of the iron should be placed over the bud and turned in a half circle several times to burn a dented circle round the bud.'

I could feel the heat of the iron near my face as I bent down. The poor little calf was beginning to struggle, sensing the impending operation. But by now the area was numb so it couldn't really feel anything.

I twisted the hot empty tube-like gadget over the bud and it singed the remaining hairs, a few of which actually caught light for a split second.

'Now dig the bud out by pressing the upper edge of the iron firmly inwards and downwards . . .'

I did as I was told.

'. . . and done correctly the horn won't grow back. Okay, Gay, let's see . . . no, not quite . . . try again.'

I did.

'Well, this sometimes happens,' Stan said kindly. 'We'll have to remove it with the scissors.'

He took the curved scissors I had used to cut the hair and snipped the top of the bud. Phewt! Phewt! Blood squirted all over my face, my glasses and hair and jacket.

'Quick, apply the iron to cauterize it.'

'I can't see . . .' But I moved as quickly as I could.

'Okay, that's fine . . . it's done.'

'Right, the other side and see if you can do it without the scissors.'

Wiping the blood from my glasses with a tissue from my

pocket I did the left bud perfectly. The poor calf was released and after shaking its head a few times ran back to join the others. I was amazed that it did not appear to be in any distress – just a little surprised.

'Right, you others have a go and then it's castration time.'

When we moved to another pen I hung back. It's not that I'm squeamish but I was covered in enough blood.

'Right, three methods. The rubber ring, the burdizzo and the knife . . . and I'm going to demonstrate all three.' You would, I thought.

We spent the next hour seeing three bull calves becoming bullocks. The ring method involves using an applicator with a very tight rubber ring, similar to the way a lamb's tail is removed – by slow strangulation. The burdizzo is a large, gruesome hand tool which looks as if it was used to extract human teeth in the sixteenth century.

'The calf suffers no stress and this is also, like the ring, a bloodless method . . .'

Stan was doing this himself. 'I'll demonstrate the cut it has.' He held up a piece of straw and the top end of the burdizzo cut it cleanly in half.

'Now the idea is to hold each testicle in turn and manipulate it to the bottom of the scrotal sac . . . see? Have a feel . . . that's right . . . feel it . . . hold one spermatic cord against the side of the sac like so . . . The castrator jaws are applied about three-quarters of the way up, like so . . . and you see I'm holding the cord just below the jaws of the castrator. Now close to grip the scrotum lightly – now firmly closed . . . and the cord is crushed like so.'

Dick was crossing his legs. The three lads had stopped smiling. The girl was touching and feeling as instructed by Stan. And I, having just about heard the moment of truth, felt sorry for the little chap!

But that was not all. Three other crushes had to be made to complete the job. Life just isn't fair for the animals.

'Next, the knife.' Stan showed a shiny stainless steel scalpel like an exhibit in a courtroom drama.

Another victim was selected.

'I bet your animals just love these courses,' I said to lighten the proceedings a little.

'Right, prepare for incision,' Stan was now sounding like a surgeon with a group of medical students, 'having first cleaned the scrotum and swabbed with antiseptic solution. Grab hold of the testicles and manipulate to the bottom of the scrotal sac . . . okay . . . with me . . . right . . . cut here with one positive stroke across the bottom of the scrotum.'

Blood starting pouring out. Dick, who hadn't looked well for some time, slipped away without a word. No one else said anything either. Silence.

Stan's hands were now quite red.

'Pull each testicle away . . .' he was straining a little, 'like so, but twist the cord and blood vessels . . . cut and there you have it.' He picked up the testicle as though it was exhibit number two.

I had already decided that this was a job I'd always leave for my vet! I'll have a go at anything but I didn't want any poor little calf to suffer while I was learning.

So there I was. In my best bib and tucker, all done up to the nine-pins, and Peter was in black tie. As soon as we walked into the pub's back room I realized what a mistake I had made. The room was packed tight with white-tablecloth-covered trestle tables, plastic stacking chairs, people and smoke.

I was expecting a little welcoming committee but instead someone said without introducing themselves: 'Oh you must be the stand-in – you're over there.'

Practically everyone was sitting down back to back in long rows ending at what appeared to be the top table. I could see two empty chairs crammed right at the far end of the top table which I assumed was where we were supposed to go.

I turned to Peter: 'Let's go before anyone else realizes we are here.'

'You're joking,' he said, 'dressed like this we're the most conspicuous people here tonight. Anyway, we've come this far.'

We had to squeeze our way past everyone on the top table to get to our seats.

I couldn't see all the room for smoke but every man appeared to be sitting down to dinner with a pint of beer and the women with glasses of sherry, Guinness or orange.

'Would you like a drink?' said a blonde woman with big dangling earrings shaped like beer bottles, in a black dress and pink apron.

'Can we see the wine list?' ventured Peter.

'Red or white house wine. That's all we have.'

'White then,' said Peter.

'That will be five pounds fifty. I'll take the money now, luv, save me a trip.'

I looked at Peter. He looked at me. The man in the middle of the top table who I assumed was the chairman was looking at his notes and hammering on the table with his spoon.

'Okay, let's have some hush,' he began.

'. . . oh yes,' he was finishing at last after twenty minutes, 'we *do* have a speaker tonight. Unfortunately Mr Harris of the Electricity Board couldn't make it at the eleventh hour. But we do have . . .' He looked at his notes for the two hundredth time. 'Is it . . .' he looked across at me, 'Mrs . . . oh yes . . . Mrs Gay Biddlestone . . . who is going to talk to us about . . . wine!'

That was a dinner I will never forget. It was like being back at my primary school in Battersea. We started with large bowls containing one spoonful of watery tomato soup. Then the waitress brought round huge dull aluminium trays containing lukewarm lumps of what I thought was chicken in a kind of pasty yellow sauce, served with huge overboiled potatoes and mushy stewed vegetables.

'At least the rolls are nice,' said Peter, trying to make the best of things.

Red jelly, tinned fruit salad and long life, pressure-whipped cream completed the meal. As watery coffee was being served the chairman rose to his feet again to introduce me, this time correctly.

I leant across and whispered in Peter's ear, 'This isn't going to work.'

'Over the top,' he said in his Hancockian voice.

And over the top I went. So over the top that I don't think anyone understood anything I said and certainly did not appreciate the puns. I did tell them what I was doing and spoke a little about the history of English wine. Every time I came to a pun or joke I slowed down to get it across better. Each time my brain was saying: 'Hurry up and get the hell out of here.' Each time Peter laughed extra loud to give the cue. And each time one or two people chuckled politely, taking Peter's lead. A number of people at the back, meanwhile, were chatting amongst themselves.

'To finish,' I said, sensing everyone's relief, 'I would like to tell a joke.'

Don't bother, my brain was telling me. Get out fast.

'. . . I ordered the claret. The waitress said, "I will have to go down the cellar to get it." I said, "Won't it be rather cold then?" To which the waitress replied, "Oh, that's okay . . . I'll put my cardigan on!"' Peter laughed loudly.

I sat down but wished the floor would swallow me up.

Peter clapped extra loud and everyone else half-heartedly joined in.

As soon as we could we left.

'I'm never giving an after-dinner talk again,' I fumed as we drove home.

'You were very good!' said Peter.

As it happened that was the first of many, all, I am glad to say, far better delivered and far better received. Now I give so many talks both at the vineyard and at various functions that that first evening is like a bad dream.

Oddly enough, several weeks after I gave the talk I was walking along Heathfield High Street when a middle-aged man in a grey suit stopped me and said: 'It's Gay Biddlecombe, isn't it? Thought your talk the other evening was fantastic. So funny. We all decided it was the best talk we'd had in years!'

CHAPTER FOURTEEN
Nun's the Word

It was pouring with rain as I drove with Elsa sitting next to me in my new old Mini-van through the big black wrought-iron convent gates just down the lane from the vineyard. It was the first time I had visited an enclosed order of nuns.

Peter, always full of bright ideas which usually mean more work, is a Catholic. He had been attending mass in the convent's tiny chapel and had been chatting to the 'out sisters' – the ones who act as go-betweens with the outside world. Then out of the blue, I got a phone call asking me to pop in and see the Reverend Mother.

'They're not going to try and get me to join you lot, are they?' I asked Peter.

'Of course not. They probably want to buy some milk or . . . hey, maybe they're interested in some altar wine!'

I didn't know what to expect. Half of me thought they might be innocent, gentle old ladies who had had enough of life and just wanted to end their days in peace and quiet. The other half dreaded a bunch of religious fanatics all hell bent on converting me to The Faith!

The convent turned out to be not your usual convent or church building but one of those oh-so-grand country houses that had obviously seen better days. Verity, next door in the village pub, told me once that years and years ago it was owned by one of her family. They were rich enough to build a huge driveway throughout the grounds so that on Sundays everybody could go for a ride in their horse-drawn carriage without ever getting their feet wet or leaving their own land.

Today, completely surrounded by a six-foot-high wooden fence to keep us out or the nuns in, it had all changed. The only part of the house that could be properly seen from outside was a small annex.

I rang the bell. The door was opened almost immediately by a happy, jolly Irish nun, Sister Monica. She looked about fifty to fifty-five although I discovered later she was well into her seventies. She had a wonderful Irish accent. She was very quickly joined by another nun, Sister Bridget, who this time had a Scottish accent. They were the two out sisters.

'I've come to see Mother Superior,' I said.

They asked me to wait a few minutes just inside the door. As I did so I could hear bells ringing all over the house. They were obviously trying to find Mother Superior and the bell ringing was a signal. A ginger cat jumped over the wooden fence and strolled up to the door. I bent down to stroke it. It purred and curled itself around my leg. Behind me I could now hear shuffling and lots of unbolting of doors.

'Cats,' sniffed Mother Superior in an Australian accent, bustling into the hallway, 'I'd put them all in a sack and drown them. Like we used to when I was at home.'

The cat turned and ran. This was not the Mother Superior I was expecting. Instead of a soft, dreamy, gentle old soul this was a brisk, tough, no-nonsense down to earth lady who seemed to crackle with energy although her face was heavily lined and she looked as if her office was a burden. I thought she was in her sixties.

'Peter has told the sisters all about his farming,' she began.

I laughed.

'We have so much grass here,' she went on, 'and it's such

hard work for us to look after it. I was wondering if you could bring some of your cattle here to graze it down? It would be free grass.'

'Well, er, yes.' I was surprised. I had been expecting a lecture on the future of my soul. 'Delighted to help.'

Then, like a businesswoman rushing off to another meeting, she was gone.

'Sister Mary Theresa is busy now. She'll call you later,' said Sister Monica.

Outside, the ginger cat was hiding in one of the apple trees.

Back in the vineyard we'd just started side-shooting, taking out the little side shoots and leaving only the main stem with its leaves. The theory was that by restricting all but the main growth the vine would develop a stronger root system in its build-up to more fruitful days. The job had to be repeated for three years or until the vine was strong enough to bear fruit.

'Gay, quick,' Ruth called all excited halfway along a row of Reichensteiners.

'Look at this. Our first bunch of grapes?'

'No, but it's good, isn't it,' I said. 'It's a bunch of flower buds. If we left it on it would become grapes but these all have to come off, for the next two years.'

'Seems a shame.'

I'd planted the vines in May and it was now August. The tiny little plants had grown to about three or four feet tall. They were almost to the top of the bamboo canes and every single one of them had side shoots at every leaf join. And every single one had to come off.

Lots of people say most vineyard work is boring and repetitive. It is repetitive to some extent but never boring – not to me anyway. But with side-shooting and quite a few other jobs you have to be gentle. Perhaps that's why foreign vineyards use a lot of female labour, I thought.

'This is going to take ages,' said Debbie, looking up and across the field.

'Not as long as it took us to plant them,' said Ruth.

I gently pulled each little side shoot off with my fingers.

'There you go; it's easy and we'll get quicker as we go,' I said in a matter-of-fact but encouraging way.

I told them about my visit to the convent as we moved along the rows. Elsa, who had disappeared on the scent of a rabbit, came back covered in mud. She looked as though she'd chased the rabbit down into the middle of its burrow. She knocked half a dozen vines sideways with her tail and ran off again.

When I got back to the house Dennis was waiting for me.

'Your sister rang,' he said.

'My sister? I haven't got a sister.'

'Well, she said sister.'

I thought for a second.

'Sister!' I exclaimed. 'That wasn't my sister. That was one of the nuns.'

I called the convent. Sister Mary Theresa wasn't there. Could I call again when they'd finished their prayers and before they all went in to lunch? On the dot I called back.

Sister Mary Theresa said, 'We're all excited. But make certain you bring them at eleven o'clock. We have a break then and can help.'

'I'd have to look at the grass first. Then the fencing. See if there would be any problems,' I explained.

'Fine,' she replied. 'Come this afternoon at two. I'll show you around.'

That afternoon Elsa and I leapt over the wall. Well, not exactly. After going through the ritual of the front door and hearing the bell signal, I was asked to go to the big wooden gates. After a few minutes I heard at least three locks being unlocked and four bolts being drawn back. As one of the gates swung open Sister Mary Theresa was there. In the distance I could see a statue and what looked like a lovely big garden. Sister took me everywhere. She showed me their orchard, which was full of old, broken-down apple trees badly in need of care and attention. I met Sister Cecilia, one of the young nuns, who was in charge of the huge vegetable garden.

'I try to grow as many vegetables as I can. Organic, of course,' she explained. 'But there are so many other things to do.'

'What? In here?' I was surprised.

'Prayer and contemplation,' she smiled.

I saw the big house and driveway that Verity had told me about. The house was obviously not at its best but the lawns were still immaculate.

'They're a problem,' said Sister Mary Theresa. 'Cutting all that grass. None of us are getting any younger.'

'You ought to get a small tractor with a mower like me or some animals. How about geese? They would eat the grass,' I suggested.

'Wouldn't that be lovely, Sister?' said Sister Cecilia to Sister Mary Theresa.

I promised to send them details about tractors and grass cutters.

We then visited the former stable block with its big square in the centre. Three sides were stables. Over the front entrance was a wonderful archway with a family crest.

'We keep all our bits and bobs here,' said Sister Cecilia, 'and this is where a lot of our practical work gets done, carpentry and so on.'

While some nuns were responsible for cooking, the laundry, even book binding, others painted, embroidered, even made candles which were then all sold to help pay for their keep. They tried to be as self-sufficient as possible.

Inside, the stable was a treasure trove which contained everything from paintings, mirrors, tables, chairs, brass candlesticks and pews to a couple of looms and a spinning wheel.

'You see,' Sister Mary Theresa explained, 'when a nun joins us some of her worldly goods come too. If they are useful we use them but otherwise they get stored away.'

There was a large pile of white china water bowls and jugs – genuine Victorian.

'Until recently we had to use them for washing but now we have proper facilities.'

I saw three enormous thick metal grills leaning up against one wall.

'They're our metal grills. Used to protect us from the world,' she grinned. 'Now we have less severe ones.'

My tour over, we agreed some minor repairs to the fencing. I said I would then deliver the calves the following afternoon, at 2 p.m. precisely.

As we were walking back about four young nuns came towards us. One bent down, pulled the bottom of the back of her skirt forward collecting the front of her skirt and tucked them into her big black leather belt from which a rosary and huge silver cross hung. She revealed eight inches of thick-black-stockinged leg and black brogues.

'Come on, Elsa,' she called as she ran off into the garden with Elsa barking and giving chase.

'How did she know Elsa's name?' I asked.

'Oh, we hardly get any visitors and news travels fast, even in here. Sister Margaret Mary couldn't wait to see Elsa. She loves dogs.'

The other nuns asked me question after question about the vineyard, the calves, what I was doing. Then suddenly there was the sound of the chapel bell.

'We'll have to leave you. Please see yourself out.'

Elsa and I then leapt back over the wall. At last it had stopped raining.

Next day I thought getting the calves into the horsebox would be easy. No way. It was as if they sensed they were being sent off before their time to you-know-where and they just wouldn't budge. We tried patting them and coaxing them but to no avail. We tried bribing them with buckets of their favourite nuts but that didn't work. Elsa barked till she was hoarse but they just wouldn't move. In the end we literally had to drag and pull and push them into the box. Inside the box I saw for the first time the original meaning of the phrase, 'scaring the shit out of you'.

I drove slowly out of the farm gate, turned left into the lane, along under the trees, past Lydia and Edgar's. I turned right towards Foxhunt Green and the convent. I was frightened to drive too fast in case they stumbled, fell over and broke their legs.

As I got near to the convent's inner sanctum gates they opened wide for me, before I had a chance to stop and go through the bell ritual. I was expected, of course. Gingerly I drove through the convent grounds and backed up to where I wanted to unload them on the roadway bounding the orchard.

It was raining again but all the sisters were there to welcome us.

'Mother Superior gave us permission,' Sister Cecilia grinned.

'How many have we got?' Sister Margaret Mary asked.

'Ten,' I replied letting down the ramp.

Only nine came out.

'But . . . but . . . but . . .' I stammered. 'I counted ten in.'

Why were there only nine?

'What are their names?' an elderly nun asked me. 'I hear you gave them names.'

'Whisky, Shandy, Gin and Tonic,' I began pointing to each in turn.

They all laughed.

'You mean they are all called after drinks?'

'Yes, of course,' I replied. 'Whenever anything happens to any of them we always have the drink the calf is named . . .'

A bell rang in the distance. Immediately the nuns all turned round and filed back to the convent.

I ushered all the calves into the orchard and they ran around as though they had never been on grass before. Their heads and tails held almost erect they tore around in circles bucking. I had to leave them to it.

When I got back, Ruth came running up to me.

'Pina Colada,' she panted. 'He's here. He leapt over the top of the ramp when you drove off. I thought he was dead. He just stayed there.'

'Bloody hell,' I said, 'why didn't you call me?'

'I chased you all the way to the corner but you didn't see me.'

'Must have stunned himself.'

'But he's all right now.'

'Poor thing,' I said. 'He obviously didn't want to leave us and Crystal.'

I went down to the field to have a look at him. As soon as he saw me he came running up to me and started nuzzling me. He was obviously glad to be at home so he stayed.

For the next couple of weeks the weather was fantastic. Elsa and I spent most of the time in the vineyard with Ruth pruning and about an hour a day at the convent. Every morning after milking and feeding our ever-growing number of animals I had to go there to give the calves their breakfast of calf nuts, top up their water, make certain there was nothing wrong with them and check the fencing. Then every evening after milking the same ritual had to be gone through. Usually everything was all right. A couple of times I noticed some of the calves had scratched themselves with barbed wire but it was nothing serious. All they needed was a quick spray of wound powder or purple spray (gentian violet) and they were fine. But once I went down there and noticed two of them had milky and runny eyes. On closer inspection there was a white spot in the middle of the eye.

I called the vet. It was New Forest disease carried by all the flies. They had to have injections in the eye, something I really didn't relish. But because I had to hold them with my fingers stuck up their noses to keep them still the vet had that job. In the end they all got it. If you leave this condition an animal can go blind.

Suddenly one day, just after I'd fed and checked the calves, Reverend Mother, who was strolling the grounds, asked me if I wanted anything from the enormous pile of things they had stored in their stable block. I didn't fancy the big heavy metal grills but I agreed to have a look anyway.

'What about these?' she said, pointing out two enormous brass candlesticks. 'And these?' Two big flower stands. 'And these?'

In the end I said I'd buy the candlesticks, the wrought-iron flower stands and an old stool. I said I'd try to sell the rest for them, including two huge looms.

I even bought the big metal grills in the end. I thought they might be useful in the big barns when we eventually came to storing all our wine. They would create the château atmosphere. But I also felt sorry for the nuns, who obviously needed the money.

One afternoon, after a last spurt in the vineyard to finish the side-shooting and another assault on the grass and weeds, I swung through the six-foot fence into the convent grounds and almost collided with one of the sisters driving her new tractor at full speed.

'Hey, steady on,' I laughed.

'It's fantastic,' she said. 'I get everything cut in half the time and it's fun!'

Somehow, whenever I went, some of the nuns were always there. They seemed to have adopted the calves.

'We love your calves,' Sister Cecilia said to me. 'It's the fatted calves we don't like!'

She took me into her little hide-away in the old Coach House where she spent her free time melting down left-over bits of wax from the candles in the convent and making very colourful modern ones.

Others told me why they had become nuns. One said that she had loved wild parties, travelling and generally having fun. She also admitted, to my surprise, that she liked the company of men. But she could not resist the calling to be a nun. Again to my surprise, she said she did not agree with everything about

Catholicism but being a nun in the convent was the only way she could find peace and serve God, as well as being the only way to change things.

An elderly nun told me that theirs was the convent in Rumer Godden's famous novel, *In This House of Brede*.

'She came and spent a long time with us,' she said. 'Then went away and wrote her book.' She sighed. 'We never saw her again.'

'Cuts the grass well, doesn't it?' Sister Mary Theresa cried as she zoomed past on the new bright red machine.

'Wonderful,' I shouted, 'we'll have to call you the red peril!'

And she was gone in pursuit of more grass to cut.

'Reverend Mother was talking about you this morning,' Sister Margaret Mary said as I clambered out of the car with Elsa. 'She wondered if you wanted to buy our big metal gates.'

I was stunned.

'You mean the big entrance gates on the road?'

'No,' she laughed. 'We have another pair just like them. They're in the shed in the garden.'

They were perfect. Just made for an impressive entrance to a vineyard. They were seven feet high and together about sixteen feet across, quite old and a little rusty but nothing some good black paint wouldn't put right.

'I'll take them,' I said. 'How much?' I could picture my new grand entrance to the vineyard once we had wine to sell.

'Like everything else, whatever you think is fair.'

On the way back to the car I met the nuns coming out from one of their services. They all made a fuss of Elsa. Sister Luke promptly hitched up her long black skirt and leapt over one of the flower beds and took Elsa on a non-stop run around the gardens.

'I love the countryside,' one of the other nuns sighed. 'I'd love to go for a gallop again.'

'Why don't you?' I said.

'More important things to do,' she replied with a smile.

The nuns asked me how the vineyard was getting on and told me I was often in their prayers.

I told them about planting the vines; how we all had broken backs; how we learnt to drive a tractor; how we were pruning. I told them about all the cats, the chickens, the geese and about Crystal.

'I'd love to come and see everything,' said one of them.

'Well, come,' I said. 'No problem. We're just around the corner.'

'It's not as simple as that. Mother Superior wouldn't let us.'

'Don't tell her,' I said.

They all laughed.

They seemed to want to chat. Maybe I'd got the timing right and this time they had longer between prayers.

They asked me about my family. I told them about the ruby wedding celebrations I'd organized for my parents; how when they arrived I'd arranged, as a surprise, for all their relatives and friends to be waiting for them and how my mother spent the evening saying, 'I don't believe it. I don't believe it.'

'We'd love to come and see you,' they said.

Then the bell rang summoning them and they all disappeared like a whiff of smoke.

The next few weeks I spent practically the whole time in the vineyard keeping on top of things. The vines were now taller than the canes and swayed gently in the breeze. And I was facing a dilemma.

If I was to do the job properly, in the first year I should have started putting all the posts and wires in to support the vines. This was going to cost another arm and a leg. So I decided to risk it and leave the job till next year. My worry was that if we got very windy weather the vines might snap at the top where there was no cane to support them.

Because it was the first year, I didn't have to spray with fungicide which was just as well because the side-shooting, tying up, weeding and grass cutting took so long.

We managed to tame the vegetable garden and at last started eating our own fresh food. And Crystal was a wonderful foster mother. All the fresh milk kept the calves in perfect health. And with the cream we were all beginning to put weight on.

Then one morning I woke up at about 5.45. It was raining cats and dogs. The phone rang. It was the convent. All the calves had escaped and were running round the grounds. They were all over the lawns and were eating the flowers. They were everywhere.

'Thought we would see you today,' Sister Monica said as soon as I arrived, already dripping wet, with Elsa to begin the round-up. 'This morning in chapel we had a reading from the bible about a woman running her own vineyard.'

CHAPTER FIFTEEN
Posts, Wires and Kenward Jars

'No,' Peter said adamantly.

'But why?'

'Because we can't afford it.'

'But I can't live in a house like this with all this . . .' I waved my arms at the neat little Edwardian fireplace, the picture rail and all the heavy flock wallpaper. 'There's probably oak beams behind all this . . . this . . .'

'After we've established the vineyard.'

'Well I'm going to do it in any case.'

We were sitting in what we still called the dining room. When we bought Cross Farm it really was the dining room and had an elegant Regency table, eight elegant matching chairs and not a speck of dust anywhere. Now it was more our centre of operations. Instead of the Regency table and chairs I'd bought an old oak refectory table, more in keeping with the age of the house and its character. An assortment of old oak and wicker chairs and an old oak coffer stood where the Regency side table had stood before. In another corner was an old mangle I'd picked up for ten pounds at Heathfield market. The inglenook was now home to a wood-burning stove. There was a big bookcase in one corner where I'd started to put my growing collection of wine, gardening and farm books. Old prints and paintings hung on the walls. There was brass and copper everywhere – my collection grew every time I went to market or visited antique shops. I am a compulsive collector and hoarder.

We'd started by discussing the stakes and wires we needed for the vineyard. The vines had survived their first year tied to bamboo canes. Some had been practically flattened in the storms during winter but overall they had pulled through. Now we had to start thinking of giving them more support.

'We're training them in the Double Guyot method. It looks a better system to me.'

'What's this Geneva Double Curtain method like? Isn't it cheaper?' Peter was always thinking of our increasing overdraft.

'I don't like it,' I insisted.

'How do you know?'

'In the past two years I've seen quite a bit of it – several people are using the system but it's still new to England . . .'

'So is English wine.'

'In any case we've planted now with the spacing for Double Guyot,' I insisted, 'and I'm not going to undo all our work to save some money.'

Other vine growers were split down the middle. Some said I should use the GDC system and others said the traditional DG or double bow. If I was to change my plans now it would mean taking out every other row of vines to create wider spacing.

'And I'm just not going to do it.'

Unfortunately whatever system I chose, the posts and wire were going to be expensive. Peter was still moaning about the overdraft.

'Look. Do you want . . .?' I raised my eyes to the ceiling in despair. Which is when I saw the single oak beam above my head.

'I've been thinking,' I continued. 'If there's one oak beam here there's got to be others. I mean they're probably all resting on each other. We should pull all the ceiling down and reveal them.'

First thing the following morning I did two things. I called

Dennis and told him I wanted to start pulling down the ceilings and exposing all the oak beams. And I started working out exactly what stakes and wiring I needed for the Double Guyot system which I'd decided to stick with.

I'd need one post every fourth vine. They would have to be about eight feet tall allowing for about two feet to be below ground and they would have to be treated so they would last longer. They would need to be at least four inches in diameter because of the weight and strain they would one day take. That would be at least 1,250 posts, allowing for extra for rows of different lengths. At the end of each row the posts would have to be bigger and angled against the strain, with anchor wires held fast in the ground with cement to keep them from moving. There were 64 rows so that was an extra 128.

As for the wire, I needed one strand eighteen inches up from the ground, another single strand a foot above that, then three sets of double wires – to train the vines against and to hold the vines in – to the top. There would have to be a further strand nailed to the top of the posts to support future netting but that could wait until we needed it.

I'd need different thicknesses but after several attempts I calculated I would need about sixty thousand yards.

Extra and thicker wire would be needed for the anchors. Two anchors per row. Then there were the wire adjusters to tighten the wires, link chain adjusters, hooks so the wire would be movable, post nails, staples. Last, but not least, a post driver and lots of help.

By now my head was swimming with figures. I decided to take Elsa for a walk around the vineyard. Working out the figures on paper was one thing, but seeing the actual area we had to cover with posts and wire was something else. I went back to the house and double checked all my figures.

During the next two weeks I looked at all the alternatives for my trellis system: chestnut stakes, old telegraph poles, railway sleepers which an old farmer told me you could pick up cheap and they would last for ever. Or concrete posts. I'd read an article saying that Italian vineyards were now switching to concrete posts because of costs. Although more expensive initially, they never needed replacing and never moved in the wind. But in the end I came back to treated chestnut stakes. The Post Office couldn't guarantee me a regular supply of old telegraph posts. Then, if they did, I'd have to saw them up into the lengths I wanted. Railway sleepers were definitely cheap but somehow I couldn't see myself hammering them into the ground.

One afternoon I went to the woodyard in Heathfield. I just wanted to see what I was ordering.

'The treated ones – how much?'

'An extra forty-nine pence per stake,' the foreman said. 'But you can waterproof them yourself.'

'We'll waterproof them ourselves,' I said, quickly saving myself a few hundred pounds.

'You know how to do it?'

'No,' I admitted.

'It's quite easy,' he said. 'First you dig a pit eight by four and two feet deep. Line it with heavy duty polythene or rubber. Then you fill it with . . .'

'You do it,' I said, quickly losing the money I'd just saved.

As soon as I got out of my van I heard George giving his warning and Elsa ran round to the old barn barking her head off. There was an old man wandering around inside. He must have been about seventy years old though his arched back made him look even older. He was smartly dressed in grey flannels and a tweed sports jacket.

'I used to play here as a kid,' he said, doffing his tweed cap to me as I told Elsa to stop barking. 'In those days, of course, it was all different. Here,' he said, banging his stick on the wooden floor in the centre, 'was where they did the threshing. The horses used to come in this way.' He waved his stick out through the door towards the paddock where George and Bettie and the calves were nibbling grass. 'And out this way,' he turned and pointed to the facing wall and behind it the courtyard, 'is the oldest tithe barn in East Sussex they say.'

In the old days, he said, Cross Farm used to be the biggest farm in the area. All the farm workers lived in the village. He showed me some photographs taken when he was a child including a picture of his father in a top hat and smock with another man in a smock taken outside the barn nearly a hundred years ago.

He asked to see the old stable. As we walked up the slight ramp he said: 'Many's a time I led old Bobbie in here. He was a grand horse was Bobbie.'

When we got inside he took his hat off again and rubbed his forehead.

'Well, I never . . . it hasn't changed much. Still got the old earth floor – that's good for their feet, you know.'

I let him ramble on since not only was he giving me bits of information for my history file but he was obviously enjoying himself. Several times his old droopy eyes went red with emotion.

'Oh my goodness, it's still there,' he said.

'What is?'

'See that up there . . .' He was pointing to a small boxed-in shelf with a trap door right up against the roof beams. 'That's where I slept when I was a lad.'

We had noticed this before but had not known what it was and since the stairs had either rotted away or had been removed and our ladder did not stretch far enough we hadn't investigated further. That was one thing we had decided to leave till later.

'You slept there!' I exclaimed.

'Seems all wrong now, don't it,' he said, 'but I was glad of it at the time.'

I could see that the shelf would just about take a small man lying down.

'It was filled with straw, above all the straw and hay stored on this,' he pointed to the ceiling or first floor. 'With the horses below, I was snug as a bug in a rug. It was my job, you see, and I had no home. Me and Bobbie were great pals.' He blew his nose.

It was fascinating. We walked back into the barn.

'See that,' he said, pointing at the big metal rod which was helping to hold up the timber part of the wall facing the road. 'I remember when they put it in. And that . . .' He pointed at the thick metal bar buried in the wall holding the rod in place. 'That is the axle from a gun carriage they built for the First World War.'

He went silent for several minutes but kept shaking his head.

'I'm going over to the churchyard to pay my respects,' he said. 'Do you know, from the church tower you could see the flashes of light from the guns at the Somme and sometimes you could even hear them.'

He was fighting back tears again and he looked very frail. A lump was gradually forming in my throat too.

Just then there was an enormous crash from the house.

'Oh my God,' I cried. 'I'll be back. Please don't go. I would like to chat more.'

I ran with Elsa across the courtyard, up the steps and into the house. Dennis was standing in the kitchen in the middle of a pile of rubble. There was dust everywhere.

'Oak beams,' he choked. 'Oak beams. Hundreds of them.'

'Fantastic,' I coughed back. 'Fantastic. Carry on.'

When I got back to the barn, the old man had gone.

I went to see George and Bettie. George knew I was the boss but he didn't like anyone else. And everyone else didn't like him. He came up to me and said hello. He now had a few more geese to boss so he had not entirely lost face. The donkeys came across and joined in. I wandered into the field to see the calves. Pina Colada came bounding over. We gossiped for a few minutes about the problems of the world. The old man had made me feel so sad. I wandered into the vineyard.

Decision time, I said to myself. Decision time. We'll go ahead, sod the expense. The grand scheme had to forge ahead. I would order all the materials tomorrow. But better make sure of my figures first. I went back to the house and my calculations.

'But that can't be right,' I thought. 'That's much too much.'

Eustace leapt on the desk and settled down on my pile of papers. Elsa opened one eye, closed it again and went back to sleep.

It just seemed a lot of wire.

The following morning, of course, there were problems. Some of my new baby calves were playing up. I was now an expert on baby calves and all their problems. Instead of rushing for the telephone and the vet as I used to do I would do most of the work myself, except the de-horning. I hated all that blood everywhere although the calves didn't seem to mind much. One calf – I called him Mai Tai – was worse than the others. So we moved him into our emergency ward complete with new bales of straw and infra-red lamp. Instead of using a cardigan I tore up an old blanket and wrapped it round him with some baling twine. The other animals were all right but it seemed to take longer to feed them.

Ruth and Debbie were going down to the vineyard to carry on our unending battle against grass and weeds. I went to make my telephone call. Then there came another crash. This time I found Dennis upstairs in one of the rooms overlooking the church. As the cloud of dust settled and all the cats started sniffing among the rubble he grinned.

'I've found a fireplace,' he coughed. 'It's a smashing inglenook.' Behind the tiny nondescript Edwardian fireplace was a genuine inglenook with a huge bressummer beam.

'How could anybody hide that?' I coughed. 'It's crazy.'

I rummaged around inside it. Leaning up against the wall was the original fireback. They had not even bothered to move it when they blocked everything up.

Dennis hacked away at the wall alongside it. It came away in pieces. Behind it were more oak timbers. He scratched away at the surface.

'This is the original wattle and daub made with straw and dung.'

'And we're looking at it all now for the first time in over three hundred years,' I said as I noticed Eustace was also in the middle of the dust and rubble, celebrating in his own particularly feline way.

A few days later as I came back from SCATS I reckoned I was becoming an expert on wire. When I first started working out how much wire I needed for the vineyard I thought wire was wire. No longer. There are different types and thicknesses of wire. And I reckoned I knew them all.

'Look, darling,' said Stan, my friend behind the counter at SCATS, when I told him I wanted some wire. 'You tell me what you want the wire for and I'll tell you the type of wire you want. Been in farming all my life. Reckon I know the right wire for the right job. Couldn't be fairer than that, could I?'

'I want it for a vineyard,' I said.

He looked at me.

'Never heard of that,' he said, scratching his head. 'Reckon that's the first time I've heard of that. In this country? You want to plant a vine yard?' He separated the two words. 'Here? In this country? I thought you started a farm?'

'Yes,' I smiled.

'I'll have to talk to head office.' He scuttled away behind a mountain of bags of pony nuts and chaff.

'Reckon we'll send you some information,' he volunteered on his return, 'and prices.'

In the meantime I telephoned two vineyards to see what wire they used and how much.

'That sounds an awful lot of wire,' Peter said that evening as I showed him our new fireplace. 'Are you sure?'

'Are we going to do it properly or not?'

'I'm just thinking of the cost. That's all.'

'Like you kept thinking of the cost of redecorating the house . . .'

'It's only because . . .'

'. . . but I bet you're glad we did it.'

'I just said . . .'

'Your study will be the best room in the house.'

'But we've got to stop spending.'

I turned round, stamped out of the room and slammed the door. The wall alongside it suddenly shivered. Some of the plaster crashed to the ground. Behind it I could see the original oak beam door to the room.

The following morning I finally ordered the stakes, the wire, everything.

As Elsa and I were walking back from the post office in the village, two old ladies in floral dresses and cardigans were looking over the gate at the house.

'We used to play here as children,' they said. 'There were lots of places to hide.'

'I can remember the inglenooks,' the smaller, more fragile lady said, 'and the bread oven.'

'Is the oast house still there?'

I asked them to come in, wanting to know more.

One of them was a Kenward, a descendant of the family that once owned Cross Farm. She must have been in her sixties and spoke very slowly and clearly with a slight Sussex accent. She still lived in Sussex but loved coming to Waldron to relive her childhood days. She could only come, though, if a friend or son drove her.

Quite a number of her ancestors were buried in the church-yard opposite. One tombstone is my particular favourite, that of

George Kenward who sadly died in 1873 aged thirty-seven. His headstone reads:

> All ye who pass this day along
> See how sudden I was gone.
> The Lord does little warning give
> And so be careful how you live.

I had already guessed that the Kenwards grew hops in Hop Garden but now my visitor told me that there was an oast house at the bottom of our garden at one time, although all I could find on a later 'dig' was the stone base of the roundel.

I took the two ladies into the house and showed them the Kenward jars I had bought at Heathfield. There's been a produce market there for many years and on Tuesdays there were also antique and bric-à-brac stalls as well as an auction of antiques and second-hand goods from furniture to tea chests full of books.

I had previously managed to collect some old farm implements in the auction but on this particular morning I spotted a box underneath an overladen table, full of large stone beer jars. What caught my eye was the name Kenward written on the top of one. I bent down. The box was too heavy so I picked the top jar up and underneath the name N. Kenward was indented in the jar: 'wine and spirit merchant. Heathfield Station 160'. There must have been at least six of them in the box and they all said the same but had different numbers. I just had to have them. They were Lot twenty-two so, knowing the speed of these auctions, I would not have to hang around for long. Further on was a large metal chest with the name Brigadier Rupert Warham Shaw-Hamilton, Command Paymaster painted in white letters on top.

Inside were hundreds, probably thousands, of photographs – black and white, hand tinted and colour prints. There were also fifteen old albums and odd bits of photographic equipment. But it was sad. Here was a man's life in photographs, including his childhood, his army days, travels and his dogs. All his memories were here and no family at all to care.

I did not have time to inspect all the contents of the chest but the colour photographs were all local – wonderful, expertly taken and beautifully printed photographs of scenes from the South Downs up to Scotney Castle in Kent and Sheffield Park in West Sussex. There were photographs of local churches, landmarks and rural scenes and close-ups of flowers, tree bark and pebbles. The Brigadier obviously loved nature. These deserve a good home, I said to myself. Right . . . Lot thirty.

'Okay, let's start off . . .' said the elderly auctioneer. He was standing on the same level as all of us and surrounded by the bidding hopefuls. Pointing to Lot one he was off. Within twenty minutes he was at Lot twenty-two.

'Okay, a box of stone jars,' he called. 'Anyone for a beer!' His assistant picked one of the jars up and held it above his head to display it. 'There's seven of them. What am I bid? Come on, start me off then. Five pounds a piece.'

Silence. No one seemed interested.

Good, I thought, here I go.

I lifted my hand. 'Two pounds,' I called.

'Okay, it's a two pound start from Mrs Biddlecombe.' They were beginning to know me by now. 'I thought it was wine you were brewing, not beer!' he laughed.

Silence.

Then suddenly a man's voice, 'Three pounds!'

'Four.' I tried to sound casual.

'Five.' He sounded determined.

'Six,' I insisted.

We were the only two in the running and he sounded as keen as me. At last –

'Seventeen pounds, Mrs Biddlecombe?' the auctioneer said unbelievingly. I nodded.

'Any more?'

Down came the hammer. 'Mrs Biddlecombe. Lot twenty-two, seventeen pounds each.'

Within another fifteen minutes we were up to the Brigadier's chest. That was easier. Either no one had noticed it or no one was interested. I did think one or two of the bric-à-brac dealers would go for it because the photographs, split up, could be sold at 50p each and would fetch quite a bit. But I had only one half-hearted competitor who backed out at twelve pounds.

All in all it was a good morning.

As I paid the cashier he said: 'You bid high for the stone jars, if you don't mind me saying, Mrs Biddlecombe.'

'I know, but I live in the house where Mr Kenward began his beer-making business so I had to have them.' I added: 'Who was the man bidding against me – any idea?'

'Oh, he has a small shop the other side of Battle. He buys the beer jars quite a bit. Sometimes paints them and turns them into lamps. He doesn't normally bid that high though – he probably thinks you're doing the same.'

'God forbid,' I said as I picked up my receipt to collect my goods.

The Brigadier's collection told an interesting story of a career soldier who travelled extensively but mainly in Malaya and who always returned to Sussex. Some research showed that he was born on 7 April 1908 and joined the Royal Artillery in 1928. His last apparent posting was in Singapore from 1947 to 1948. From the photographs he did not appear to be married although he was a dashing man. But he did have two dogs.

Some of the photographs of Sussex hang now in my office and I like to think that his life's work and love of photography have not gone to waste.

The Kenward jars now sit on a shelf in a room of the house which overlooks Hop Garden Vineyard.

*

The two old ladies still had vivid memories of the house as it was in their day.

'This was the old kitchen – and look,' said Miss Kenward, 'the old meat hooks. They used to hang the hams here.'

Miss Kenward turned to her companion. 'This was quite a place for smugglers in the real old days. Do you remember the tunnel?'

'But we're miles from the sea,' I protested.

'Not in those days,' she continued. 'Waldron was a centre for smuggling.'

'So where's the tunnel?' I asked.

'You know the cellar?' she asked.

Know the cellar? One of the first things we had done was to clear out the cellar, put in our own wine racks and start stocking it.

'Alongside the cellar was another room just as big. It used to be a meeting room . . .'

'From there,' said the other lady, 'the tunnel goes under the road into the church grounds.'

They took me to the garden wall by the side of the house.

'Dig up the earth by the wall,' they said, 'and you'll see where the tunnel is.'

Tommy was working in the garden and doing odd jobs about the farm that week. I got him to do the digging for us. It was true – about two feet below ground level the bricks in the foundations of the wall curved as if there was a tunnel underneath.

'What did we tell you?' they said.

Just then Peter came by. He'd been out on Laddie, his new horse, who was panting, wet with sweat and mud all up his legs.

'What a ride!' he said. 'He's fantastic.'

I introduced him to the two ladies.

'They say there's a tunnel running from the cellar to the church,' I said. 'Look.' I pointed at the bottom of the wall. 'I think we should . . .'

'No,' he said.

'But why?'

'Because we can't afford it.'

'But it would be so exciting to discover the tunnel,' I began.

'It will cost too much. Be . . .'

'Just think of what it might contain,' I argued.

'And just think of how much the vineyard is costing . . . think of all the things you need . . . tractors, a sprayer . . .'

'. . . a cutter, post driver . . . yes, I suppose so,' I conceded. But as he trotted down to the stable I called: 'When I've made enough money selling my wine I'LL DO IT!'

CHAPTER SIXTEEN
A Friend for Crystal

Animals are like people, they need and enjoy company. So after a while we decided to get Crystal a friend.

Although she enjoyed having calves about her, when she was out in the field we thought she looked lonely. After all, she had come from quite a big herd. And as we now had over forty calves, we needed the extra milk.

'We're going over to Friesians,' said the Sussex accent at the end of the line. Our vet had told me of a farmer at Chiddingly who was selling off his Jerseys and I rang him almost straight away.

'Why?' I asked.

'People are getting too figure-conscious. It's you ladies that are doing it. No one buys the Jersey milk or cream any more and there's all this stupid propaganda about dairy food and heart attacks. I've lived on Jersey milk all my life and look at me.'

Well I couldn't so I wasn't able to judge, but I arranged to go and see him. Ruth and I went off early after milking. Ruth had turned Crystal out saying: 'We might bring a friend back for you today,' but I don't think Crystal understood. She put her head down straight away to start producing the next gallon for the evening milking.

As we drove down a long dirt track towards the farm we could see Friesian cows grazing on lush green grass either side. When we got to the end a wide concrete square opened up with the farmhouse on one side and the cattle sheds directly opposite.

At the far end was a huge hay store with a tractor parked outside. A collie leapt straight out of the tractor and ran to us barking.

'Down, boy!' Immediately the dog stopped and lay down wagging its tail.

The instruction came from a large man who must have been over six feet tall and at least sixteen stone in weight. He had four other collies walking to heel. At a quick silent signal all four lay down instantly as he approached us.

'You're come to see Joycey, then?' he asked.

'Well I thought you had several Jerseys,' I said.

'I did that,' he replied, 'but most of 'em have gone. I'm keeping a dozen to boost the Friesian milk a bit – wishy-washy stuff! How many cows do you run?'

'Well we only have one. We haven't got a dairy herd,' I said.

'Oh, what do you do then . . . if you want another?'

'I'm really establishing a vineyard . . .'

'What, wine!' he exclaimed, looking surprised. 'Here, in Sussex?'

'Yes. We're starting with four acres and then, well, who knows. But we've got quite a bit of land and we're not only trying to be self-sufficient but we're rearing calves. I also want to sell the cream at the farm gate.'

'So you know all about vines, then?' He was suddenly very interested.

'I wouldn't say that, but I'm learning.'

'It's just that I've got a vine in an old greenhouse – bloody thing's everywhere. I want to chop it down but the missus insists we keep it. I don't know the first thing about them.'

We were walking through the milking parlour with the five dogs close behind us. At the end there was a large pen with at least twenty or thirty cows inside.

'Jack! Ben!' the man called as he opened the gate to a field. 'Get them out.'

Two barking dogs moved to either side of the back of the

pen. As the dogs started herding the group out the man called, 'Joycey!'

A large light brown, almost yellow, Jersey looked up, tossed her head and stood still.

'Skip, get Joycey,' he called.

A third dog, liver and white instead of the usual black and white collie, ran over to Joycey and with Ruth and me looking on in amazement guided Joycey round the rear of the moving group towards us.

'I've never seen dogs herding cattle before,' Ruth laughed.

'I use them for the sheep and trialing really but I like the cattle to get used to them. The cows know what to do but now and again it helps.'

'I noticed Skip didn't bark like the others. Didn't he want to scare Joycey?' I asked.

'No,' he smiled. 'He can't bark. Got kicked in the neck by a bull when he was a puppy and hasn't been able to bark since. But he's a good 'un. I won the South-East Trials with him last year.'

Joycey was now nudging the man and eyeing us closely. She was six years old. As Ruth and I started stroking her she tossed her head and gave the tiniest skip with a not-so-full udder swinging violently beneath her.

'She's a real character,' the farmer said, 'likes a bit of mischief.'

She then started chasing Skip around the pen. It was obviously a game they had played many times before, with Skip daring her to chase him by spreading his front legs, putting his head down, wagging his tail and obviously saying, 'Come on, catch me if you can!'

For her size and shape Joycey moved quite fast and clearly enjoyed the fun.

'If she moves any faster,' I laughed, 'the milk in her udder will turn to butter!'

We fell in love with her and she seemed to take a shine to us.

So after we had a few pulls on her teats to make sure all was well we agreed on £275 including delivery.

'Come and see my vine.' The farmer was walking back towards the house with all the dogs keeping close and watching his every move. We walked around the side to the back and there was a large old Victorian greenhouse that had obviously seen better days. He had to force the door open and inside was a giant of a vine which must have been as old as the greenhouse with a huge main stem – almost a tree trunk. It had taken over completely in a huge tangled mess of old and new wood. Green stems and new leaves were just beginning to sprout all over the roof, the sides, across the door and even hanging down to the floor.

'We were told to leave it so it would produce lots of fruit but it's hardly given us any, bloody thing. Taking over, it is.'

I gulped. My reputation – not that I had one as yet – was at stake. I just wanted to turn round and leave.

'Well,' I said, 'it has been neglected, hasn't it? What variety is it?'

'I haven't the foggiest,' he replied, 'but the grapes are black and not bad – if you can get one. If the missus was in she could tell you more but she doesn't really know what to do with it. Chop it down, I say.'

'That would be a pity.' I was beginning to see it as a challenge. 'But it does need a lot of pruning – now, before any more growth appears. It's a bit late but by the time summer comes you won't be able to get in here. And the air circulation in here is poor. You must keep all the windows and door open. Judging by the size you could get quite a lot from this. It's probably a Black Hamburg.'

I was now in full command. Though Black Hamburg is a favourite dessert grape this was really an educated guess.

'Look,' the farmer said, 'I'll make a deal. You prune it for us and I'll knock the price of Joycey down. How's that?'

I wasn't looking for more work and I could tell by Ruth's eyes that she was thinking, 'You've got enough to do, leave it.'

So I said: 'Okay, you're on. How about fifty pounds?'

'Done!'

I had got my first consultancy contract!

Elsa suddenly started twitching and I woke up. It was almost 3.30. I had gone out just before midnight to look at Bambi, one of our new animals who was in the emergency ward. I had brought many calves back from the brink. But this one was different.

I'd bought him for twenty-five pounds at Hailsham Market the previous week. Bambi was the only Charolais calf at the market. He was beautiful with a white and blue-grey coat and gorgeous soft doe-like eyes. I'd bought him partly because he was so very thin and I'd felt sorry for him. I put him in a pen of his own with lots of clean straw and gave him some sugar water, made with warm water. Cold water straight from the tap might have been too much of a shock for him. He drank it all in one go which was a good sign.

Over the next few days we finally took delivery of the stakes. After I'd placed the order I suddenly thought I should have bigger stakes every fifth row in case I had to put up wind protection, so I rang the suppliers up and made them change everything. I had seen a few vineyards who had fixed thick plastic netting every fifth row throughout the vineyard to reduce the bad effects of wind – which not only brings down the temperature but can be destructive, as we were to discover in later years.

Poor Bambi didn't seem to be getting any better. His scours had stopped and he had graduated from sugar water to milk and water. I'd even given him some real pure milk from Joycey which I thought would be better for him because it was less rich and creamy than Crystal's. He lapped it up like mad but it still didn't seem to make any difference to him. He was certainly perky and would wag his tail and jump up and down in the pen whenever I went in to see him but he was still as thin as the day I got him.

The vet suggested an energy booster so I gave him a series of vitamin injections but that didn't help either. You could still see his ribs. He had not put on any weight at all.

It was in the early summer of 1981 and earlier that evening, after another hard day moving the stakes down into the vineyard and laying them out by the vines ready to be hammered in, I'd gone in to see him. For the first time he was huddled up on the straw looking sorry for himself. He waggled his ears when he saw me but made no effort to get up.

Oh no, I thought. Please let him be all right.

I called Ruth and Debbie. Quickly we built a new emergency ward for him. I fixed the infra-red lamp overhead then I picked him up and gently carried him from his pen. He didn't protest, or twitch or kick. I laid him down under the lamp and he just stayed there and didn't move. I tried him with some milk but he wasn't interested. I mixed him some sugar and water. He played with it a bit but hardly drank anything.

I had another look at him after we'd milked the cows and fed all the animals. When we first started, feeding the animals meant giving the donkeys an apple and some hay. Now we had geese, chickens, ducks and, of course, calves. It took Ruth and me over an hour every morning and every evening to feed them all.

Poor little Bambi was still the same. He was still curled up on the straw. He looked so sorry for himself I thought I'd go out and have another look at him before I went to sleep.

Peter was somewhere in Africa on business. Elsa and I were all by ourselves.

When I went back Bambi was curled up in the same position. I sat down next to him and started to stroke him. He twitched his ears from time to time. Even Elsa gave him a couple of sniffs then licks.

Christie, an Irish farmer Peter's mother had married after being a widow for many years, had told me that some calves never get over the shock of being taken away from their mothers when they are only a few days old. When they are born, calves should be put straight on to their mothers to get their first milk which is full of colostrum and builds up their antibodies. The milk is no good for anything else so a farmer has nothing to lose. At the same time it makes sure that a calf gets a good start in life. And I have always felt that it is cruel to both cow and calf to separate them this early. All mothers, whatever the species, need to look after their young.

Calves are not supposed to be sent to market until they are seven days old and there are supposed to be checks at the markets to make sure the law is complied with but I've seen it broken. Many calves are taken off their mothers after just two or three days and sent to market, sometimes the same day! Farming can be cruel and whilst most farmers love animals, I have met some who have absolutely no regard for their animals' welfare. Many calves, Christie said, could be born during the night or early morning, have their first sup of milk from their mothers in the morning; be packed off and auctioned by ten o'clock; and then transported maybe forty or fifty miles to a new home by midday. I was determined little Bambi was going to be all right. He had a good home and I was going to look after him.

All that week I spent a lot of time with him. In the mornings I would muck him out and give him new straw. Then I'd try to get him to drink. Sometimes he would, sometimes he wouldn't. I tried getting him to suck my fingers and then lowering his head into a bowl – a bucket was much too high for him. I even used a wine bottle with a teat on the end. I think he was probably the only calf in the country to drink out of a champagne bottle.

I've done it, I thought, I've done it. He's going to be okay.

Then an hour later he would be curled up on the straw again refusing to move. The vet tried everything and so did I.

On the Saturday afternoon I had to leave him for a while. I wanted to buy some pigs. The vegetable garden was becoming more and more of a problem. In the first two years it had been great growing all our vegetables and being self-sufficient. But the vineyard was taking up more time, as I had anticipated. I would have to reduce the size of the vegetable garden by at least two-thirds. The animals were also taking up much more time, which I had not anticipated.

First I thought of just letting it all grow back to grass again. Then Christie said to me, 'Pigs. Get yeself sum peegs.' Or words to that effect.

'They'll do thee job for ye. Turn over all the ground, break it up and manure it. Ye've got two cows. Ye can feed them with any milk ye've got left over. They'll be right fine creatures for ye. A handsome meal at Christmas.'

'But what about looking after them?' I said. 'I haven't got any sties or anything.'

'Glory be to goodness. Do you hear this lady,' he laughed. 'Pig sties! Not at all. You throw them out in the vegetable garden, let them live there. They'll turn up all the ground for you and dig out all those old roots. Get some corrugated iron. A shelter's all they want – three sides and a roof. They'll be the happiest pigs alive, to be sure.'

The previous day I'd seen an advert for piglets in the *Friday-Ad*. I rang up and arranged to go and see them on the Saturday morning.

The farm was about ten miles away at the back of Mark Cross on the way to Tunbridge Wells. And the farmer was a typical old pig farmer. He wore a greasy old brown coat held together with bits of baling twine. He had a big red nose with large nostrils and on his bald head was a rather grubby cap.

'They your first pigs, lady,' he said as soon as I arrived in the Land-Rover. I thought the Land-Rover was more appropriate for buying pigs than my little old van. 'Fattening them for Christmas, are you?'

We walked through his pig house. Pen after pen of hundreds of little pink piglets were running around non-stop. An enormous fat old sow was actually giving birth in a farrowing pen.

'This old lady ain't no trouble at all. Knows what to do. No trouble at all,' he said affectionately, leaning over to give her a pat. 'Given us lots of piglets haven't you, old girl.' She lifted her head off the concrete as another one popped out.

'Like clockwork, she is,' he added.

Four-week-old piglets were the best, he said. 'They've got over their mother and are able to stand on their own. Give you no trouble at all. Just throw them out in the open and they'll look after themselves.'

I said I'd take two.

'Two,' he exploded, spitting into one of the pens. 'Ain't worth having two. Not with the petrol coming here to get them.' He grabbed one piglet and started stroking it like a cat. It squealed so loudly I was nearly deafened. 'How much land you got?'

I told him about the vegetable garden and the milk from Crystal and Joycey.

'Cows? You got cows? You goin' to give them that Jersey milk?' He took a long breath. Another spit. 'You need ten. Ten at least. Maybe more. Gor, they'll thrive on that.'

In the end I took six – which seemed like a fair compromise. 'I'll come back for them,' I said. 'I'll get the trailer.'

'Come back?' Another spit. 'You take them now. Save on the petrol. What you got?'

'A Land-Rover.'

'Soon have them in the back.' He started picking up the squealing piglets at random.

'But I haven't got any . . .'

'Straw? You don't need straw. Who needs straw?'

'But won't they . . .?'

They did.

The drive home was, I think, the most hair-raising I've ever made in my life. I had six tiny pink piglets running all over the Land-Rover. They were all over the back, all over the front, and even under my feet while I was trying to drive. I had to stop several times but I was frightened to open the door in case they escaped. And the noise! I reckon they were squealing non-stop the whole way. You could have heard us in Tunbridge Wells.

'You have to get a grill or dog guard fixed to this,' I kept saying to myself all the way – again.

When I finally got back to the farm my head was singing.

I backed the Land-Rover up to the vegetable garden. Ruth, Adrian and the children were there. Peter wasn't. He was out riding again.

'Say hello to our new arrivals,' I said, throwing open the back door of the Land-Rover.

Suddenly the piglets stopped squealing. Instead they all ran to the back and huddled together.

'Come on,' I shouted. 'You're home. Come on.'

They huddled even closer together.

'Come on,' I shouted again. 'You've got nothing to be frightened of. Lots of milk. Come on.'

Not a movement.

As Stuart and Alexis' excitement grew the piglets huddled closer still.

'Let's be quiet,' I barked, 'then maybe they will come.'

Half an hour later they still hadn't moved.

'I think you're going to have to pick them up,' said Ruth slowly. 'They're never going to jump down from the Land-Rover. They'll hurt themselves.'

'Okay,' I said. 'Let's all get one.'

Everyone took one step back. I thrust my hand in to grab hold of one of the piglets. Immediately there was the most piercing, ear-splitting shriek you've ever heard in your life as six little pigs literally went berserk. They ran, jumped and leapt everywhere – on the seats, on the dashboard, in the tool compartment. They went everywhere except out of the Land-Rover and into the vegetable garden.

'They're making a right mess,' Dennis laughed as he came to see all the fuss.

'I'm not cleaning the Land-Rover,' said Ruth firmly.

I turned round, my nerves in shreds. My hand was still shaking.

Peter came riding in.

'Problems?' he asked, jumping off.

'That's typical,' I said. 'Going riding and leaving everything to me.'

Peter tied Laddie to a nearby post and jumped into the back of the Land-Rover. The piglets screamed even louder. I thought my ears were going to melt. He grabbed the one on the dashboard by its back leg. It screamed the scream of a thousand devils. Then it squirmed and twisted out of his hands and threw itself back on the dashboard. He grabbed it again. It tried the same trick again but with no luck. Peter handed it to me. In a second it was out of my hands. But it was in the vegetable garden.

Dennis jumped in to help Peter amid even more squeals. They grabbed the piglet standing on the tool box. Again it shrieked – probably a thousand times louder than its companion. This time they both held it tight as they passed it to me. I managed to hold it for at least two seconds before it leapt for its life. But at least it also leapt into the vegetable garden. The children were squealing just as loudly but with laughter.

The third piglet was scuttling across the back of the Land-Rover one second, next it was flying through the air. Then it was in my hands and immediately it also joined the pack. So did number four and number five. The sixth just did not want to go anywhere at all. The only way we caught it was by closing all the doors and windows and chasing it from rear window to windscreen, from tool box to front seat, from under the pedals to the top of the seats. In the end we won – more by exhaustion, I'm ashamed to say, than by skill. But did it scream? It screamed and squealed and bit and spat at us more than all the others put together, and for longer. Because, of course, once we'd caught it we couldn't open the doors and Ruth and Adrian wouldn't come anywhere near the Land-Rover because they thought we were going to give it to them.

Once it had touched dry land again, however, it was as sweet as pie. It rushed to join its little friends, presumably to get a copy of *Animal Farm*.

So began my attachment to pigs. I was growing very fond of the cows and calves who are far more intelligent than people think. But pigs are even more so. They have a lovely nature and contrary to what I – like most people – had thought, they are very clean. It wasn't until later that the friendship with all these animals made me finally give up eating them. Would you eat your friends?

After the piglets settled in, Peter went to groom Laddie. Ruth and Adrian turned the cows out on to grass and I went back to have another look at Bambi.

I couldn't believe it. He was standing up in his emergency ward full of beans. His ears were twitching and he was waggling his tail like mad. I rushed to give him a little glucose and water which he drank down in one go. I gave him some milk out of a wine bottle and he drank it non-stop.

Fantastic, I thought. I've saved him. I went down to help put up the stakes in the vineyard.

'He's better,' I told everyone.

'Probably frightened out of his life by all the noise the pigs were making,' Adrian said.

We must have put up over a hundred stakes that afternoon. Sometimes I would hold the stakes and Ruth would drive the tractor with the hired automatic hammer attached. We had to wear crash helmets because the hammer came down on the top of the pole with quite a force. Sometimes Adrian held the stakes and I drove. Holding the stakes was like being at the end of a pneumatic drill – you shook violently. It was almost five o'clock before we stopped and Elsa started barking for her dinner.

This time, however, when I looked in the calfhouse Bambi was poorly again, lying on the straw, looking tired and miserable. I was up at six o'clock the following morning, Sunday, and he was just the same.

I decided to call the vet again. On a Sunday. Which meant paying double time. Our usual vet was not on call but the stand-in vet came straight away. He examined Bambi and took his temperature.

'He should be eating. I don't understand it,' he said.

I asked him for more vitamin injections, perhaps some tonic.

'Do you know how much this is costing?' he said.

'I don't care,' I said. 'I'm not going to lose him. I think he was taken away from his mother too soon, maybe without getting his colostrum. What do you think?'

'Maybe. It does happen,' he said. 'That would account for the problems. With his injections, my visits, and being called out on a Sunday, you must have spent over forty pounds so far, if not more. Are you sure you want to carry on?'

'Sure,' I said. 'I'm not going to let him die.'

He gave me the vitamins and more tonic.

'Are you sure there is nothing we can do to help him?' I asked him.

'I've done everything I can,' he replied.

Why don't I ask one of the local old farmers, I suddenly thought. There might be some traditional cure. The two I rang couldn't help. Maybe Christie would know. When he was staying with us he helped us stop the calves from getting too much milk off the cows and making themselves ill by tying a flower pot over their faces. The holes at the bottom allowed them to breathe. They could still run with the cows. The cows were happy but it meant we could regulate their milk supply. Maybe he had another idea which would help.

'To be sure, what's the weather like over there?' he said when I got through to him on the phone.

'Fine. Fine, Christie,' I said.

'Soft. 'Tis very soft here.'

'I was wondering if I could ask you about Bambi?'

'Lambs by . . . You have lambs? I didn't . . .'

'No. No, Christie,' I screamed down the phone. 'Bambi. Bambi. Not lambs, Bambi.'

'You're going to buy lambs?'

'No. No. I have a calf . . .'

'You're buying half . . .'

'No. No.' I took a deep breath. 'I have a calf. It's very ill. It's not . . .'

'Let it die.'

'I'm not going to let it die.'

'How much did it cost you now?'

'Twenty-five pounds.'

'Let it die. You can't afford it. It's not worth spending . . .'

'But it's such a . . .'

'Now are you a farmer or are you wanting to be keeping pets?'

'Yes. Well.'

'Then let it die. No farmer can . . .'

'Yes. Yes, Christie,' I said putting the phone down.

I went back to have a look at Bambi and give him another drink. At first he looked a bit more chirpy but then he went back to his listless old self.

Each coil of wire was heavy – twenty-five kilos (we were working both in metric and imperial depending on what the supplier used, which didn't make things easier). Peter and Adrian had gradually brought the coils down to the vineyard and the rest of the day I spent helping with the wiring. First we tried unwinding it direct from the big coils it came in which didn't work. The wire kept twisting and tying itself into knots. It was crazy.

Instead Dennis came up with the solution. He built a turntable on top of one of our big wheelbarrows and put the wire on it. We then unwound the wire as we went along the rows and fixed it directly to the posts. By four o'clock when we finished we'd wired up six rows complete with adjusters to alter not only the height of the wire but to loosen or tighten it; strainers to hold the wire taut; and the anchor wires, which were extra thick and tied around the end posts and connected to the anchors we had already placed in the ground so that they took the strain and stopped the weight of the vines pulling the posts and wire out.

After milking, feeding the calves and giving the donkeys an apple I checked on the piglets who were now thoroughly at home running around the vegetable garden. They loved their fresh creamy Jersey milk which we poured into long feeding troughs. Seconds later the troughs were also filled with piglets! I had another look at Bambi who was still looking thin and weak and miserable. I gave him another injection and tried him with some milk fresh from Crystal mixed with some warm water. He played with the bottle a little at first then just ignored it.

I wondered whether to call the vet again but he couldn't do anything. He'd given Bambi all the injections he could. In any case I didn't feel I wanted his advice. I began to think that the kindest thing to do was to put him to sleep – like a dog.

After dinner, I went out to have another look at him. He was still stretched out on the straw but he'd obviously been moving around, maybe even standing up. I sat down next to him in the pen with Elsa and started stroking him. He waggled his ears. We were in contact again. He opened his big brown eyes and looked at me. I carried on stroking him. He really was a lovely little calf. Once he was better I could see him running around the fields. I wanted to take him into the house with me and all the cats and dogs. Why should he be left outside? He shifted closer towards me, and I pulled my cardigan up round his neck to keep him warm.

The next thing I knew Elsa was nudging me. It was after midnight. I'd fallen asleep again stroking Bambi. I looked at him. He was dead. I'd lost my first calf.

CHAPTER SEVENTEEN
Cry God for Harry, England and St George!

'So what about William Shakespeare?' Debbie said to me while Elsa and I were checking the vines one afternoon.

'Erm. Well. Erm. I don't know,' I mumbled.

'William Shakespeare's Olde English Wine?'

'Erm.'

'William Shakespeare's Choice Vintage English Wine?'

'Oh, no!'

You might think that planting the vines, pruning them, hammering in over a thousand stakes and tying up over forty thousand yards of wire was difficult. Forget it. Choosing the name was the most difficult job of all – honestly. It took me months before I came up with what is obviously the best name anybody could choose for an English wine.

'Charles Dickens English Wine?' Ruth suggested as we were milking early one morning.

'Erm,' I mumbled.

'Mr Pickwick's Choice English Wine?'

'That's awful.'

'Scrooge . . . ?'

'No. I don't think so.'

I thought of a thousand different names. And every name I thought of I tried out on everybody I knew.

From the beginning I knew what I didn't want. Most people

take the easy way out and name their wine after themselves. But somehow Biddlecombe English Wine did not have the same ring about it as Baron Philippe. Okay if I was producing cider. Biddlecombe is, after all, a West Country name – ideal for Scrumpy! Others call the wine after the area they live in. Again Waldron was not exactly on the international wine map. And many favour the name of their farm or estate. But Cross Farm English Wine did not have much class about it.

Wherever I went I was thinking of names. Whatever I was doing I was thinking of names. Whoever I spoke to it was always at the back of my mind.

It was so important.

A name and a presentation – in this case a label – helps to sell a product and also create an image. Get it right, I kept thinking, and it's half the battle. True, if the wine was awful it perhaps would not matter. But my wine was going to be good. And it would have to be selected not only for its taste but for its appearance.

'Do have a taste of this Biddlecombe' did not sound very impressive.

With all the stakes in and the wiring finished we had seen the end of the heavy work, and at last the vineyard was beginning to look like one. But there was still plenty to do. The grass had to be kept under control and so did the weeds. The first year had been back-breaking – and often knee-breaking as well, as we literally had to crawl along the rows of vines pulling the grass and weeds off them and cutting them back – only to repeat the process two or three weeks later. For weeks on end neither Ruth nor I could stand up straight. It's a wonder I can even today.

'Back-breaking English Wine,' Ruth grunted one evening as we finished weeding the last row of the vineyard. We burst out laughing. 'It would be a good seller.'

At the start of the second year, in January 1981, we had pruned each vine down again to two to three buds. We would have to repeat the process of the first year. If we allowed the vines to bear fruit before they were ready we would exhaust them and they would die. But they were getting stronger. The weeds were still a problem. The black polythene was a godsend but after the first year we used a knapsack sprayer filled with contact weedkiller along the edge, leaving us a clear path to mow down without damaging the polythene.

The knapsack held four gallons. It doesn't sound much but having that strapped to your back all day and having to walk twice down sixty-four rows is pretty back-breaking too!

We had to tie the vines up again, side-shoot and remove the flower buds. It seemed an endless task.

The third year seemed a long time coming. I had decided that because the growth in the second year was strong, next year would be our first vintage, at least for most of the stronger vines. The weaker ones we would de-flower again to give them another year to catch up.

'At last,' said Ruth.

'Can't wait,' said Adrian.

'Perhaps we'll get some money in,' said Peter.

By the start of the season – in those days it was January but now because we have so many more vines we begin in December – the wood of the vines had hardened well. The idea was to go for a small crop so as not to overwork them, all part of the building-up process for future years.

At the beginning of the third year we trained the main stem up to the first wire and then almost at right angles along it, tying it in several places to keep it down. And we left from two to eight buds. The amount of fruit we would allow each one to bear would depend on the individual vine's performance. Weak ones would not be allowed to bear any fruit. The strong, vigorous ones, I thought I would let have two bunches, perhaps three. At the end of the day the climate would help sort this one out. If we have frost at bud-burst time – April – the risks are high. You could lose every bud. Result: no fruit.

Nowadays, with such well-established large vines, we leave

two canes to tie down with one loose one as a spare so that if the frost catches too many buds on the tied canes we use the spare one instead or in addition, hopefully to end up with the right number of buds.

The pruning, bowing down and tying up took Ruth and me longer than we thought. Bending the canes wasn't easy until we realized it was a job best done either after it had rained or while it was raining, as the moisture kept them pliable. In the early spring sunshine they became brittle and as we bent them over it was almost a case of crackle, snap then pop. So we had to slow down to take more care or leave the work until it was raining or damp again.

We got used to crouching in the rain tying the vines with water trickling from a wet hat down our backs and wet hands and knees. Ruth wore rubber gloves to stop her hands getting wet and over her jeans she wore waterproof trousers. I couldn't wear either. I couldn't feel the vine properly with gloves on, and the trousers, while they kept the knees dry, ended up by giving me a Turkish bath. They were like those plastic clothes used as slimming aids in the 1960s which made you sweat!

Debbie had now left us and gone to work in a bank in Heathfield. The call of a centrally heated office, nice clothes and high heels was too great!

In her place we had the part-time help of Thomas who was seventeen and in a youth training scheme. He was tall, very slim, looked older than his years and was very quiet. But he was fast and energetic and a good worker. He would turn his hand to anything and had obviously been used to working on the land and with animals.

He had apparently been adopted by a couple with a small orchard and farm on the other side of the village and his heart and soul were obviously in the countryside. He seemed to be particularly interested in wild birds.

Ruth and I were glad to have someone who would do some of the heavier work.

'Backpack English Wine?' Thomas laughed as he raced away with the spray along the rows.

'No!'

'Vineyard English Wines,' Ruth added.

'Of course it's from a vineyard,' I said. 'Where do you think it's from? An antifreeze manufacturer?'

So 1982 would be a milestone in my grand scheme. It was the year we pruned for our first fruit.

We started the pruning on 3 January after the Christmas and New Year break and celebrations. To me a vineyard always looks good. It's at its best when the sun is shining and there are lots of lovely ripened bunches of grapes to be picked. But the winter has its own charm. The vines are bare but the dark mature wood, sparkling with dew or frost on a crystal clear day, and the winter sky of soft pinks, blues, greys and gold make a lovely picture. And working in the vineyard, well wrapped-up (especially with foot warmers in your wellies) is a pleasure. Even in the snow, when the colours are better still.

It is so peaceful and quiet, with only the sound of the birds, the occasional aircraft, perhaps the distant hum of someone's tractor to distract your mind. Occasionally the bells of the Visitation Convent can be heard calling the nuns to prayer. The inevitable robin keeps you company, darting here and there, and sometimes a rabbit pops up to nibble the grass.

Some of the people who work for me now use headphones with their transistors to listen to music to entertain them while working. I like the peace.

And the smell of the countryside in winter is different too. Gone are the wild flowers of summer and the perfume of the roses we now have in the vineyard to make it more attractive for our summer visitors. Instead the air is fresher, cleaner, sharper – so much so that it seems to heighten your other senses.

And when you stop pruning to stand upright and stretch your aching back for a few minutes you can see further than when you do the same while de-leafing in summer. There are no leaves on the trees or in the hedgerows to obscure the surrounding countryside. Often the air is so clear you can even see the division of the fields on the South Downs with their different browns and greens, as they slope down the hills fifteen miles away.

The hedgerows are a vital part of our vineyard in summer. Their dense foliage protects the vines from the winds far better than netting and they look nicer too. In fact I have a 'thing' about hedgerows. They are one of the most typical, beautiful, varied and evocative aspects of the English countryside. They are a rich habitat for wildlife (twenty-three species of birds regularly nest in hedgerows) and plants (250 species of flowering plants) and insects. When I get on my hedgerow hobby-horse, every time a visitor asks me about ours, I never fail to point out that England has lost and still is losing its hedgerows – at something like four thousand miles a year! So I feel we are conserving nature as well as our vines for the good of all of us!

Back in 1982 the winter work in the vineyard began in bitterly cold conditions. But Ruth, Elsa and I didn't mind. We could see bottles of wine at the end of every row! We were usually joined by one or more of the cats. They didn't want to miss any of the fun, particularly Hilda who seemed to spend most of her days there winding herself around our bent legs. Come-on often came too, talking all the time and jumping up to brush the top of her head against our hands as we pruned. We began to call them our anti-rabbit patrol. Eustace and Squeaky always stayed in the warmth of the house, usually curled up together.

Our feet were cold no matter how thick our socks and no matter how many we wore. Even Elsa was grateful for the log fires in the evening to thaw her frozen paws.

'Okay. Okay,' I said to Ruth. 'Now this is how you prune a vine.' I went through it all over again. 'Make sure the main stem is nice and straight and be careful how you bend it over the wire. If you're not sure how many buds to leave I'm right next to you.'

No questions.

'Okay. Let's go,' I said briskly.

Snip. Bend. Tie.

'Isn't it exciting,' said Ruth.

Snip. Bend. Tie.

'We've got a long way to go yet,' I said.

Snip. Bend. Tie.

'But won't it be great to get some fruit after all this time?'

Snip. Bend. Tie.

'Wonder what it will taste like?'

Snip. Bend. Tie.

'Celebration English Wine,' said Ruth as we finally pruned, bent and tied the last vine exactly thirty-two days, five tins of Elastoplast, ten packets of fruit drops, two pairs of secateurs, two pairs of gloves and several swear words later.

The job had taken longer not only because we were being very cautious and careful, but because of the time spent milking, feeding and caring for all the animals. We had bought a milking machine to speed things along but while it got the milk out quicker it took about twenty minutes to clean!

Another time saver, or so I thought, was my new mobile phone. When you're half a mile away you can be forgiven for not answering the phone direct. But there I was in the vineyard taking my calls and pruning at the same time. I was getting ready for the days when I would be taking wine orders!

But at least we'd finished the first real pruning for fruit.

'Finale English Wine,' said Ruth, looking at her hands. 'Do you remember, Gay,' she asked, 'when we had nice soft hands? Look at these blisters!'

I just collapsed in a heap on the ground and prayed that one day the feeling would come back to my arms.

Later, as the strength returned to my right arm – my left arm still didn't belong to me – and I was catching up with my office work and beginning to think of wine making, the front doorbell rang.

'English Bells English Wine,' Ruth shouted out.

I was expecting Major Sanderson from the Country Land Owners Association. We were buying more land in the village and I wanted some advice. I opened the front door. It was Sister Margaret Mary.

'I thought you weren't allowed out,' I stammered. 'I mean I thought . . .'

'I know. I know,' she giggled almost like a schoolgirl. 'I had to go to the dentist in Lewes. So as it's on my way back . . .'

'But Lewes is not this way,' I butted in. 'It's the other direction. It's . . .'

'I know. I know,' she laughed. 'The driver got lost. So I wondered if I could telephone the convent in case they are worried about me?'

She wanted to see everything and meet all the animals. Hilda wanted to sit on her shoulder like a parrot. Round and round the garden she ran with Elsa. We saw the horses and Sister Margaret Mary said she'd love to go for a gallop but much as I tried to persuade her, she didn't. I relished the thought of seeing a nun in full habit galloping through Waldron! We went into the cowhouse where Ruth was skimming the cream off the milk.

'Blue Nun,' Ruth laughed as soon as she saw her.

'What's all this about Blue Nun? I think it's awful,' Sister said.

'We're trying to find a name for our wine,' I explained. 'Any suggestions?'

'Saints,' she declared.

'I'll think about it.'

We walked round the vineyard with her throwing sticks for Elsa all the time. I introduced her to Thomas.

'Black Nun,' he whispered to me as we left him.

I invited her to stay for lunch but she said she had to be going. A cup of tea? She had to get straight back. I took her back to her car and the driver who couldn't find the way home from Lewes. Then I remembered.

'The telephone,' I said. 'What about the telephone? I thought you . . .'

'Best not to worry Reverend Mother!' She waved as the car headed back to the convent.

It was now spring again and still I hadn't thought of a name.

'Rose and Crown English Wine,' Ruth shouted out as we passed a pub on the way to Lewes cattle market.

'No.'

'The Sussex Downs English Wine.'

'Nice, but no.'

I bought some little Friesian calves and two big sturdy red Sussex calves. The best breed at the Smithfield Show the previous year had been a Sussex from Lewes, so I wanted some. There were some nice Charolais there and at a good price too but I didn't buy any. They reminded me too much of Bambi.

'Pedigree English Wines,' Ruth whispered as I was bidding for the calves.

'Ruth,' I said. 'Not now. I'm . . .'

'Thirty pounds I'm bid,' the auctioneer waved his hammer at me.

'Now look what you've done.'

'Thirty-five.'

'If only you'd . . .'

'Forty.'

'. . . keep quiet.'

'Sold to Mrs Biddlecombe. Next lot: four Hereford Friesian crosses. What am I bid? Mrs Biddlecombe?'

I ducked down and ran for the exit.

'Pedigree English Wines,' I shouted at her once I was out of range of the auctioneer. 'Pedigree English Wines! What a name! And you made me bid for three more calves than I really want.'

It was now getting into summer and still we had not found a name. Dennis had finished most of the redecorating. We'd uncovered all the original oak beams and found old oak floors that must have been made from old ships' timbers. We'd even discovered a secret room we didn't know we had.

The core of the house is its huge Elizabethan chimney and most of the main rooms surround it on the ground and first floor. But at some stage in the past, either deliberately or because it was simply easier, false walls had been put in. We were measuring up to paper between the oak beams when we realized the outside wall measurements were a lot bigger than the inside wall was. At first I thought Dennis couldn't add up properly.

'Dennis,' I kept saying to him. 'Surely these numbers can't be right?'

He measured the walls again. And again. And again. Still the same figures.

'Well you must be doing something wrong,' I said.

'The only thing I can think of . . .' he said slowly as he started measuring the walls again, 'is that there is another room.'

And there was. A tiny room. It was between Peter's study on one side of the chimney and our bedroom on the other side. There was now no window in it and clearly it was part of another room because it also had a false wall which led into another small room on the outside wall of the house. It was getting quite complicated! But presumably when the house was built back in 1622 and either priests or smugglers were on the run it may have been home to somebody.

'Smugglers English Wine,' Dennis said.

Mr Bishop and his two sons, who ran the traditional polishing service in Crowborough nearby, then came to polish all the oak floors. Before they would do as much as lift a duster they made us literally empty the house of everything. And I mean everything. They sealed all the windows and doors.

First they sanded all the wood, creating huge clouds of dust in the process. Next they collected all the dust up in enormous vacuums. Or, at least, as much as they could. Then – finally – came the polishing.

'Bright and Beautiful English Wine,' Ruth said.

'Slippery . . .' added Thomas.

'Thomas,' I shouted, 'go and cut the grass in the vineyard.'

But in the end, when we moved everything back into the house again, it was worth it. At last the house was beginning to look the way I had always imagined it.

'Fantastic, isn't it?' said Peter over a bottle of Cheval Blanc '47 that evening as we celebrated.

'What, because I can't think of a bloody name?'

'I mean at last we're getting everything sorted out.'

'Sorted out? What do you mean sorted out? I can't even print any labels yet. Why can't you think of a name? I mean, we haven't heard from you on the subject.'

'What about St George? St George's English Wine.'

'Well . . .'

'It'll mean we'll have our own flag.'

'Umm . . .'

'We'll have churches and cathedrals and hotels . . .'

'Oh, don't be . . .'

'. . . named after us. We'll be the only English vineyard with our own special day. Nobody will have that.'

'Ye-es. It's . . .'

'We'll even have some Shakespeare as our slogan. "Cry God for . . ."'

'"Harry, England and . . ."'

'"St George's English Wine",' we both said together.

That night I had a brainwave. The following morning I stood on the steps in the courtyard.

'Everybody. Everybody,' I called. 'Everybody.'

Ruth came plodding through the farm gate from the cowhouse. Thomas dragged himself out of the barn.

'Everybody,' I said. 'Everybody. We've thought of the name.' I paused for effect. 'St George's English Wine.' Another pause. They just looked at me blankly. 'Well, what do you think?'

'Yes. It's all right,' Ruth grunted.

'But can't you see it's a bloody good name? We'll have our own flag. We'll have a special day. We'll have Shakespeare as our . . .'

'Yes. I suppose,' she said, turning round and heading back to the cowhouse.

'It's also good because it will help to distinguish us from British wine. It stresses that our wine is English and not made from imported grape juice and merely bottled here,' I called after her.

'Yes . . . you're right,' she said, disappearing through the door.

English wine producers have had a bad time, what with our climate and consumer and trade resistance. But one of the biggest problems we have had to face is this confusion between English and British wines. British wine is made from imported juice and I have not met anyone yet who has liked it. The fact that it still exists shows the power of marketing. And British wine companies have always ridden on the backs of the English producers because slowly we have created an up-market image for English-grown, English-made wines. The fact that the inferior juice, usually the left-overs of the European wine lake, could be called British at all is an indictment of our labelling laws and trading standards. It still confuses the public today.

I turned to Thomas.

'So what do you think?' I asked him.

'Well I don't know,' he said slowly. 'I always thought that wherever you had a St George there was always a . . .'

'Ye-es. And you're looking at her! Get on with your work.'

My mind was made up. I knew that if they liked the name, it was a good one!

I got quite excited. At last we had a name. We would have to find a logo for St George, something different from the usual rearing horse on top of a dragon. The quest was on.

Once I'd found my St George, with the red Cross of St George prominent, I could then swing into action designing the label and the letterhead for our new company: St George's English Wines Ltd. And I had made up my mind – no dragon. Just to be different, so that people would notice, comment and perhaps remember the name and the wine as a result. In any case, I thought, there isn't room for two of us!

I wanted a sign outside the vineyard telling people who and what we were. After a few phone calls I found a flagmaker and ordered a flagpole and some St George – or shall I say English – flags.

'Being an English vineyard,' I said proudly, 'I would have to fly the English flag.'

That evening, over a bottle of Muller Thurgau from New Zealand, which I'd bought to see how it compared with an English Muller, I told Peter what I had done and my ideas for a label.

'When will we know if they'll accept it as a company name?' he said, studying my rough design.

'I've sorted it all out with the accountants and our solicitor.'

'Do we really need the flagpole? And the flags? They're expensive – our overdraft . . .'

'Yes.'

Soon everything was organized. I'd registered the company as St George's English Wines Ltd. We had our first company meeting over a bottle of Muller Thurgau from East Anglia and one from Baden, Southern Germany. I opened a bank account.

I had now seen numerous St George's – in books, old paintings, stained glass windows, on pub signs, posters, even a housing estate prospectus. I had asked a designer Peter used occasionally for his clients to come up with ideas. In the end an old coin in the British Museum gave me what I wanted – an overall shape that would look good on a wine label, brochure, letterhead or anything else I needed it for.

And now I had chosen with my printer a typeface in keeping

with the image I wanted. I had a sign made for outside the vineyard gate. Flags were flying over the barn. The letter heading had been printed and labels were being designed. And my latest white Mini-van had a gleaming St George on the sides with St George's English Wines painted boldly in red underneath.

As I drove through Heathfield and Horam I noticed people looking at the van. Cars would slow up as they passed the vineyard. I even got one or two telephone calls asking about vineyard tours. St George's was beginning to make an impact. But one result of this was far from expected.

One afternoon, when Elsa and I arrived at the convent for our regular visit to the calves, Sister Bridget was waiting for me.

'I've got some bad news for you,' she said. 'Reverend Mother says can you please stop coming to the convent?'

I was shocked. 'But why? After all this time.'

'Because she says people see St George's English Wines written all over your van and think you keep coming here delivering wine for all the sisters. We might get a bad reputation!'

CHAPTER EIGHTEEN
The Family Gets Bigger

P
Pie in oven. Add frozen chips.
160 for 25 minutes.
Yogurt in fridge.
G

Now that I had a name I was legitimate. Having already joined our local Weald and Downland Vineyard Association, I'd decided to join the National English Vineyard Association. I wanted to find out what was happening in the growing world of English wine. I wanted to see who the other owners were, what kind of wines they were producing and, more importantly, who they were all selling to.

I had also joined beekeeping classes at the local Heathfield School. I thought that vineyard honey would be a great idea. Perhaps it would have the sweetness of honey and the flavour of grapes – like Château d'Yquem on toast! Then there were my art classes, riding lessons, animal husbandry courses, poultry classes . . . Hence all the hurried notes I kept leaving for Peter.

And on top of everything else, Elsa had just become a mother. After she came to us via the Rescue Society we received her pedigree papers and as a result the society were happy for me to mate her. I returned to Mrs Lowe and she agreed to use one of her dogs. Elsa tolerated him but was obviously glad when it was all over. I felt awful, as though I had organized a rape! Still, he did want to run around and play games to woo her first.

She made a lovely mother. But the arrival of her puppies had its moments, not least because we lost two which were born dead. On the morning of the second day after the others were safely born, I noticed one puppy lying very still, looking blue with cold to one side of the box. I thought she was dead. She obviously had been pushed aside by the others and hadn't been able to get any milk. Elsa licked her and looked at me with her big dark pleading eyes.

I picked the puppy up quickly and rushed into the kitchen with her. She was breathing . . . but only just.

I wrapped her in a towel for warmth and made up a hot water bottle to lie her on for extra heat. I had in reserve, in case of an emergency, some powdered replacement bitch's milk and a pipette so I made up a feed. The blind little bundle no bigger than the palm of my hand weakly took the first few drops.

Within three hours she was taking the small amount of milk as though her life depended on it – which it did! For three days and two nights that little puppy went everywhere with me, wrapped up in the towel on top of the hot water bottle I changed every hour to keep the temperature constant. I fed her with the pipette every two hours and after the first day – and night – she was squealing for her feed. I carried her around in an old shopping basket and I never let her out of my sight. At nighttime she lay by the bed with a quickly-made wire cage over the top of the basket so none of the cats would lie on top of her! After three days she was obviously strong enough to join her brothers and sisters.

By now she had caught up and was back to being a pink blind bundle of life. I marked her belly with a blue felt-tip pen so I could distinguish her from the others and make sure she got her feed. As I returned her to Elsa, who had watched her progress with obvious interest, I put her straight on to a teat. She sucked furiously as Elsa licked her.

We were to keep Blue – as she was called from that day – and another bitch we called Honey. And my three girls became my constant and devoted friends.

One evening Ruth and I went to a WDVA meeting on pruning techniques.

I'd finished doing the milking with Ruth. The new milking machine was an enormous help although we kept debating whether it was quicker to milk by hand. I'd said Goodnight to the donkeys, George and Bettie and the rest of the geese and all the calves and given Elsa her dinner. I'd scribbled another note for Peter. And Ruth and I shot off across the border to Kent in my little van. Sometimes the WDVA meetings were interesting but most of the time I found them quite boring. Everyone – about 20 of us – would discuss action for ages then decide nothing. Sometimes I made suggestions but there was a little clique of growers who obviously felt the whole set up was for their benefit only. They were the first ones to grow vines and they all had sizeable vineyards. They rather dismissed the smaller growers and I actually heard one of them say 'if we help everyone, we're doing ourselves out of business.' But at least we finished the evening on a high note, tasting each other's wine, and it gave us a chance to compare growing notes with some of the other beginners.

But I didn't think any one of them had had the problem I had later that night.

I woke up at about 2.30. Hilda had jumped on the bed and was licking my face. It was a bright full-moon-lit night, the sort that looks like a black and white negative photograph. I put my arm out to stop her. She struggled a bit but I managed to pick her up and put her at the bottom of the bed. She edged her way back up. And then I thought I heard something.

Nothing. Then again. No. It couldn't be. I was dreaming.

Just as I was beginning to fall asleep it came again.

I woke up immediately, instantly wide awake. I lay there straining to hear the slightest sound.

Then it came again. A long, deep, rich, mellow mooooo.

'The cattle!' I shrieked. 'I can hear cattle in the vineyard. Oh my God, no. Cattle. Quick. Quick.'

Peter leapt out of bed, mumbling he couldn't hear a thing.

I rushed for the phone.

'Ruth. Ruth. Cattle. Cattle. Cattle in the vineyard. Quick. Quick. We'll need help.' I was practically incoherent.

In two seconds I was hurtling downstairs. Then I saw them through the windows at the front of the house – cattle. But they were cattle in the churchyard opposite, walking all over the graves and eating the flowers.

I grabbed the phone.

'It's okay, Ruth,' I said. 'They're in the churchyard. I made a mistake. They're not in the vineyard.'

We all heaved a massive sigh of relief. But we still went out and rounded up all the cattle together in one corner, away from the graves. I telephoned Edgar, the local farmer whose land bounded the churchyard, and we helped him take them back. We couldn't get them to go back through the gap in the hedge and had to walk them down the lane to the farm and into the field through a proper gate, all of us in pyjamas, dressing gowns and wellingtons!

We got back at about four o'clock and had just got into bed when I thought I heard something again. Nothing. Then again. No, it couldn't be. It couldn't possibly be.

As I sat up it came again. A long, deep, rich . . .

'Oh no,' said Peter, 'it can't be. This is crazy. What's gotten into everything tonight?'

'Cattle,' I shrieked down the phone to Ruth. 'There really are cattle in the vineyard. No, seriously, I'm not bloody kidding.'

Ruth moaned. I could hear Adrian saying: 'Tell her to take a running . . .'

I grabbed my dressing gown and ran for all I was worth. I

got to the vineyard gate. I opened it. There facing me were all our cattle. They'd broken through from Barley Gratton and were tucking into the grass and – I couldn't bear to look. I could see that Ruth, with a reluctant Adrian, had come down the other side with a torch.

I started to shout 'Ruth' but stopped. If I shouted I'd frighten them. If I frightened them they could trample the vines to the ground. I could see all our hard work going to waste.

Ruth started to call. 'How are we going to get . . .'

'Shhh,' I said in a loud whisper.

'. . . them back . . .'

'Shhh. We don't want a stampede.'

I motioned to Peter and the others to get behind the cattle who fortunately were facing the gateway into Hop Garden. Nora, Gladys and most of the older ones just looked at us, mooing quietly from time to time. The others kept munching the grass. None of them were looking at the vines.

'Shhh,' I whispered. 'If Pina Colada sees me . . .'

And, of course, at that moment, he looked up from the grass. He turned and started to run straight towards me down between two rows of vines. Keep calm. Keep calm, I kept saying to myself. If you panic it'll only frighten the other cattle and then who knows . . . He was picking up speed. He's only playing. He only wants to say . . .

There was nothing I could do. I leapt out of his way just as he careered past me. The others had caught on by now. It was time for the rodeo. We had our first stampede and it was in the vineyard!

Oh bloody hell . . . I was almost resigned. Not the vines. Please not the vines.

I couldn't see Peter, Ruth and Adrian. But I could see two torch lights going up and down rather fast.

As the cattle rushed out of the various rows they were in, kicking and bucking and having a great time, they all turned to follow Pina Colada who was rollicking his way into Hop Garden. I saw a torch light hit the ground.

'Oh hell . . . bloody animals.' It was Adrian's voice.

I then heard Ruth scream as the other torch light hit the ground.

'Quick. Quick,' I shouted. 'They're out.'

'Never mind "quick, quick", I'm covered in mud,' Adrian moaned. 'This is the last time . . .'

The torch lights had now gone out.

'It might have been the lights that started them off,' said Peter.

'That's right, blame us,' said Ruth. 'It was Gay's voice – they always run to her.'

'Well either way,' I interrupted, 'let's leave them in here until the morning then we'll get them back to Barley Gratton. And find that bloody hole in the fence.'

The cattle had stopped and their heads were down munching the grass. They were panting as much as we were. We heard the church clock strike five.

'What's that smell?' Peter said as we all started walking back.

'Wonder what got into everyone tonight?' Ruth asked. 'Maybe it was the full moon. Golly, yes. Something hums.'

'Blimey, Adrian.' I moved away.

'Bloody hell,' shrieked Adrian. 'It's all down my trousers.'

Peter laughed. 'Couldn't you wait or was it all the excitement?'

'Oh shit.'

'Ye-es.'

I got back to the house. Elsa was in what we now call the dog room, all her little puppies huddled together fast asleep in a big whelping box Dennis had built for them. As soon as I went in, her tail started wagging like mad. She stood up to say hello, knocking all seven pups all over the place. But most of them stayed asleep.

Being just a few days old the pups were still only the size of my hand. I picked them up gently, one by one. They were all pink and warm. They nestled softly in my hand, their eyes closed. I put them back on to Elsa and they all started nuzzling away like mad. It was a wonderful sight.

The morning after the rodeo I checked the vines. I could not believe it but not one leaf had been eaten or damaged! When I got back I could hear an enormous lorry drawing up outside. It was a big tractor with front bucket and dumper. I wanted us to start landscaping the area in front of the barn and turning ourselves from a farm into a vineyard.

We'd already moved the chickens, turkeys and ducks to their new home next to the pigs in the field, and taken up the post and rail fencing around the paddock. But the ground was still very bumpy and uneven, with lots of old tree roots and stumps. Our old Massey was not powerful enough. We needed a big earthmover.

I wanted to take down the old wooden farm gate and put up the big double metal gates I'd got from the convent. I'd also got some big metal railings from a demolition site which matched the gates perfectly and which I wanted to put alongside. But if I was going to do this I had to create a proper entrance. The tractor would level off the ground where the gates were going as well as the whole area in front of the paddock.

We unloaded the tractor and I told the driver exactly what I wanted.

'Level off all the bumps by the hedge. Use the earth to fill in the holes near the front where the post and rails were. Then level off the entrance.'

'Right. Right.'

Harold Cottingham, a Sussex man who runs a nursery in Godstone and who had helped me landscape my previous garden at Oaklands, then arrived with a lorry full of plants and shrubs and trees. There is nothing he does not know about plants and gardening and he taught me a lot. I'd already started cleaning up the old tithe barn. I'd had a new concrete floor put in, either side of the wooden threshing floor. I'd also had toilets built. Now I wanted to start landscaping the area outside. After all, having decided to open to the public one day I had to make the place look welcoming. And the sooner we began, the better it would look when we started selling.

I helped him unload. He'd brought over a hundred different shrubs and trees, knowing I didn't have time to go to his nursery some twenty-five miles away.

The phone rang and I rushed off to answer it. It was my beekeeping teacher, Robin Symington. He'd been offered some old hives. Did I want them? I jumped at the offer.

By now I was learning more and more about bees. What a fascinating subject. I must confess that in the past I had never given much thought to bees or honey. I simply thought bees were insects collecting pollen and honey was the end product.

But there are all kinds of bees: nice, friendly ones and nasty, vicious ones. Their whole existence revolves around the queen and different bees do different work to keep the colony going. I had never looked into the gastronomic benefits and health claims of honey nor the different flavours. It fascinated me that honey eaters were just as serious about their subject as wine tasters or tea drinkers. They can tell you what the bee fed off and, like a master of wine extolling the virtues of this or that vineyard and identifying the slopes where the vines were grown while sampling a wine, a beekeeper can do just the same tasting honey!

Even the health benefits of being stung amazed me. I would never suffer from arthritis if I was stung by my own bees, I was assured. I soon discovered that beekeepers are a breed apart. They are fanatical about their subject, totally immersed in it and that's probably why they are often thought just a little bit 'odd' by non-bee people.

The whole new world of the bee was unfolding. I went to bee meetings and bee sales, read books and even wrote to the famous beekeeping monk, Brother Adam, at Buckfast Abbey in Devon who is one of the world's leading authorities on bees.

'Beekeeping is really a way of getting something for nothing. It is free food,' I had read.

I had rather fancied catching a swarm of bees. It was, after all, the cheapest way to stock my two bargain hives. But in the end with the help of Robin I had to buy a queen and a small colony of bees. The old hives had cost me next to nothing, but all the other equipment plus the beekeeper's hat, gloves, all-in-one dungarees and the special 'smoker' to lull the bees into a sense of security cost me a small fortune! But my beekeeping days did not last long. One evening I took my hat and gloves and went with Elsa for an inspection. Realizing where I was going Elsa turned round halfway to the vineyard and flopped down to wait for my return. As I lifted the top of the hive there were just a few bees wandering around. No queen bee. In the distance I heard a great humming noise. As I followed the sound I realized my bees had swarmed. Someone else would definitely find 'something for nothing'. As for me, I decided against having another go.

Outside, the paddock was a mess. There were enormous holes by the hedge and a giant ridge running along the front where the post and rail fencing used to be. The driver was sitting in the lorry drinking a cup of tea.

'But that's not what I wanted,' I interrupted him. 'I said level off the bumps by the hedge. Use the earth to fill in the holes near the front. That's not what you've done.'

He looked at me.

'In a minute, lady,' he grunted. 'Just finishing my tea.'

'Tea,' I screamed. 'I haven't even had my breakfast. And I've been up since three o'clock.'

Harold waved at me.

'You want the lavender here or over there?'

The rest of the day was spent arguing with what must have

been a dyslexic tea-addict of a tractor driver who just couldn't get anything right, and helping Harold with the planting. In the end it all worked out the way I wanted: the levelling off because the tractor just ran out of wrong places to shift all the soil and the planting because Harold is one of the best landscapers I know.

By the time I'd finished everything was a mad rush. I zoomed down to the convent to check the calves. Reverend Mother was now happy with my van. I'd told her none of the villagers thought the nuns were drinking wine all day. I'd told them they were all drinking gin instead!

It was now gone six. I had to leave by ten to seven. The WDVA meeting started at 7.30.

At 6.30 I left Ruth doing the milking.

'Sorry, Ruth,' I shouted. 'I've just got to go!' I left Peter another note.

My parents, who had recently retired and moved to Eastbourne, came to the vineyard – we were now calling ourselves a vineyard not a farm – once or twice a week to help. They helped with the planting and gave us a hand with some of the farm work. But most of all my father looked after the Land-Rover and the van while my mother did all the washing and ironing for me. I hate housework. I would have been lost without their help.

'You should watch all that acid. Eats into the paintwork. Then you get rust. Once you start getting rust . . .'

My father was cleaning the van in the courtyard.

'. . . you can say goodbye to your van. It's all those pigeons.'

'Doves, Dad,' I said. 'I keep telling you they're doves.'

'Doves pigeons. Pigeons doves,' he shouted across at the church the other side of the lane. 'What difference does it make? I keep telling you, you should watch it. Ruin your van, they will.'

'Yes, Dad,' I replied. 'But what can I do? I can't stop them from flying over here, can I? Anyway I like them and you're exaggerating.'

'I'm only trying to help you.'

'Yes, I know, Dad. Thanks. What I mean is . . .'

'I don't have to come here, you know. Your mother and I can easily stay . . .'

I looked up at the church. There did seem to be a lot of white doves around. They were sitting on the main roof of the church as well as on the chapel. Not exactly like Hitchcock's *The Birds* but it could have been a dress rehearsal. Some were flying in and out of the belfry at the top of the main church roof. But they did look nice and gave the church a peaceful air rather than a dead look. They often flew over us and down into the barn where we kept our straw and hay and I liked to see them about the place.

Dad picked up his bucket of soapy water and his sponge and stormed off mumbling.

The phone rang. It was David Westphal. Now I was legitimate the next stage of my plan was to visit as many other English vineyards as I could to see what they were doing and maybe pick up some tips on wine-making equipment. As his father, Bob, virtually started me off in the business, their vineyard seemed the best place to start. We agreed a date and time.

When I first visited Penshurst, what seemed like fifty years ago, they had just gone into production. Now they were fully established. They had a proper winery with stainless steel tanks and all the necessary equipment.

We walked around their winery. It seemed very organized and compact. They even had a big oak barrel which they'd had made in Germany, complete with their name carved in English on the front. Something didn't look quite right.

'That's not how you spell your name,' I said.

'German spelling mistake!' grinned David.

We discussed the different equipment I'd need – and the prices. It was becoming clear I could not afford it all. 'You could buy second-hand,' said David, 'there is some around.'

It was about this time that I met a brilliant German wine maker, Karl-Heinz Johner, who made wine for several English vineyards as well as his own in Baden. In his time he put many vineyard names on the map and what he didn't know about wine making wasn't worth knowing. He was also an agent for several German companies supplying anything from vines to the most modern winery equipment. He had helped David a lot and the English wine industry would not be where it is today if it had not been for this short, slightly overweight, leather-jacketed German who was nicknamed 'Chubby'.

He was always happy to give his advice and help and since he travelled all over the world looking at vineyards, meeting wine makers, learning everything there was to know, he was much sought after. He commuted between Germany and England and when he was here he was on the road visiting vineyard after vineyard and making wine, in the end, for other thirty vineyards.

He is now back in Germany concentrating on his own business but I valued his advice and help which he gave whenever I needed it. It was he who helped me plan my modern winery of today.

He was sometimes criticized simply for being German. A few English growers felt that English wine should be made the 'English way' and this was at a time when German wine was beginning to get a bad reputation for being poor quality and too sweet. But the Germans produce some wonderful wines and have been growing for longer than we have. Their technology is so advanced and we still have much to learn. While there now is an English style typified by light, dry, fresh, clean and fruity wines with English garden bouquets, it can be argued that in many cases Chubby showed the way to creating it. It always seemed odd that a German wine maker had such a strong belief in the future of English wine. He certainly inspired me with great confidence as well as solving lots of my initial problems.

David and I walked out towards his vineyard and I spotted his Soay sheep and wallabies.

'You should have some,' he said.

'What, wallabies?' I laughed. 'No thank you. I'm an English vineyard, not an Australian one!'

'No, Soay sheep,' he said. 'They're good for the grass, delicious to eat and quite a lovely character. They're a rare breed.' Soays are smaller and of more delicate build and foot than other more common breeds. Their wool is dark brown and curly and is sought after.

After three hours I left – with three of his Soay sheep, one ram with large curly horns and two females.

'Well, every vineyard has to have its mouton,' I said wryly to Peter that evening.

In those early days many vineyards in the South East, in Kent, Sussex, even in the Isle of Wight, seemed to be very casual and homely. A lot were run like someone's hobby rather than a business. They were almost surprised and embarrassed to find themselves actually selling English wine. They also seemed to be taking the visitor very much for granted.

One vineyard I remember in particular. I walked in through the gate straight into a field. There were no signs, no notices, nothing telling you about the vineyard. Nothing at all. I wandered around and eventually saw a caravan parked in a corner. I knocked on the door.

'Excuse me,' I said. 'Is this the . . . ?'

'We're closed,' an elderly, scruffy man barked at me.

'I was wondering if I could buy some wine?'

'No, we're closed.'

He slammed the door. I couldn't learn anything here, I thought.

The vineyard at Horam owned by the Merrydown Cider

Company was the exact opposite. Jack Ward, one of the men who founded Merrydown from a garage in Horam, was one of the pioneers of English wine. Ted, the old 'strawberry vine' man who looked after it, always had plenty of time for you. You could ask him anything about growing vines and he would help you as much as he could.

I got back late one afternoon from talking to Ted and found my parents sitting in front of the television. My father had cleaned all the copper and brass in the house and was watching the racing with Eustace sitting on his lap. My mother was fast asleep.

'He caught one of those pigeons.'

'Doves,' I said.

'Whatever you call them. Brutus . . .'

'He's not Brutus. He's Eustace.'

'. . . caught one of those doves.'

'Did you get it off him?'

'Woman came in today,' my mother woke up, 'said everybody in the village is complaining about them.'

Upstairs, calmly sitting by the door of the study was Come-on.

'Hello, precious,' I bent down to stroke her. 'How's my little . . .'

I looked again. Half her jaw was hanging off. I rushed to the phone.

'Ruth,' I said, 'Come-on's face is smashed to pieces. Didn't you see her?'

'See her,' she said, 'see her? I didn't get a chance to see anything. Those bloody sheep. We spent all day trying to get them out of the vineyard.'

'Out of the vineyard? How did they get into . . .'

'They kept jumping in. That's what they did.'

'Jump? What do you mean?'

'Jump. I mean jump. JUMP. J-U . . .'

'I've got to go. Come-on. I've got to take her to the vet.'

I picked her up gently. She didn't even murmur. I wrapped her in a towel and carried her back to my van. Elsa jumped in. She thought I was going up to the Downs but as soon as she saw where we were heading she started shaking and tried to hide in the back of the van. Lloyd the vet was marvellous. He operated on Come-on there and then: put a wire support in her jaw, stitched her all up, gave her some antibiotics.

'A couple of days and she'll be right as rain,' he said. 'She'll have a twisted smile though.'

I was wary about going out again in case anything else went wrong. Instead, I carried on with the landscaping and the planting. Ruth was right. A couple of times the sheep got into the vineyard and we spent hours rounding them up and trying to get them back. I didn't realize when I got them that Soay sheep can jump over normal fences.

'Didn't you ask if they could jump when you got them?' Ruth kept asking me.

'What do you think? And in any case, David has them all over the place,' I replied.

I also rescued goodness knows how many pigeons – doves – from Brutus – Eustace.

My next piece of vineyard research took place on the Isle of Wight. I arrived during Cowes Week. The sun was shining and I spent three glorious days visiting all the vineyards on the island.

I had got used to the idea that any time off or so-called holiday for the next decade or more would be a busman's holiday. And having seen quite a number in the South of England mainland and only heard of the success of the Isle of Wight's vineyards I thought it was about time I took a few days off to have a look.

Most of them were small, just a few acres. One of them, which was larger, had just sold all its produce to a foreign wine company which, though obviously financially useful, must have taken the fun out of selling it.

Another was in a very prestigious site and had been written about in newspapers a few times. But all I saw was badly pruned vines covered in mildew. There was nothing to be learnt there.

One was in a delightful spot and offered lots of information and even a tiny show of old wine-making equipment. Then I heard an Italian voice offering a visitor a pizza. The image was destroyed!

I had tasted all their wines and was glad I was growing in Sussex. Since then, I hasten to add, their wines – as everywhere – have improved beyond all recognition.

Back home, the first thing Ruth said to me as I got out of my mini-van was 'They've blocked it up.'

'They've what?' I mumbled.

'Blocked it up. Everybody's very angry.'

'They . . .? Who . . .? What . . .?' My mind was reeling. 'Who's blocked it up?'

'The church,' she shouted. 'The doves. They've blocked them up. In the church roof. A lot of them are trapped inside. Others keep flying into the blocked window and injuring themselves. It's awful. Look.'

I turned round. She was right. I could see doves sitting on the edge of the petal-shaped opening to the roof. It had been covered with wire netting. There were also about twenty doves sitting on the roof of the church and side chapel. It was becoming more than ever like *The Birds*.

'But they can't do that,' I said.

'Apparently they say there is so much muck in there they are frightened the roof is going to fall in.'

I marched across to the church.

'You can't do that,' Ruth kept shouting.

'Who says? I'm going to stop this.'

Close up I could see more clearly. They had put up a grill inside the roof, stopping the doves from going in. But those that were already in couldn't get out. They were pecking at the netting. I saw one with blood down its white chest.

'Come on, Ruth,' I said. 'I'll ring the vicar or the church-warden.'

I spun round again and marched down the church path. One of the village women was coming in.

'Shocking isn't it?' she said, waving at the doves. 'And they call themselves Christians. Noah would turn in his grave!'

'Terrible.' I stormed past her, determined to get to the phone as quickly as possible.

'And all those young ones trapped inside as well, unable to get out.'

I spun round. 'How do you know?'

'It's the right time of year. Everybody is very upset about it,' she continued.

'Upset. I should say upset. I'm bloody upset, I can tell you.'

Just then one of the men who had been working on the church drew up in his van.

'Did you do that?' I asked.

'The grill, you mean?'

'Yes, the grill.'

'I was told to do it.'

'I'm sure you were, but you can see what's happening and there are babies in there. Please undo it.'

'But I can't.'

'Why not?'

'I'll get into trouble.'

We all trailed across to the back of the church. We had been joined by a few passersby who had come out of the pub to see what the commotion was all about. Doves were flying every-where and I could hear a lot of squealing and screeching. We put the ladder against the wall. The workman climbed up it while doves flew round and round him. He got to the grill and started to undo it.

'Oh my God,' he said. 'They're eating the young ones. They're actually . . .'

'That does it!' I shrieked! That does it! Take the netting away.'

I blazed my way across the churchyard, thundered across the lane and shot up the stairs to my office. I rang the vicar. He was out.

'Now look here,' I bellowed down the phone at the unfortunate church-warden. 'Do you know what you are? I'll tell you! Call yourself a Christian . . . all creatures great and small . . . If people knew . . . I don't care about the timber floor, what about the doves? They're eating each other. Can you imagine that? Mothers can't get to their babies. You should have got them all out first. Gassing would have been kinder. And you a churchman . . .'

I slammed the phone down. Now I wanted to see if the workman had undone the harm. I got as far as the courtyard when Ruth came running through the gate.

'Sheep. Sheep,' she cried. 'Those damn sheep are in the vineyard again.'

We ran down to the field as quickly as we could.

'You're going to have to do something about these sheep,' Ruth panted as we got to the vines. 'You can't have this all the time.'

'What can I do?' I said. 'Teach them not to jump?'

'Get rid of them,' she said.

'To the butcher? Never.'

'Well, give them away then.'

It took ages to round them up. There were only three but what they lacked in numbers they made up for in speed. First we'd get them all together, herd them gently towards the gate and then – pandemonium. They would suddenly leap all over the place. Two would disappear through the vines for another quick snack. One would jump over the hedge. The others would stroll in a leisurely way up to the house. Again we tried. Again pandemonium.

'You really are going to . . .' Ruth would begin.

'I know,' I said through increasingly clenched teeth. 'I know.'

Then they would disappear all over again. Eventually we got them back – by using the oldest trick in the book. We started feeding the ram, then gradually moved the bowl further and further towards the gate. Once he was through the gate, the others followed. We had them back again.

'But for how long?' said Ruth.

During the next few days I staged another of my attacks on English vineyards. I went into deepest Kent over Canterbury way.

When I got back I phoned Ruth.

'The vicar rang,' she said. 'He said he knew you would be pleased. They've got all the birds out of the church roof. But he's putting the grill back . . .'

'Where are they going?' I asked.

'. . . because they really have caused a lot of mess.' She continued ignoring my question! 'About the sheep, Gay.'

'I'll miss the doves. They are so beautiful.'

'You'll really have to . . .'

'I know.'

The following morning I went to see Jane Broster, who had planted a vineyard at Berwick on the edge of the Downs. She had two acres of thick heavy clay. She always made me laugh because she was such a pessimist. I always wondered why she planted the vines.

'Oh I really don't know,' she would say, 'look at the clay, see how the water lies on top. We get such fierce winds across the Downs. If there's frost, we'll get it. We'll never get a crop . . .'

On the way back, getting on his bicycle just outside the church was the vicar.

'Hello, Mrs Biddlecombe,' he shouted at me as I slowed down to tell him what I thought. 'Are you coming to our Animal Service on Sunday?'

I gave the dogs their dinner and a kiss each. I was off to another WDVA meeting.

I got changed in two seconds and rushed into the kitchen. No time to clear up or prepare anything. Another note for Peter:

Pie in oven.
160 for 25 minutes.
Make yourself some chips.
Yogurt should be ready.
G

I arrived at the meeting, which was in Leeds Castle, as Oz Clarke was getting up to speak. Those were the days when he was known as the actor in *Evita* who also drank wine. Nowadays, of course, he's known as probably our liveliest and certainly most colourful wine writer.

'Delicious, fragrant, effervescent . . . full of greengages, limes and elderflowers . . . a hint of autumn . . .'

I looked at the programme. I thought I'd come to the wrong meeting.

'. . . elegant . . .'

Was he talking about wine? Elegant, I could understand. But what did he mean by a hint of autumn? He sounded as if he'd swallowed *Roget's Thesaurus* and a gardening manual.

'. . . raindrops on autumn leaves . . .'

I looked at everybody else. They were either nodding in agreement with everything he said or they'd fallen asleep.

I drove back, having had just a few too many tastings, marvelling at the descriptions Oz Clarke had given to different wines. Would he, I wondered, describe my wines as elegant? Would he hail them as the very essence of Englishness? Of course he would. I had no doubts about that.

Heathfield was fast asleep as I drove home along the High Street and took the side turning to Waldron. Even the Chinese takeaway was closed. Roland Burgess' sheep looked up as the headlights caught them as I turned into Waldron.

Along the lane into the village everything was quiet. A fox dashed in front of the car just by the bridge, obviously on his way to Mike Farrant's chickens. A Cleveland bay was standing by its gate.

Around the bend and I was on the final climb into the village. Past Rafters where we'd been invited to dinner and they'd put a bottle of claret right by the log fire to warm it up! Then finally a left turn and . . . *a fire engine. Outside the house. Dr Gray's car.*

I screeched to a halt and ran into the house. There was smoke everywhere. The firemen were in the kitchen which was sooty black from ceiling to floor.

'Oven caught fire,' Peter said.

'But I left you a note telling you what to do. Oh my goodness, look at the mess!'

'It's very dangerous leaving fatty dishes or oil in the grill or oven,' said the gruff fireman in charge as he left. 'It was bound to ignite. You're lucky we got here in time.'

'Thank you, officer,' Peter said with a meek smile.

'Thank you,' I said with an even meeker smile. 'It will be salad in future.'

CHAPTER NINETEEN
Off to Devon

At last the great day was almost in sight. After all the preparation of the land. After the back-breaking agony of planting the endless rows of vines. After two years of nurturing them with such loving care and catering for their every need. After putting in all the stakes and miles and miles of wire. This was it. This was the year of our first vintage. At last. But we still had to wait till October.

After Ruth and I pruned them in January, we had tied them back to their cane, bent them over the lowest wire and tied them along the wire by the end of February. Even so there was still a busy year ahead. Not only had we to make sure we had a small crop but I had to start buying wine-making equipment.

Because it was partly an experiment – although I was determined it would succeed – and because our bank overdraft was also growing quite well too, I decided my thinking big would have to be postponed for another year. A beautiful winery with gleaming new stainless equipment would have to wait. And after all, other growers managed on less. Beggars can't be choosers. There seemed lots of reasons not to spend £50,000 to £100,000 setting up a modern winery!

'But I'll go for it next year,' I told Peter, 'whatever happens.'

'Yes, Gay.'

The spring of 1983 was fine after a hard winter. We had spent many days working in deep snow and in bitter winds and the warmth of the spring sunshine was very welcome. The vines liked it too and their buds were swelling. The first leaf buds usually start swelling in February and March and then burst open in April, depending on temperatures. In really good years when spring is early and warm, they burst as early as mid-March.

'What will happen if the frosts get the buds,' asked Ruth who, after two years and lots of lectures from me, was beginning to see the point of it all.

'Well,' I said in a matter-of-fact voice so as not to dishearten her, 'it will make it easier for us.'

'How come? I thought the last thing we wanted was frost?'

'We don't. But if the frost gets just a few buds it might save us from taking fruit off later so they don't overcrop. Anyway, think positive. Remember the rainbow and this is where the crock of gold is . . . somewhere.'

She laughed and seemed happy that either way we would win.

In fact we didn't get a frost. The buds got bigger and bigger. They finally burst mid-April, bright green leaves glistening in the early spring sunshine. With each development in the vineyard my excitement increased. First the leaves would grow, the stems get longer and then the flower buds would form. Flowering in early July would be normal. June would be better because it would give us a longer time for the grapes to ripen. It all depended on the weather.

The black polythene protecting the vines from weeds was looking a bit shabby but I decided to leave it down for one more year. In any case changing it would be a winter job. Thomas was taking a computer course so now only came at weekends but Ruth and I were into an organized routine. And I didn't mind mowing the grass until it got dark sometimes, as late as nine or ten o'clock.

Elsa, Honey and Blue didn't mind either. They would chase after me in the tractor until they found a more interesting scent to follow. Then when they had tired themselves out they would flop by the gate and wait for me to finish, usually with Come-on and Hilda sitting beside them.

On the words: 'That's it. Let's go,' they would race me back up to the house for dinner.

I had sold Elsa's other five puppies at nine weeks old, vetting all the new owners thoroughly. I didn't really want to sell any of them but Peter kept reminding me of the cost and the work. They were all gorgeous bundles of cream curly hair and when they were old enough they completely took over the courtyard and garden. Honey and Blue were inseparable with Honey being the leader of the two.

Mornings and evenings were still devoted to milking and feeding, although it had been easier this winter. Dennis, Peter and Adrian had built an open-sided pole barn out of old telegraph poles, second-hand timber and corrugated iron. We needed a building in which to keep the tractors and other equipment and winter some of the animals. The donkeys and horses had to have some kind of stabling.

Peter and Adrian are not exactly the most practical of men but apprenticed to Dennis they did their best. Dennis had got quite a lot of weather-boarding from a demolition job and we made up the rest with new timber. We needed heavy, strong and long timbers for the roof and sides and I managed to get them from a farm sale. The corrugated iron I had to buy new.

Work began one Saturday morning and it took four weekends to finish it. It was not without incident.

Dennis had dug fourteen large holes to take the telegraph poles which were to be hoisted up and cemented in. Simple. Peter and Adrian were cutting the weather-boarding to the lengths Dennis had given them. Easy. While they were laughing and joking as usual, the children were running backwards and forwards between helping in their small way and brushing the donkeys. 'Mind where you walk . . . you'll hurt yourselves,' warned Adrian. Ruth and I were nearby working on the vegetables. The sun was shining. All was well.

'Oh! . . . oh! . . . Ouch!' Adrian was suddenly yelling at the top of his voice.

Peter's laugh was just as loud. Dennis hooted.

'What's up?' Ruth called.

Adrian then let out a terrifying scream.

He had walked over to the site for the barn carrying a long piece of weather-boarding to check that it would fit the side of the barn. But he forgot the holes. One leg went straight down, the other just crumpled beneath him. When he tried to pull himself out he found he was stuck.

With tears streaming down his red face he yelled: 'I've broken my leg, I can't move.'

'Nonsense,' said Peter.

'You're shamming,' said Dennis.

'Oh Adrian!' called Ruth.

The children both chorused: 'Mind where you walk, Dad!'

But Adrian's screams got louder. The donkeys were getting restless. The cattle and sheep had lifted their heads. You could have heard him on the other side of Waldron.

Peter and Dennis ran over to Adrian and started to lift him out.

'Oh . . . ouch . . . ooo! . . . no . . . it hurts.'

'I'd better ring for the doctor.' Ruth ran off to the house.

'See if you can stand on it,' Peter said, with half of Adrian's thirteen stone weighing him down.

'No, no, I can't, I can't,' he yelled in obvious pain.

'Lay him down,' said Dennis.

Peter tried to touch Adrian's foot. More screams.

The children, who had stifled their giggling on the instructions of Ruth, started to be concerned.

'Oh, Adrian!' I was never one for soft-soaping. 'You've only fallen down a three-foot hole. Don't make such a fuss.'

'And he told the children to be careful,' Dennis laughed.

'If there's a hole,' Ruth had returned, 'Adrian's foot will find it. The doctor's on his way. We'll have to get him back to the house.'

In the end, amid yells of pain, we loaded Adrian on the trailer and drove the tractor the few yards to the house. With every bump came a fresh scream.

It turned out that he had only sprained his ankle and by the following weekend he was hobbling about helping with the barn again.

But the following weekend presented a big surprise. Peter is never ill, sick, aching or complaining. So it was considered a hoax when, bending down to cut some timber to Dennis' instructions, he suddenly yelled out. After Adrian's incident we all thought he was joking. He didn't straighten his back, just remained bent over and groaning.

'Trying to go one better,' laughed Adrian.

'Not another one!' yelled Dennis as he slapped Peter on the back.

'Ouch . . . no . . . don't do that! I'm serious. Ouch. Oh my back. I can't get up!'

Now Peter, being a very fit person, can never understand why other people sometimes feel the opposite. He could never understand, for instance, why I was in pain when I slipped a disc or suffered from lumbago. A backache . . . what's a backache?

Well, I gloated, I must confess. He had obviously twisted or pulled something and his back would not straighten. And needless to say sympathy was not forthcoming from any direction.

'Serves you right for laughing at me,' said Adrian.

'Now you know just what it feels like,' I said.

Bent over he edged his way up the path, past the paddock, past the cowhouse, round the corner, through the gate and into the courtyard. I followed. He wasn't joking and by now I realized it was extremely painful. But he didn't complain – just took fifteen minutes to lower himself on to a garden seat.

'I can't make the steps up to the house.' He tried a smile. 'Can you phone the doctor or someone?'

'You need a physiotherapist, he'll snap you out of this.'

'Oh, very funny.'

I telephoned the specialist I had used at Broad Oak who suggested I bring Peter immediately.

It took longer for Peter to get into the car than it did for me to drive the five miles to the clinic. A quick manipulation, a scream and fifteen minutes later we were on our way home – upright but sore!

'I'll never joke about backaches again.'

'Promise?'

'Promise.'

The pole barn was completed without further incidents. It might not have been beautiful, even as farm buildings go, but to us it looked terrific, especially after all the pain that went into its construction. We kept some of the animals in different pens in it and stored the tractors under its cover.

Meanwhile the bullocks were getting bigger and bigger all the time. Carrying bales of hay across a slippery mass of straw, being buffeted and nudged by as many as thirty big beefy cattle is a memory that will always be with me. Being knocked by my friendly Pina Colada so hard that I fell over and landed in the middle of an enormous cow pat is a memory I shall never forget. Elsa shared my mixed feelings. The one place she and Honey and Blue wouldn't go on the farm was in the open barn with all the cattle.

But large or small they still had to be fed and either mucked out or given fresh bedding every day, rain or shine, sub-zero temperatures or just bloody cold!

The little calves, on the other hand, were always a joy. I loved taking them buckets of warm, fresh, steaming milk. Most of them practically leapt out of their skins to get at it, and then carried on licking the bottom of the bucket for hours afterwards to make certain they hadn't missed the last drop.

I would soon have to think of selling some of the animals,

either for fattening on or for the butcher. The very thought started to horrify me.

I enjoyed farming but my problem was that I had grown so fond of every individual animal. Sadly I had already sent some of the big cattle off to 'Devon', our euphemism for heaven since my mother had woken up one day when we were talking about sending the cattle off to market and practically had a heart attack when she realized this was the end of the line for them.

'How can you be so cruel?' she kept shouting. 'Sending them to be . . . no, no, I can't say it.'

'Enjoy your steak?' I said to her after dinner.

'That's different,' she replied. 'You've got that from the butcher.'

Far worse was the first time we took some pigs to be slaughtered. At first I didn't think much of it. I ate meat like everyone else and meat comes from dead animals. Our pigs had the best home and the best food. They roamed around freely burrowing, and on hot days wallowing in mud holes. They played together and were very happy. They had all the cream and milk that was left over from us and the calves – thick yellow Jersey cream. And apart from pig food and scraps they had mountains of apples from two local orchards who let me collect all the windfalls that could not go to market.

'Pork and apple sauce combined,' Peter licked his lips.

I telephoned Mr Hobden, the butcher in the next village, Cross in Hand, and he said I could deliver the pigs to him and he would do the rest. Two hours after Peter had backed the horse box to collect two of the pigs we were all still trying to get them in, to the ear-shattering squeals of increasingly worried pigs.

We put food in the horse box. We put milk in the horse box. We put apples in the horse box.

As soon as one got its front legs in it would about-turn and run straight out. Dennis was red and sweating, having chased them round. Peter was, as usual, trying to work out some complicated scheme to coax them in. And Adrian, as usual, had fallen in one of their mud baths and was just about to give in when I said: 'Okay, I'll ring Mr Hobden and ask him how to get them in.'

Minutes later, after I had been forced to listen to hoots of laughter while feeling smaller and smaller, I returned to the pigs with the solution.

'Why didn't you think of it?' I said to Peter as I explained the method.

Two of us – Dennis and Peter – would have to hold two large boards to create a walking corridor for each pig in turn to be manually guided along and up into the box. The idea was that the pig wouldn't see an escape route on either side. Adrian would have to walk behind with another board to block the rear. And we had to keep quiet and calm so as not to get them excited.

On the first attempt it worked miraculously easily. One pig just walked straight between the two boards and right into the horse box. As soon as it saw the milk it started slurping furiously.

'You bugger,' said Adrian, 'why couldn't you have done that in the first place?'

'Quick, Ruth,' Peter shouted, 'close the door to keep it in.'

'Don't be daft,' said Dennis, 'we might be able to get the other one in. Ruth, Gay, get a gate and just hold it across the opening. *Don't let go* until we say so . . .'

Watching their attempts with the second pig had Ruth and me in stitches . . . again.

'If you can do better . . .' Adrian bellowed, very red in the face.

The second pig had seen the first performance and was not to be fooled. But she played along for the first half of the show, walking sedately between the boards. As she neared the ramp she darted straight to the left before Dennis could close ranks; the second time she darted to the right of an even slower Peter;

the third time she quickly stepped back and rammed Adrian who, after several skids and calls of 'Oh no, oh . . . aar,' finally landed with his bottom in another mud bath. Ruth and I decided to keep quiet but had to turn our heads to stifle the giggles.

'I'm bloody well going to enjoy eating you, you pig,' Adrian shouted. By now Stuart and Alexis had joined the fun and this added to Adrian's indignity so much he insisted that the next attempt was his last.

As the pig neared the ramp all three men gave an almighty roar and rammed the pig up and in, as Ruth and I lifted the gate like a drawbridge.

'Good riddance,' the three men said.

'Poor Pinky,' said Ruth.

I just felt like a murderer.

Peter drove them to Mr Hobden's farm only two miles away. The next we saw of them was two huge sacks of pork chops, belly of pork, legs and even the trotters and heads.

'Best pork I've ever seen,' said Mr Hobden. 'How did you do it?'

'It was all our Jersey milk, cream, the apples and being free range, I suppose,' I said, feeling sick looking at this mountain of food which was Pinky.

'You'll get top prices for those cuts,' he went on. 'There's hardly any fat but then, if they were free range, there's your answer.'

I must confess that the meat tasted delicious and for a while we kept up the pork production and made a little money. But after a while I decided I could not be a hard-hearted farmer, let alone a meat eater.

'Nonsense,' said Peter as he was munching some crackling with excessive relish, 'if we didn't eat meat you couldn't enjoy the animals. We can't keep a zoo.'

CHAPTER TWENTY
Flowering Time and the Winery

It was a sunny though not too warm July and there they were. The long awaited and full of promise flower buds. Over the minute flower of a vine is a small brown cap and when the anthers (part of the stamen containing the pollen) are ready to be released the cap falls off and the pollen falls on the stigma. I had heard this referred to as capfall or full bloom.

I remember seeing my first vines flowering and being amazed at how tiny the cream flowers were, no bigger than a pin head. Such a small and insignificant beginning to a fascinating and sometimes long process that ended, mostly, with such great pleasure and sometimes great ceremony.

I was feeling very pleased and unashamedly proud as I walked through the vineyard. Everything looked healthy and it became obvious as I examined the Muller Thurgaus, then the Seyvals and Reichensteiners, that if all the flowers set we would have too many grapes!

I prayed for the weather to stay calm. The last thing I wanted was rain to wash the pollen away, which would have virtually the same effect as frost on the pollen – no fruit.

Vines are self-pollinating and are assisted only by very light winds and not, as with most plants, by insects such as bees. The ideal weather for quick pollination is warm and dry and it need only take two or three days. After another two or three days flowers that haven't fertilized drop off – or 'shatter' as the professionals say – and the remaining fruit is 'set'. Since I was growing varieties with slightly different flowering times the fruit set was likely to take anything from a week to ten days.

And set I was for my first season of fruit.

One hundred days after flowering the fruit would be ready for harvesting. That was the theory. But within one week of the start of the flowering the heavens opened and we had two days of torrential rain. I nearly cried as much. It wouldn't help in the least but I kept going down in my waterproofs with Elsa, Honey and Blue, who sensed the gloomy atmosphere and impending disaster. There was nothing I could do. I just watched the rain hitting the pollen despite the protection of some of the leaves.

'But why couldn't it have waited?' I moaned to Ruth while we were putting my herd number, 'SQ 325', on tags and clipping them to the ears of some calves. 'In any other country we wouldn't have this problem.'

When the rain stopped there were huge puddles in the vineyard but the sun came out fierce and hot so that everywhere you looked steam was rising. Maybe it wouldn't be so bad. Maybe some flowers were protected by the leaves. Maybe some buds were still about to flower. Maybe we would get some fruit after all. All we could do was wait and carry on side-shooting, weeding, mowing and stem cleaning (taking off any new buds or growth that showed on the main stem and were not wanted). When the flowering finished we would have to resume spraying fungicide against the various rots and mildews that can ruin a harvest. The rain would help foster them too. The joys of powdery mildew and botrytis were yet to come!

After I'd given away our rare herd of fence-leaping, trouble-making, vine-eating sheep to the rare breed farm on Ashdown Forest, I got some ordinary conventional sheep instead. I had visited a retired couple, Jean and Bernard Jackson, who kept a sheep farm but who were growing an acre of vines near Robertsbridge. They had joined the local vineyards association and we had struck up a friendship. As they showed me round I saw two lambs on their own just bleating continuously in a small pen.

'Where's their mother?' I asked.

'She died. We haven't got time to foster them and in any case one of them is dopey,' Jean said.

'How do you mean?'

'Well, it doesn't know how to suck.'

'What will happen? What will you do?'

'Oh, it will probably be dead by morning.'

'You can't . . . I'll take them. How much do you want for them?'

'Gay, you can have them. But it won't be easy. You've got to feed them round the clock.'

'No problem.'

I picked up the two skinny little bundles and took them home, collecting some substitute milk powder and some spare teats on my way.

As soon as I got them back I put them in a small corner of the cowhouse. Joycey and Crystal didn't seem to mind. They just watched with interest as I tried to feed the lambs. They were used to unusual happenings.

I renamed dopey 'Lady' – a much better name – and the other one 'Tramp'.

Tramp took to the bottle easily and within minutes was pushing and nudging at it with her tail wriggling so fast it caused a draught. But Lady was very difficult. I could see what Jean meant. At first I thought maybe the lamb was blind. It just couldn't seem to find the teat. As soon as I got the teat into its mouth it lost it. It didn't seem to see the bottle or the teat but it was not blind. I spent hours with it trying to get it to drink but it didn't seem to know what its mouth was for.

It was, in fact, brain-damaged. It behaved like a handicapped child, without co-ordination and with much head-throwing. But I was determined. I got Ruth to hold its head while I forced the teat into its mouth until it became clear that I stood the risk of choking it or maybe flooding its lungs. I then used a teaspoon to tip little doses of milk into its mouth but most of it ended up over me or on the floor.

I even used a sponge dipped in milk to drip drops of the liquid into Lady's mouth. But this was not going to keep the poor thing alive, let alone get it thriving.

I rang Roland, just up the lane. He kept lots of sheep and always offered to help. But even he said: 'It's probably brain-damaged. Not worth it, Gay.' And he volunteered: 'Do you want me to knock it on the head?'

'Oh no!' I cried.

So day after day I persisted. I put it out on grass to see if it would nibble. Tramp took the grass naturally and gobbled away. But Lady, as hungry as she must have been, just didn't know what to do. But they both jumped and rollicked all over the place.

After several days I decided to go back to holding her head and forcing the teat into her mouth. She must have taken only about six sucks but it was one of those great moments. She *was* going to learn. Every few hours I tried again. It was a slow process but I persisted. Everyone else called her dopey but I knew different.

I had to bottle feed her for over two months and it took her weeks to grasp the idea of eating grass. She had a lot of catching up to do.

Now she must be the oldest ewe in Sussex. She has given us one normal lamb who to this day is with her. When I call Lady's name she comes rollicking across the field like a new born lamb.

I walk into her field every day with the dogs and every day she comes to say hello to me. She loves being scratched under the chin and behind her ears and she often wants to play with the dogs.

She can't, or won't, eat sheep nuts. And she still plays around with hay instead of just eating it, though she'll eat grass all day long. But she's not so daft. When it's sunny and warm she finds the coolest spot. When it's windy or wet she finds the best shelter. And nowadays in winter, when it is really cold or raining hard, she stands at the gate asking to be allowed inside to a special pen we made for her.

We made the pen after our first case of foot rot.

'Foot rot,' the vet said one morning when I called him in after finding them hobbling around the field. 'I'm afraid you'll have to bring them into the dry.'

Instead of being out in the vineyard, I then spent practically the whole day preparing a warm, dry pen for them in the open barn.

'We can't go on like this,' Ruth kept saying.

'But I can't leave them outside, can I?'

'I mean, we haven't got time for animals as well as the vineyard have we?'

'Throw me some more straw,' I replied.

On Saturdays I'd started going to the local riding school in Horam. Peter rode Laddie there and I rode Pickles. Then for one hour we were subjected to the tortures of Sheila, the owner and riding teacher.

Sheila is about my age, short and just slightly overweight. She knows all there is to know about horses having handled them since she was a young girl. She runs the riding school and stables with her husband, Brian, and she is a great believer in the theory that if your muscles did not hurt you were lazy!

'Heels down. Heels down. Thumb up. Kick. Kick,' she would holler at us as we walked, lumbered, trotted and occasionally cantered round and round in circles in the indoor school. One morning I finally managed to work up a brisk trot round and round in circles. Peter was away on business and so was unable to admire my progress.

'Trot. Trot. Trot,' Sheila kept shouting out in her best sergeant-major voice. 'Trotting. Sit up. Head up. Heels down.'

My horse lengthened his paces. Finally we'd got into that rhythm that had been eluding me all these months.

'Trotting. Trotting,' Sheila kept shouting out. 'Heels down. Heels down. Thumbs on top. Head up. Trotting . . .'

One of the stable girls ran up to the edge of the training circle.

'Gay, Gay!' she shouted at me.

'Carry on. Carry on,' Sheila bellowed over her. 'Kick him on. Use your legs.'

The girl stood by the entrance.

'Ruth has just rung. Your dogs . . .'

I was off round again in the circle.

'What about my dogs?'

'Heels down. Head up . . .'

'They've gone missing . . .'

'Pay attention and keep a hold of the reins . . .'

'Run off . . .' she said as I was back by the entrance.

'I'll have to go,' I shouted to Sheila.

'You couldn't stop halfway through a cross-country,' shouted Sheila as I guided the horse through the entrance and back to the stables.

I raced back home. Ruth was outside the gate in anticipation.

'I don't know how they got out.' She was on the verge of tears.

I shot off down the lane on yet another search for my three wayward girls. Being retrievers they were always chasing a scent. And while individually they were well behaved, when they were together they were like three children out for devilment. I often saw Honey look at Blue with a glance that said: 'Come on . . . let's go see.' Elsa would follow and catch up, more I think to keep an eye on them. They would go through or over our hedge or fence on to adjoining farmland and sometimes travel for miles. Most of the time they would come back dirty and tired and usually smelling to high heaven.

I spent the next three hours driving round and round all the lanes surrounding the farm.

If they're on the run, I thought, they must cross the roads sooner or later. If I keep driving round the chances are I'll catch them. But, of course, I didn't. Looking for a needle in a haystack is easy. It keeps still. Looking for three dogs in open countryside is a million times more difficult because they keep moving all the time. And some farmers wouldn't think twice about shooting dogs loose where there are sheep. As it began to get dark, I went home.

I hope they don't get hit by a car, I kept thinking. I hope nobody steals them. I hope they'll be all right.

When Peter got home that evening we both went out searching for them but at midnight we decided to give up. I was so worried.

'They've probably found somewhere to sleep by now,' Peter was trying to reassure me.

The following morning, no dogs. The following afternoon, no dogs. I rang the police. Nobody had reported seeing any dogs. That evening I drove round and round the lanes again. I kept stopping and asking people if they had seen three dogs, retrievers. But nothing.

I hope they're not injured, lying in a field somewhere, I kept thinking. I hope they haven't been shot by a farmer. I hope . . .

The following morning, nothing. I got in my van again to search for them, going further afield. Every time I saw someone walking a dog I stopped and asked if they had seen mine.

I was fighting back the tears. They had never been gone so long. How could they leave me? Didn't they have a good home? Maybe they were dead. Maybe someone had taken them for vivisection. Maybe someone just fancied three grown dogs! At six o'clock I decided to go back for milking. As I drove in I saw three black, muddy, dirty dogs collapsed in the courtyard. They were shattered, exhausted, hardly able to stop panting. They looked as though they hadn't stopped running for a month. None of them could stand up, their legs were so weak. They hardly had enough energy left to wag their tails. And they stank!

A woman at Gun Hill six or seven miles away had found them. They had collapsed on her lawn. She'd found the telephone number on their collars and brought them back.

'You should take them to obedience classes,' she said.

'I do,' I said unconvincingly.

They were so weary I didn't have the heart to hose them down. We were all so grateful to be reunited. I put them in their room. They drank gallons of water and wolfed down their dinners, then collapsed into their baskets. They slept for the next two days. They never ran away again – they had learnt their lesson.

After the two days of heavy rain in July we had a long spell of glorious weather. Everything was bursting with the joys of summer. The vines' leaves looked greener and more buds opened in the vineyards. We would have fruit after all. The rain had been nature's way of cutting down my crop. It had saved me a job! You see, everything always turns out right in the end.

The animals were all enjoying the weather too. Joycey and Crystal were giving the creamiest of milk and both were due to calve in September. Putting them into calf and watching the calvings fascinated me. It wasn't organized rape like the mating of Elsa. It was very clinical, by artificial insemination, with no handsome bull to perform the necessary. I telephoned the AI man when both cows were ready.

I had asked the Ministry of Agriculture for information on the service and they gave me a telephone number in Maidstone. 'AI man' sounded a lot better, I thought. Fancy being at a social gathering and being introduced as the artificial insemination expert!

'What breed,' said an elderly man's voice at the other end, 'or do you want sperm of the week?'

I thought he was pulling my leg.

'I've never done this before, so I'm not sure what's best,' I said.

'Okay, leave it till one of us comes down and we'll go through it with you.'

The following morning the AI man arrived. He explained the whole procedure, examined Joycey and Crystal and told me what was on offer.

'We have a bull of the week – a prize bull and a full allocation of his sperm. This week it's . . .' He was getting out a clipboard from the boot of his car which was filled with disposable polythene gloves which came up to the armpit, his 'plunger' for getting the sperm in, wellingtons, overalls and lots of tubes containing, I suppose, sperm. '. . . Duke of Burgundy the Eighth, a Charolais, or Harry for short.'

'Well, I don't know,' I admitted. 'I don't want it to be difficult for them. Aren't Charolais rather large?'

'Yes, but they seem to cross well with a Jersey,' he said.

'What other options do I have?' I asked.

'We have every flavour there is madam,' he laughed. 'I tell you what,' he added kindly, 'we'll do one with a Jersey and the other with a Sussex. You'll have no problems unless the Jersey is a Bobby calf when it won't be any good for anything. But you should get a female with this sperm because the ratings are high.'

Every time I went to the cattle market I was saddened by the sight of some of the calves, particularly the male Jerseys – Bobby calves. If a male Jersey calf was born it was usually sent off to slaughter straight away. It was seldom kept even for veal because there was never much meat on a Bobby calf. Fancy being born and cast away within hours.

The insemination was quick and both Joycey and Crystal hardly stopped munching their hay. In went the arm with the long insemination tube and a little feel around for the right place.

'Bob's your uncle,' the AI man said, 'it's done.'

★

And of course there was hay-making which I loved. I had discovered that farming is very hard work but it is rewarding. Hay-making was also fun. And the smell of new cut hay and quickly dried hay is gorgeous. If there is one smell that typifies the country for me it is the smell of hay-making – fresh, green wild flowers and grasses, a sweet, earthy, sunshine smell.

We all enjoyed hay-making, so much so that by the third year we had to toss a coin to see who was cutting, tossing and rowing up. Needless to say it was 'Make hay while the sun shines'. The timing can be crucial. If you cut the grass when the weather is unsettled you can lose it all. You have to know when you cut it that you're going to get several days of warm, sunny weather. The hotter it is the quicker the grass dries and the better the hay.

Great Meadow is now a vineyard but in those days, along with Barley Gratton, it was our best acreage for hay since there were different meadow grasses in it and virtually no weeds like docks and nettles.

We had to cut the grass going round in circles from the outside of the field to the inside, preferably before the grasses seeded. But so much depended on the weather. It was better to let it seed than to risk the cut grass getting and staying wet. As I drove the tractor round and round with the sun shining down on me and the smell coming up, I could think of nowhere else I would rather be. One summer it was so hot we were hay-making in our swimming costumes and shorts. It's a better way of getting a tan than lying prostrate on some beach.

Once cut the grass was left to dry on top.

We all liked the job of sitting on the old open Massey in the sun bumping around the fields with the spinning rake whirling behind us. This tossed the grass in the air, got the sun and air through it and left it in fluffy mounds all over the field to continue to dry.

The dogs liked this stage best and they also enjoyed the smell, I could tell. They would run around, helping unknowingly to toss the hay, and then roll in it from their heads to their tails.

Ecstasy! Elsa in particular would lie on her back with her legs in the air just enjoying the sun on her belly and her nose in the hay!

Every evening we 'rowed' it up and both Adrian and Peter would volunteer to do this if they were home. Using the spinning rake at a different setting we drove round and round in decreasing circles from the outside of the field to the middle. The rake collected all the hay and left it in high rows, the idea being that if it rained it would be more protected than if it was spread out.

There is a strange thing that sometimes happens at this time of year which I first encountered in 1989, another hot summer. By then we were open to the public and looking much more posh than we did in the early days. It was hay-making time and the day was particularly hot. I looked up in the sky and there in the distance was a whirlwind of hay. It was literally a mass of hay that had been caught up in a hot wind and was spiralling around in the sky. It must have been sixty to eighty feet high and it was shaped like a cone, coming to a point at the bottom and wide at the top.

It whirled over us, shedding some of its hay in the process. Large chunks fell on our rooftops, in the field and on the vines. The rest of the cone sped on its path westward. If it fell on a field, no problem. But I could imagine the mess it would create if it fell on someone's house or garden or even the road.

When I asked an old farmer what it was, he said he had seen many a time hay lying in a field being whipped up by the wind and then lifted and kept flying by the thermals.

When our hay was rowed up for the last time ready for baling, Roland, one of our near neighbour farmers, came with his baler on the back of his large tractor. He would drive slowly over the rowed-up hay with the baler chug, chug, chugging away. The baler would collect the hay at one end and at the other end would come out a neat oblong tightly-packed bale of fresh green, sweet-smelling hay all tied up with bright yellow or orange baling twine. It would eject about six bales one after the other and move on slowly. One year we made nearly two thousand bales.

If all of us were available, we would follow collecting the bales and lifting them on to a trailer. If it was just Ruth and myself and the weather looked good, we would pile them up two on top of two ready for collection later. One year we had the use of a grabber which grabbed the bales and placed them on a trailer for us. When we took the trailer up to the pole barn we then had to unload and stack the hay as high as we could.

Usually it was all hands on deck for collecting and stacking the hay, sitting on top with Elsa as we made our way up to the pole barn. I remember the first time. Adrian insisted he would drive the trailer up. All but Dennis decided to walk up behind. None of us felt like a ride which looked so precarious. Dennis sat on top shouting, 'Take it steady . . . go slow. Hey, look at me, folks. You can walk if you like but . . .'

As Adrian got through the first gate he suddenly accelerated, forgetting all about Dennis. While Peter, Ruth, Roland and Thomas watched, the top two layers of hay came tumbling down with Dennis, whose laughter had suddenly turned to swearing. From then on Dennis drove the tractor and we all sat on top without further incident.

So hay-making was always done when it was warm and sunny. We would get sunburnt, hot, sweaty and dirty from the dust of seeds. Ruth and I in particular would have aching backs and the coarse grasses would scratch our arms as we handled the bales. But it was a great job with everyone laughing, joking and working together, and the dogs enjoying all the fun and getting exhausted. And all the time there was the lovely sweet smell of hay and summer. Afterwards we would all go round to the pub for a long cool beer.

Towards the end of August the vineyard was looking like a vineyard. We actually had grapes, bunches and bunches of them.

After fruit sets the rate of growth is amazingly fast. Within a short time there are tiny, hard green grapes which by the end of August look like large peas. Some vines did not have any and we did not have to remove many bunches to ensure that the maximum any vine would bear would be two bunches.

We were still weeding, mowing, side-shooting and spraying fungicide. Also, by now the vines' shoots had reached well over the top wires so we had to trim them down. If you don't top the vines they will just keep growing, using up lots of energy and nutrients where you don't want them. In later years the topping was also necessary because of the netting we used to cover all the vines to stop the birds eating the grapes.

I had two hedge trimmers which we used to clip the top of the vines off. It was not so bad for Ruth since she is nearly six foot tall but the lack of those extra five inches meant I was stretching more all the time to cut off the tops, some of which must have been over seven foot tall. It took us two days, after which we felt like a couple of orang-utans with long arms in the air.

By now I had also cleared another small outbuilding at the back of the cowhouse to make way for the rather primitive second-hand wine-making equipment I was gradually getting together. I was tentatively planning to make some wine myself and send some grapes to another winery – to guarantee that we would have some drinkable wine! It would all depend on the harvest which was still a long way off.

The conversion of my 'winery' went a lot smoother than building the pole barn. It was not so much a winery, more a building I was going to attempt to make wine in. The difference might appear subtle but looking back to my little shed with its very basic equipment and comparing it to the large purpose-built winery with the latest stainless steel equipment I have now, the difference is tremendous.

The shed was part of the cowhouse complex but I had used it more for garden tools and potting. The three sides that were built on the old brick wall of the cowhouse and old stable were timber which had been painted green. The sloping roof was covered in felt and tar. Dennis had put on a new door and to give some insulation we used special insulating panels across the ceiling and walls. The floor was concrete and sloped towards a gully. It was basic.

I had been on the lookout for second-hand equipment. I even had a few calls from people trying to sell me what they thought was good wine-making equipment. I went on several wild-goose chases. One call was from an elderly Italian man offering to sell me a press. He had read about us in the local paper and he assured me the press had produced some excellent wine from Italian grapes he had purchased from Covent Garden market. I drove to the other side of Tunbridge Wells only to find it was a very small hand press that had been painted blue and stuck in the garden for decoration! Another call sounded more promising. A couple had purchased a farm and found two huge wine vats made of fibreglass. The previous owner of the farm imported French wine in bulk and bottled it for local restaurants.

'They're in good condition,' I was told on the phone.

'How big are they?' I asked.

'Very big,' the man's voice said.

'Yes, but what capacity are they?'

'Must be a total of twenty thousand litres.'

Well, that was more than I was going to produce but it was worth a look. As soon as I drove into the farm near Burwash I said to myself, 'You're wasting your time!'

It was more like a junk yard. There were all sorts of things everywhere and most of it looked dirty, rusty or just clapped out. I was shown round the back of a large agricultural building. And there stood two enormous sand-coloured fibreglass tanks. Not only were their doors missing but they had no other fittings and one of them was split!

Luckily I had discovered a firm who welded stainless steel

and after some discussions found it would be fairly simple and not too expensive to convert stainless steel milk tanks. Second-hand milk tanks were going fairly cheap so it seemed a good idea.

'I'd like to get into this wine vat business,' said the eager middle-aged man who answered my enquiries. 'There are one or two vineyards in the country and I gather you have to get the tanks from Germany.'

With some help from David Westphal, Karl-Heinz Johner and one or two others I gave the company specifications and after supplying a very competitive quote they went ahead with the conversion of two second-hand tanks I bought from a farm just outside Lewes. I ordered a small press through Karl together with other items I could not get or borrow or convert here.

In those summer days I usually started between 5 a.m. and 6 a.m. and collapsed into bed feeling shattered but satisfied at about midnight. Elsa would slump down by my side of the bed, too exhausted to get on top. Honey and Blue preferred the sofa downstairs. Within seconds at least two of the cats would jump on me and settle by my side or across my feet. At last they had me to themselves, too weak even to lift them off! I would have maybe ten to fifteen minutes to read up either about wine, pigs or fungicides or just why my yogurt had trouble setting before my eyes would give in to sleep. Somewhere in the distance was Peter's voice: 'So what have you been doing today . . . anything?'

The warm days of August quickly merged with the equally warm days of September. The grapes were beginning to ripen. Hard and bright green at first, they gradually got bigger and turned paler with a hint of yellow, becoming translucent as well as softer.

Autumn is a lovely time in the vineyard – an artist's or photographer's delight. The morning mists give it a mystical look. There are dewy cobwebs and dewdrops on the grapes and leaves. And the leaves themselves take on their autumn colours of yellow, gold, rust and even bright red on some varieties.

Nowadays we net the grapes against birds but in that first fruiting year we decided to risk it. Maybe the birds around here wouldn't notice the fruit in the first year, I thought. How, I do not really know, but that first year I don't think I lost one grape to a bird. I knew some other vineyards netted but reasoned that there was so much fruit in the hedgerows the birds would be happy enough without touching my grapes! It would also save me two thousand pounds. Now they would eat the lot if we let them.

My little winery was coming along nicely, and would be ready for the first vintage in October. The only new piece of equipment was the small hydro press from Germany. Looking back I do not know how we managed but we did.

Peter and Laddie spent all their time together going at full gallop across the South Downs or through the forest at Cross in Hand. Honey and Blue were, at least, taking their obedience classes seriously and even out in our fields were staying, sitting, lying down and coming, whatever scent was in the air. And Joycey and Crystal were about to calve.

'Keep them quiet and calm,' said the vet, with his arm inside Crystal and her rump pressed firmly against his cheek. 'Everything is in the right place. Let her do it her way but call me if you need me.'

I had read four times the book *TV Vet No. 2 for Stock Farmers* which was all about calving and even had photos to help. I was glad we didn't seem to have any malpresentations when I saw the methods for dealing with them. I didn't fancy the idea of putting an arm inside Crystal to try to turn a calf rightside up!

I knew the theory. There were three stages. Firstly the cow begins 'labour', she is restless, she strains, loses all urine and dung and eventually lies down. Secondly she gives birth and finally there is the afterbirth.

'Quick, Gay,' Ruth shouted, 'Crystal's started!'

It was fortunate for Peter and Adrian that it was a Sunday afternoon. Like Ruth and me they both wanted to witness this great happening. None of us had seen a cow giving birth before.

'We must be quiet,' I said, stationing myself on a bale of straw with Ruth behind the fence.

'What's that?' I exclaimed loudly as I saw a tree in the hedge move violently.

'Oooooohaaaaaa. Damn!' Crash. I heard Adrian's voice.

'What's he doing?' I asked Ruth in a low voice, agitated at the noise which made Crystal look up.

'He thinks Crystal wouldn't like us watching,' explained Ruth, 'so he's behind the hedge on a ladder – or off the ladder, it looks like.'

We chuckled as his head slowly appeared over the top of the hedge. The children crept up behind us whispering.

'Ssh,' Ruth hushed them.

Just then a loud clip-clopping announced the arrival of Peter and Laddie.

'Smashing ride,' he shouted. 'My little lad went like a bomb.'

'Ssh. Keep quiet.'

'What's going on?' He was still shouting.

'Sssh,' said all five of us, almost as loudly.

'Well I only . . .'

'For goodness' sake, Peter,' I shouted exasperated, 'Crystal is giving birth. Please *be quiet*.'

Just then Dennis drove in and hooted his horn.

'This is ridiculous,' I said, running up to see him. 'It's like Piccadilly Circus out here.'

Dennis joined us and we all sat there in different hide-aways watching Crystal for over an hour.

'I'm going back to the house to do some work. Call me when it gets exciting,' said Peter.

Another hour passed.

'We're going to play in the hay,' said Stuart, dragging Alexis behind him.

Another hour passed.

'I've got to go,' said Dennis.

After half an hour, just as Adrian was complaining of getting stiff, Crystal lay down. Her water burst and we could see two hooves just sticking out. I raced to the house as quietly as I could. When Peter and I got back the head had already appeared just behind the hooves. Its tongue was hanging out.

'Oh no,' said Ruth. 'It's not . . . ?'

'No,' I said, 'that's how it happens.'

After several strains and what felt like several hours but was only about twenty minutes, a beautiful wet, dark calf slithered into Cross Farm. Crystal almost jumped to her feet with the afterbirth beginning to hang from her and started licking her baby furiously. As she licked the calf we could see the reddish-brown hair of the Sussex breed becoming clearer. It was a wonderful sight, a sight that many farmers probably take for granted. But we marvelled at it and couldn't get over how quickly the calf got to its feet. Within ten minutes it was standing – or rather, with Crystal's still fierce licking, it was rocking on its unsteady legs. And within half an hour it had found the teats and was sucking the precious colostrum that so many market calves didn't seem to get, while Crystal was eating the nutritious afterbirth.

Joycey's calving four days later was much more difficult. She was straining for a whole day and still nothing happened. The vet came several times and in the end what I had been dreading had to happen. We had to help her by pulling the calf from her, tying a rope around the calf's feet and pulling while Joycey remained standing. You would think this was easy and that with the pulling force of a grown man the calf would just slide out. In fact it was more like a tug-of-war. As the calf finally appeared I had to catch it and help it down. It was wet, slippery and both the vet and I were exhausted but it was a terrific feeling when I wiped all the mucus away from the calf's nostrils and mouth and it struggled to get to its feet. Joycey appreciated the help but there was more drama to follow.

The vet had left but I kept making checks on Joycey and her new baby. Joycey did not look at all well. She had been through a lot and I put it down to exhaustion but the following morning she was down.

'It's milk fever . . . quite common,' the vet said as he started to drip calcium into her intravenously. Almost within minutes she was up and back to her old self.

'What's that?'

'It often happens within twenty-four hours of calving. It's caused by the sudden increase of milk straight after the calf is born.' He was feeling her teats when she gave him a quick kick with a back leg.

'She's recovered quick enough!'

Over the next two weeks I called the vet out three times. Joycey was eating okay – she always raced her cow nuts down – but she did not look happy and alert. She was usually full of mischief but now she was listless and just not interested. She let her calf, whom we called Blondie, suck but when we tested her milk she never seemed to have much.

She had vitamins and antibiotics but the vet seemed mystified. On his last visit, two weeks after the calving, he said: 'There's no point my coming back. You'd be better off calling the knacker man.'

'What?' I yelled.

'Well, there's no point. I don't think she's going to get any better. In any case, it's not worth spending all this money on a maybe.'

Ruth shed a few tears when I told her.

'But I'm not giving in. I'll get a second opinion. She's not going to Devon – not yet.'

I rang another local veterinary practice in Uckfield, five miles away.

'It's unethical . . . we can't take over another vet's patient,' said the young man's voice.

'It's private medicine for animals, isn't it?' I demanded.

'Well, yes.'

'I pay the bills, right?'

'Yes.'

'Well I don't give a damn about ethics. I am paying the bill. My cow needs a second opinion before she dies. So you're coming?'

'Yes.'

The young vet was only minutes with Joycey. He was obviously guarded in what he said but I could see the surprised look increasing as he examined her inside and out.

'She's septic. There is some afterbirth left and she has ketosis.'

'Why and what's that?'

'I don't understand why there is afterbirth there. It should have . . .'

'Well?'

'Well it's difficult for me to say. It's unethi . . .'

'. . . ical,' I finished the sentence with a nod.

'The ketosis or flow fever is a metabolic disease.'

'Please explain in layman terms.'

'Well, basically she has to produce glucose and she can't. She had a fatty liver at the time of calving.'

'So what's the treatment? You will treat her – that's not unethical?'

He smiled. 'No, not now. She just needs a drench. It's quite simple.'

By the evening she was her old self.

CHAPTER TWENTY-ONE
What a Vine Day

The great event was approaching fast. But plans had to be made.

Guessing the weight of the grapes we would end up picking was difficult. I had no experience and while I knew that vines in England could crop about two to three tons to the acre in an average year, I also knew that because it was our first and because we had restricted the fruit it would be nowhere near that figure. I decided not to guess, just wait and see.

Most of the bunches looked healthy and I used my new refractometer so I could test the grapes for their natural sugar levels. I knew wine making was not a simple business but I had the minimum of equipment and no experience – the ideal formula! After all I had planted the vineyard and nurtured the vines for three years without any experience. The grapes were ripening but even I realized they needed more sunshine. They tasted bitter – high in acid. So far there had been no bird damage and no disease to worry about. The weather was still fine for September and the great wine god in the sky was smiling down on us!

We had received a few leaflets about fruit-picking containers used by soft fruit farms but to save money Ruth, who had finally plucked up her courage and learnt to drive, made several trips to Heathfield in the van and bought ten buckets and ten large dustbins. The little winery was ready and waiting. Everything had been cleaned – the two second-hand tanks several times.

'Can we come down for the great event?' It was the Geordie accent of my Aunty Joyce. 'We can help you pick.'

All my mother's four sisters still lived in or near South Shields and being a close family we had a lot of contact. They had commiserated with my mother about her rather eccentric daughter but as the big day approached they were keen to be part of the action. 'Yes, it would be great,' I said. 'Who's coming?' I was beginning to worry about where to put them and how to feed them. It was the last thing I needed to think about during harvest.

'Well, just me and Walter,' she said, 'and . . . well, if it's okay . . . Olive and Bob.'

Uncle Bob, who had had a stroke and was now partially paralysed, had to be in a wheelchair all the time. I liked my Uncle Bob and I had very fond childhood memories of him.

I was surprised but said: 'Great. The more the merrier.'

The simple practicalities concerning the wheelchair did not occur to me until Peter asked that evening when he got home from London. But Dennis – where would I be without Dennis? – came up with the idea of making small movable ramps to fit against all the steps in and outside the house.

More food had to be bought in, beds made up, secateurs bought. Everything was on standby.

'Why don't we pick now?' said Ruth on the first day of October. 'The nights are getting so cold.'

'I know, I know.' I was a little irritable. 'But the days are still good. I really want the best grapes and the sugar readings are only about sixty-five. They should be seventy-five or maybe eighty-five or better still ninety-five . . . I don't know.'

I rang David Westphal.

'We've started picking,' he said in a rushed, I'm-really-too-busy voice. 'Just watch the frost warnings . . . must go.'

I decided to wait till the weekend when everyone would be here.

'I might get up to seventy,' I said optimistically.

Mum and Dad were alerted. Joyce and Walter were on their way with Olive and Bob. Adrian had booked some time off on the Monday if it was needed. Alexis and Stuart were given strict instructions. Their jobs included carrying the buckets and carefully picking the grapes. Peter had arranged to get home early on Friday so he could ride Laddie at least once that weekend. Dennis had fixed the trailer to the tractor and made certain everything was oiled, tightened and working.

On the Friday afternoon my sugar levels averaged seventy. Not brilliant but not disastrous. Although it was still fine during the day-time, frost warnings were being given for the night-time in most of the country.

I made gallons of vegetable soup, bought a huge lump of Cheddar cheese and put ten French sticks in the freezer for our 'harvest lunch'. Ruth had bought a few packs of Elastoplast. Waterproofs were ready but the weather was still fine and there was no sign of rain. I had also organized a timetable.

'Right,' I said that evening when the whole family – all twelve of us – were together. 'Remember to pick the grapes carefully by cutting the stalks. Don't cut anything else. Be gentle.'

We were all excited.

'I'm going to bed,' said Dad. It was only 9 p.m. 'And you all should do the same. We'll have an early start.'

'Let's see the weather forecast first,' said Peter switching on the television for the nine o'clock news and weather.

When the house was quiet and everyone had gone to bed I telephoned the weather station for the South Coast region: 'It will remain fine and dry until Sunday evening. Night temperature will be above freezing, no frost.' Great!

'Rain. It's bloody raining!' I shot up in bed. Cats flew off in all directions. Elsa started barking for her life, Honey suddenly howled like a she-wolf and Blue tried to crawl under the bed.

'Bloody rain,' I yelled. 'It couldn't wait, could it? Of all the sodding days of the year it has to bloody rain.'

It was 6 a.m. and barely light. I dressed, put on my anorak and wellies and sloshed straight down to the vineyard. Everything was soaked. All the vines were bowed over. There were puddles everywhere. And still it was coming, chucking it down.

'Just one more day. Just couldn't wait, could you?' I looked up at the sky as I shouted. I kicked a vineyard post hurting my foot. It shuddered and the vines showered me with more rain. 'Couldn't bloody wait.'

Ruth had already started milking. As I walked into the cowhouse she said: 'I know. I know. Did it have to be today!'

'But the forecast . . .' I started.

'Don't listen to them, they never get it right.' She had almost finished.

'Well, what's the verdict?' asked Peter as he came in.

'What's happening?' echoed Adrian, still half asleep.

Just then Dad and Walter turned the corner and shuffled in.

'Well?'

They all looked at me.

'Let's go for it,' I said, 'it's only water.'

'Right.'

'Okay.'

When I got back to the house Bob was up and in his wheelchair. Mum, Olive and Joyce were wondering about their hair.

'You're wearing waterproofs,' I said. 'No one's going to see you.'

'But you'll be taking photographs,' Mum pointed out.

Harvesting is always different. Some years it's glorious. We've spent five weeks picking delicious warm grapes in brilliant sunshine – like in 1989 and again in 1990. But 1987 was different again. That was the year of the hurricane – one harvest I will never ever forget. But the first harvest is the one you always remember, especially if it rains all day long. Now we never pick in the rain. It does no good for the grapes – or the pickers! The sugar levels go down in the rain so now we try to pick only on fine days. And we don't worry about a little frost, either!

I went round and unlocked all the barns. Dennis arrived.

'I knew you'd go ahead,' he laughed.

He got the tractors out and hitched up the trailers. I got the buckets and bins out and handed out the secateurs.

We looked an odd bunch to say the least. A very odd bunch. We had put Uncle Bob in his wheelchair in the back of the transport box of the Massey tractor and Dennis had tied it with rope to make sure it would not slip. Bob was covered in a big waterproof cycling cape and holding an umbrella. Everyone else was in green waterproof jackets and trousers or yellow oilskins and sou'-westers. Dennis and Adrian drove the tractors down to the vineyard. Peter was in the transport box holding on to Bob. The rest of us were walking behind splashing with every step.

Mum, Joyce and Olive started 'Hi, ho. Hi, ho. It's off to work we'll go . . .'

Walter preferred: 'I'm singing in the rain . . .'

The dogs barked and jumped up thinking it was all a game. The rest of us laughed. Later a neighbour told us that she heard lots of singing and laughter all day and wondered what on earth was going on.

We must have appeared mad – even madder than when we first arrived with plans to plant the vineyard!

The wet ribbon blew in the stiff breeze. I had hung it from the first post in the vineyard across a row to the second post.

'You can't ever say we don't have a sense of occasion,' I beamed, handing the red-handled kitchen scissors to my Uncle Bob whose wheelchair was still tied to the tractor's transport box which Dennis had backed right up to the ribbon.

'Please declare the first harvest,' I said.

With the rain streaming down his cape he cut the ribbon with great aplomb.

'I declare this wine to be St George's and may all who harvest here never stay sober!' he said in his twisted, slow and slurred voice.

'Hip, hip, hooray!' we all shouted.

Since Mum had planted the first vine it was only fitting that Dad should pick the first bunch in the first row of Muller Thurgau. With a great cheer it was cut and put gently in the black bucket below. Mum picked the second bunch, then we were off.

The traditional panniers or buckets you see in those sunny photographs in wine books were definitely out. This harvest was not for the photographers! But I did record the great event for posterity with my little automatic.

Now we pick one person either side of the row and we pick variety by variety. But this first time, because there were fewer grapes, I decided to pick everything in one go from the start of the vineyard to the top end.

'Right, let's get cracking,' I said. 'Split up into teams, four to a team.'

'Yes, Sergeant Dhargenou!' roared Adrian.

'Two each side of the row and off we go.'

Dennis drove Bob back to the house. It was too cold and wet for him. Olive was more than grateful to go back to keep him company.

'I'll keep the fire going and put the soup on for lunch,' she said, waving as she went. All three dogs, looking twice as slim because their curly coats were soaked, also deserted us at the mention of the word 'lunch'. Dennis' job when he got back was to collect our buckets and empty them in the dustbins on the trailer and to join the row that was not keeping up.

Now the picking is more organized simply because we have so much to pick and it takes so long. We now even do 'selective' picking – taking only the best bunches.

'Don't pick any that look rotten,' I said, 'and none of these tiny hard green ones.'

'Yes, Sergeant Dhargenou.'

Peter and Adrian were cracking jokes about each other the whole time as usual.

'I'm looking forward to seeing you on top of the Christmas tree this year.'

'Concentrate,' I shouted.

'You won't. There isn't room for two of us.'

'Please concentrate!'

Snip. Snip.

'Here, Adrian, your mother's been coming to us at Christmas for ten years now.'

'Oh yes?'

'But this year we'll let her in.'

'Ouch! Oh bloody hell.' Adrian had cut his finger. He was bound to be the first.

'Serves you right for not concentrating.'

'I'm wet through,' Mum moaned. 'I think I'll see if Olive and Bob are okay.'

'Oh Mum . . .'

Occasionally one of us would say: 'Look at the size of this bunch!' or 'There's nothing on this vine!'

By 12.50 we had finished all the Muller Thurgau and half of the Seyval.

'We've got seven dustbins-ful,' said Dennis, to slightly less noisy cheers than before. We were all so cold. The rain had not penetrated our waterproofs but it found its way up our sleeves and down our necks. My hands were bright red, tinged with a delicate shade of blue. Ruth had had the sense to wear a pair of bright pink plastic kitchen gloves.

'Let's go and have lunch,' I said.

When we got back Stuart and Alexis, Honey, Blue and Elsa were keeping Uncle Bob amused. Olive and Mum were asleep by the fire. The huge pan of vegetable soup was simmering in

the kitchen. And as we walked in the warmth and the smell of
the soup made us realize how much we were aching and how
cold we were.

'Oh my back,' said Ruth.

'It's my knees,' said Adrian.

'It's my neck,' said Walter.

'We both have a pain in the neck,' chorused Adrian and Peter.

The only person who didn't complain was Dad. He just kept
jollying everyone along.

'We've got half an hour,' I said. 'Don't forget, it gets dark
early.'

'It's hardly worth getting dry,' laughed Dad.

I had a quick mug of soup then Dennis and I emptied out five
other dustbins, three of which contained the horse feed and two
the cow nuts. We lined them with new black polythene sacks.
The rain had stopped by the time we finished and the sky began
to brighten. With red cheeks and thawed hands we started back.
As I left the house the phone rang.

It was a Colonel Somebody or Other from Hertfordshire.

'Well now, my dear lady,' he said, his voice dripping with
old world charm. 'We have some delicious grapes we thought
you might like to buy for . . .'

'What type?' I butted in.

'. . . quite certain that you'll want to . . .' he continued.

'Look, I'm very busy,' I said. 'I'm picking today and I'm
afraid I haven't got much time. What type are they?'

'Well, my dear, I do believe they're possibly some type of
German variety.'

'Look,' I said. 'How can I buy any grapes when I don't know
what type they are? If you want to sell me grapes you'd better
find out the variety. I can't make a decision now.'

'Can I call you in a few minutes? It won't take long.'

'Okay but I can only wait for five minutes then I must get
on.'

Four minutes later, as I was putting my wellingtons on, the

phone rang. A few extra grapes wouldn't do any harm, I thought. Good practice.

It was the Colonel again.

'My dear Mrs Biddlecombe,' he oozed. 'I am delighted to be able to tell you that I am informed . . .'

'Yes. Yes,' I said trying to hurry him.

'. . . that I am reliably informed by my colleagues, whose expert knowledge of vines I can assure you is . . .'

'Yes. Yes. What are they?'

'. . . second to none in the country, that our vines are Miller To Go.'

'Muller Thurgau.'

'Yes, my dear lady. Miller To Go.'

'Muller Thurgau.'

'Miller To Go. Exactly. So my dear, you do want them don't you?'

Well maybe, I thought. 'How much do you want for them?'

'Want for them?' he shouted, affronted at the thought of money. 'You mean money?'

'Yes. Money. How much do you want?' I had no idea what they would be worth.

'Well . . .' There was a long silence. 'How much do you pay?'

'How much do you want?'

'My dear lady,' he said, 'I'm afraid I'll have to discuss the matter with my colleagues. I'll telephone you back again if I may?'

Back in the vineyard the picking was going like clockwork. The two teams on either side of the two rows of Seyval were picking like mad. My father was now replacing full buckets with empty ones and emptying the full ones into the dustbins. There was lots of laughing and joking – 'Don't go too fast or you'll get a speeding vine' – and the occasional shout of 'Bucket' – at least, I think that's what they were saying. And Dad kept making sure everyone had a fresh bucket every time they needed one.

The bins were getting fuller and fuller. Stuart was driving the small tractor up and down the rows for all the world like a professional, even though he was only eleven years old.

'Everybody, everybody!' I shouted. 'Let's try and get it all picked today.'

'Yes, Gay,' they murmured with varying degrees of enthusiasm.

I'd discovered the best way to pick: kneeling on both knees in front of the vine. It still played hell with my back and hurt my knees like mad but not as much as any other way. Plus it had one added advantage: I could see what I was kneeling on.

Adrian flopped down beside me. I lost my balance and grabbed a bunch of grapes that was home to the only dozy wasp left in Sussex. But its sting was pretty dynamic.

'You *!?* idiot,' I hollered. 'Look at what you've done!'

Stuart came skidding up to me on the tractor. 'Quick,' he shouted. 'You're wanted on the phone.'

I jumped up and ran. I splashed along the row to the edge of the vineyard, into Hop Garden, along by the hedge, past the cowhouse, into the courtyard only to meet Stuart there on the tractor.

'Oh Stuart!' I panted. 'You could've given me a lift.'

'You didn't ask me,' he said.

I grabbed the phone.

'My dear Mrs Biddlecombe, I hope I'm not troubling you?' It was the Colonel again.

'Yes,' I said.

'Yes? I am troubling you?' he said even more slowly.

'No. You're not. It's all right.' He was slowly driving me crazy.

'But you . . .'

'Yes. How much?' I shouted down the phone. 'How much? How much do you want?'

'Oh yes, the price,' he said winsomely. 'The price. My colleagues and I believe that it would not be too unreasonable to, perhaps, consider as much . . .' a nervous cough, 'I mean as little as . . .' I slammed the phone down. My hand was on fire. My head was singing. The wasp sting had just taken effect. I slumped on the nearest chair.

Mum and Olive were fast asleep by the fire with two cats on each lap. Uncle Bob had joined them with the three dogs lying flat out by his feet. All were snoring.

The phone rang. As I stood up my head seemed to clear. I was all right again.

'I think the line went dead,' said the Colonel.

'Yes. Yes,' I mumbled.

'We thought we would have to check the market price independently,' he said, 'so we'll call you this evening.'

As I put the phone down I shouted: 'The idiot. He called me all the way up from my first harvest just to say . . .'

'Ssh,' said my mother, 'you'll wake the cats.'

We seemed to harvest the rest of the vineyard a little quicker. I was not sure if it was my soup that was responsible, the fact that there were fewer grapes or that the rain had started again. Probably a combination of all three!

By 3.30 we had just four rows to go. But it was getting dark.

'Come on, everyone,' I rallied. 'It's the final push.'

'Over the top,' said Peter in his Hancockian voice.

'Tally-ho,' said Adrian.

Walter made the sound of a hunting horn.

'I can barely see what I'm doing now,' said Ruth. 'If only the rain would stop.'

Right on cue it came down in torrents. As we got to the end of the last row, almost in darkness, there was an almighty cheer. Dad led the 'hip-hip-hooray'.

'Gay, you pick the last bunch,' said Ruth.

'That's right,' said Adrian, 'then she can say she did it all by herself!'

We had picked fourteen dustbins-ful and three buckets. I calculated that we had harvested about a ton of grapes – maybe a little over.

With aching back, sore knees, numb feet and hands and a very weak wrist I cut the last bunch in the dim light. The rain had stopped and the darkening sky had cleared of clouds. The moon was already clear. Everyone cheered. We were very cold, very wet and aching everywhere but we all agreed it had been a great day.

'But I hope the harvest won't always be like this,' said Ruth who went home to change into dry clothes for the milking.

'No,' I said slowly. 'In future it will last a month.'

Now our harvests do last a month. And instead of one ton it can be anything between forty and ninety tons.

Mum was running across the courtyard.

'Phone. Phone,' she was shouting. 'Quick. Quick.'

I ran to the house and picked up the phone.

'My dear Mrs Biddlecombe,' that voice oozed again. 'Have you decided whether you wish to avail yourself of . . .?'

'Tell me,' I interrupted, 'I forgot to ask you. How many grapes have you got?'

'Well, my dear lady,' I could almost see the treacle coming out of the phone, 'the vine does stretch all the way down one side of the house as far as . . .'

'Traitor!' I called as Peter opened two bottles of champagne. After all the aches and pains had mellowed in hot baths and by the heat of a huge log fire the family collected together to celebrate our first harvest. Even the cats and the three dogs joined us.

'Well, we've got English with our dinner,' Peter assured them.

'Wait till it's our own,' I said.

I didn't really want to stop for food but everyone else did and

I didn't want to spoil the celebration. Everyone had certainly earned it. But after dinner in the library – the largest room in the house – I got up from the two trestle tables and our dining table which we had moved into the room to take all thirteen of us, including the wheelchair.

'Well I'll be off,' I said.

Everyone looked at me in amazement.

'Leaving us to do the dishes!' said Ruth.

'We've all had a hard day, Gay,' said Mum, who hadn't.

'We haven't had coffee yet,' said Peter.

'Someone has to make the wine,' I said.

'But it's ten thirty,' Ruth said. 'You're surely . . .'

'There's too much to do,' I said. 'I can't leave the grapes standing too long.'

'You must be mad,' my mother said.

I put on a dry coat to a half-hearted chorus of 'Do you want any help?'

'No thanks. Don't wait up. It's going to be a long night – for me anyway.'

That first night of my first vintage making my first wine was a long, cold, lonely one. Well, not so lonely. Elsa left her place by the fire to come and see the next stage.

Because the night was so cold most of the grapes would stand quite happily outside in their bins for pressing on the Sunday. But I had to start and finish by Sunday night or their quality would deteriorate.

My little winery with its two converted stainless steel milk tanks and the small new hydro-press was almost full once I had brought in four bins to start my pressing.

'If my calculations are right,' I turned to Elsa who opened one eye, 'we should end up with about 800 litres. Divide that by 70 centilitres and we'll have . . . 1,142 bottles, Elsa! And that, divided by twelve, is . . . wow! Elsa, we'll have 95 cases of wine!'

That thought spurred me into action. With fourteen pressings and with two hours for each pressing, time was of the essence.

I emptied the grapes into the press. This was a cylinder-shaped stainless steel cage on four legs with a heavy duty black rubber bag inside. The grapes had to go between the bag and the cage. After sealing the lid I slowly filled the bag with water via a hose connected to a fitting at the bottom of the cage. The cage itself had lots of holes to enable the juice of the pressed grapes to trickle through and fall into a wide rim around the bottom with a spout at the right height to stand inside a large stainless steel bucket. I used the two stainless steel buckets we normally used for the milking.

As the water expanded the rubber bag it pressed the grapes against the side of the cage and the juice would begin to flow.

'Idiot,' I screamed. Elsa jumped up.

'Oh no.' I was drenched – again.

I had forgotten to screw the top down tight and was so engrossed in watching the first juice being squeezed out through the spout at the bottom that I was squirted with water shooting out of the top like a mini geyser. But the juice tasted delicious, even at that stage. Elsa liked it too!

I was tempted to run into the house for everyone to taste it but I noticed the lights were all out except one by the back door. And I didn't want to leave the pressing in case something else went wrong.

I worked through the night completely engrossed in what I was doing. The only noises were Elsa's snoring and the drip, drip of my liquid gold slowly filling bucket after bucket which I then emptied into one of the tanks. It was a very slow process and I laugh now when I think of it.

I didn't notice the dawn but Elsa needed to go outside at 6.30.

'Golly,' I said to her, 'I hadn't realized the time, Elsa.'

As I went out for some fresh air I could hear footsteps.

'You were up early,' Peter said, looking smart in his tweed jacket and jodhpurs. He was picking his way carefully to avoid getting his shiny black leather riding boots dirty.

'Oh, well, ye-es,' I replied, wiping my sticky hands across my jeans, 'you could say that.'

'Washed your hair? It looks a mess.'

'No. But it's a long story.' I suddenly felt tired. 'Want to taste the juice?' I asked.

A quick slurp. 'Wonderful. I must go – got to get Laddie ready. Have fun.'

I looked at Elsa. She gazed back at me with what looked like a frown. I was about to turn back when Ruth arrived for the milking.

'I slept like a log. I put the electric blanket on and off I went – lovely. Your hair's a mess, Gay.'

'Thanks!'

I went back to the pressing and after ten minutes didn't feel tired any more. Honey and Blue joined Elsa and after some early morning warm milk all three took themselves off for a run around Hop Garden. At 9.30 Ruth appeared with a mug of steaming hot chocolate.

'You've been up all night!' I wasn't sure if it was a question or a reprimand.

'Well, this is what wine making is all about,' I said. 'In any case I've enjoyed myself. Here, taste this.'

· All through that Sunday Ruth and I took it in turns to press the grapes and we became so engrossed that the day went quickly.

Now, in our modern winery we press a ton at a time and it only takes two hours.

At noon I added some yeast.

'How do you know how much?' Ruth asked.

'David Westphal said about . . . um . . . and it's on this packet – in German and English – ten grams per hundred litres.'

'Oh I can't think in litres,' moaned Ruth.

I had to climb a stepladder to put the juice in the tank, add the yeast and then put the airlock in.

We went on pressing and emptying the juice until milking time.

'You're not going on tonight,' Ruth said as she kissed Crystal and Joycey good night.

I heard Peter's voice. 'Bloody hell,' I said, 'I've lost track of time doing this.' I was about to stop for a break. The trouble is, when you stop you really do feel tired.

'You should have seen Laddie. He was going like the wind – what a mover. What are you doing?'

'What does it look like?' I said.

'You should have come out riding with me. It was fantastic on the Downs! You should have seen him go . . .'

I looked at Elsa. Elsa just barked. It was time for food.

'Have we got a bottle of our wine with dinner . . .' Peter joked, 'or shall I open something less pretentious?'

In fact all I stopped for was a quick cheese sandwich and within ten minutes I was back with my grapes. This time I left Elsa in the warm having dinner with Peter, Honey and Blue and the cats and took my cassette player instead. I love silence but an evening with Placido Domingo helped a lot.

By 7 a.m. the following day I had finished. All the grapes had been pressed and all the juice was in one tank. The yeast would now have to do the work.

'Have fun,' Peter called as he came out of the house in his navy blue overcoat with its navy blue velvet collar, with all three dogs – and me – forgetting that it was Monday and he was off to his office in London.

'By the way,' he said, 'you must have been late again last night. Did you fall asleep in front of the box? Watch the late night movie?'

My eyelids felt heavier than the dustbins of grapes.

'Yes. It was about a wine maker who married an opera singer.'

I slept the whole day.

Everyone else had gone home after long goodbyes and warnings about my health – and my hair!

CHAPTER TWENTY-TWO
A Lot of Bottle

After two days nothing had happened.

'But it should have started by now,' I groaned at Ruth.

'You sure you've done everything you need to?'

'Of course!'

'Can you add more yeast?' she suggested.

The eight hundred litres of our precious grape juice which I had already lost two nights' sleep over had not even bubbled, let alone gurgled into fermentation.

'I'll have to.' I was worried but didn't like to show it.

I got on the ladder and started to add more yeast. I began stirring it in with a new broom handle bought specially for the job. As I stirred I looked down at Ruth and started to joke about the broom handle.

'Quick, Gay. Look!' she yelled.

As I turned, white foam was billowing out over the top of the tank and oozing down the sides.

'Oh, bloody hell!' I shouted as I moved fast to put my hand over the hole. But as I did so the stepladder started to shake.

'Ooh . . . oooooh . . .'

'Be careful,' Ruth was shouting. 'Oh my goodness, Gay . . . be careful.'

The foam was oozing out between my fingers and now covered the front of my coat as I leant against the tank. It started squirting in my face.

Ruth suddenly screamed. A great big blob of foam had fallen into her face as she was looking up.

'Do something!' she yelled.

'Oh, bloody hell! What a mess.'

I went to grab hold of the airlock with my other hand. I couldn't find it with all the foam.

'Get me the spare airlock,' I shouted.

'Where is it?' Ruth was spitting foam out of her mouth.

Just then my fingers felt the airlock. I grabbed it quickly and put it on to the hole. Suddenly the whole sea of foam subsided as quickly as it had flared up.

'Phew. I rather overdid the stirring, I think,' I said as I climbed down.

My hands were sticky. My coat was sticky. Even my hair was sticky. I looked at Ruth and suddenly burst out laughing. She was about to explode herself when she burst out laughing instead. She had a white moustache.

'Ssh,' I said, 'listen.'

Blurp. Blurp, blurp . . . blurp . . . blurp, blurp, blurp . . .

The fermentation had begun.

'Everybody, everybody,' I shouted.

Ruth came drifting out of the cowhouse. Wendy, a bright and breezy blonde teenager who had just started helping us with the horses, did a slow trot from the stables after having used up God knows how much woodshavings mucking out the horses. Adrian looked up from where he was sitting watching the cattle. Mum jumped. Dad carried on washing my van.

'Everybody. Everybody,' I shouted again as they all gathered round the bottom of the steps in the courtyard. 'I've decided to get rid of all the animals. We're trying to do too much. We should concentrate instead on . . .'

'That's what I've been saying for years,' Ruth butted in.

'Well why didn't you tell me?'

'I did. You never listened.'

'Well,' I continued, 'I've decided to get rid of . . .'

'You mean Laddie?'

'No. Not Laddie.'

'The dogs?'

'No, of course not.'

'The donkeys?'

'No. Not the donkeys.'

'The calves?'

'Well, maybe not all at once.'

'Crystal and Joycey?'

'Well, maybe not immediately.'

'The geese? Ducks? Chickens? . . .'

'. . . turkeys? Cats?'

'No, not the . . .'

'But you've decided,' said Ruth.

'To get rid of all the animals,' said Wendy.

For the next two weeks while the wine fermented I bitterly regretted saying anything. The animals didn't really take up too much time. I mean, if you're going to get up at six o'clock every morning what trouble is it to milk the cows, feed maybe twenty calves, muck out and feed maybe another twenty bullocks? Every morning? Winter and summer? And how long does it take to feed the geese, the chickens, ducks and turkeys? The donkeys? They're no trouble at all. And the horses? Well Wendy and I looked after them and went riding together during the week. And at weekends Peter was out with them on the beach, on the Downs or in the forest for, what, six or seven hours at a time. Which is nothing really. And he certainly would never sell Laddie, his first love!

One morning, the local auctioneer wandered in.

'Heard you were selling off all your animals,' he said. 'Wondered if we could help?'

'Well not at the moment,' I said.

'Would you like to see them?' Ruth butted in. 'Just in case?'

'Yes please,' he said.

I turned round and they were gone.

The wine had stopped fermenting after two weeks and three days. I kept tasting it and thought it was the best wine I had ever tasted! Well, maybe the second best. But there was still much to do.

I had borrowed a pump to rack the wine – transfer it slowly to the second tank, leaving the sediment at the bottom of the first tank. This is done at intervals during the maturation of the wine as well.

'Looks like a milk shake,' said young Stuart.

'Would you like a milk shake then?'

I gave him a sample.

Ruth appeared. 'What's this?'

Stuart tasted the new wine. 'It's smashing,' he said.

'Well, that's it then,' I said. 'We'll plant more vines.'

'What?' exclaimed Ruth. 'Oh, Gay!'

'Well, I've been thinking. If this is a success four acres won't be enough . . .'

'Enough? But . . .'

'. . . to go commercial in a big way. I'm only thinking about it.'

'Is that why you're getting rid of the animals?'

'Well it's only a thought. I've got a lot to decide, but if I do plant more we'll either have to get more help or I suppose some of the animals will have to go.'

'How many more vines?' Ruth asked cautiously.

'Well . . . we do have fifty acres . . .'

'What?' she shouted. 'Then we will need help *and* have to get rid of the animals.'

'Anyway, it's just a thought.'

That evening when Peter got home from London I took him to taste the wine.

'It still has a long way to go,' I said.

'What finesse. I don't think it's too pretentious,' he smiled.

'In fact it's not bad at all. It has a certain – what are you doing?'

'I've got to make sure it doesn't oxidize so I'm adding some . . .'

Just then he leant over the jug I had in my hand. He pulled back so fast his glasses fell off and crashed to the ground breaking one of the lenses.

'Oh goodness.' He screwed his face up. 'My glasses!'

'It's sulphur,' I said. 'You should have asked. Better go and say good night to Laddie.'

The following weekend Dennis was working on the pole barn. 'I've been thinking,' he said. 'That old barn by the side of the road would make a nice shop. It's got lots of old timbers. Of course, we'd have to put a proper floor in and a front and back.'

'Yes, Dennis,' I said, 'it would.'

'Just thinking,' he said.

Then on the Sunday evening Peter rode in as I was feeding the geese and ducks in the pouring rain, and Ruth was in the warm milking the two cows.

'If Dennis turned that old barn into a shop,' he said, 'you could make this whole area into a mini-vineyard. Plant some vines. Show people how they're grown. It would look nice.'

Again and again I kept putting off the decision. I loved the animals. And I loved having them around. I knew in the end I would just have to do it. But not yet.

After the first racking of the wine I had to filter it to stop it looking like a milk shake. Now we have the latest technology in filter systems which filters more efficiently and certainly more quickly. We were the first vineyard in England to have one and our clever winery manager, Priska, does all the filtering now. But back in that first season it was egg whites. Mind you, the method is not to be scoffed at. It is still used today, or at least I have met some French, Australian and New Zealand wine makers who say they use the old traditional method. I don't know how but I know it works.

After all, we had our own free range chickens and all I needed for my eight hundred litres of wine was about two dozen eggs. They cost me next to nothing. My filter machine today cost nine thousand pounds!

I collected the eggs in the morning and left them in a basket in the cowhouse while Ruth was milking. Adrian had come in to see what was happening and to taste the wine. He had now gone into shift work at *The Times* printworks, which meant he was often home on weekdays.

'Can you bring me the eggs?' I shouted out of the door in the direction of the cowhouse. I could hear Adrian and Ruth laughing and chatting.

'Hello? Can you bring me the eggs please?' I shouted louder.

'I'm coming . . . I'm coming,' Adrian called back.

I heard Joycey's hooves, Ruth shouting and a yell from Adrian. I couldn't quite make it out but Adrian was cursing, 'Those bloody beams!' I heard Ruth scream, 'Well you should have looked.'

I ran round to find milk all over the floor and pouring out on to the path. As I got to the door I could see that the milking bucket was overturned. Broken eggs were everywhere. Joycey was about to add to the concoction or at least comment on the whole affair.

Adrian was clutching his head and Ruth was shouting: 'Why can't you ever do anything without . . .'

I tip-toed backwards, quickly jumped in my van and drove a mile to the other side of the village to Mike Farrant's dairy farm where he had just started up a large free range egg unit.

'Thought you had your own,' he said as he handed me a tray of still warm eggs.

I whisked the whites of the eggs, giving the yolks to the pigs, and added them to the wine.

'Yuk,' said Alexis.

Within a few weeks I would have crystal clear wine. Another racking and then I would have to think of the bottling. Because of the way I had made the wine and on advice from different people I thought I would bottle next spring. (Now I leave the wine in tanks to mature for much longer.) It seemed to be simple at the time. I now know I had a lot of luck . . . and perhaps St George to thank for it.

'Hello there. I haven't heard of you, have I?' said Mr Chapman who ran a bottle wholesale business with his father, brother and son in Clapham.

'You will as soon as I get some bottles to sell,' I promised.

'Just tell me what you want and we'll deliver. Do you want hock, Moselle, burgundy, Bordeaux, Sauterne – brown, clear, green, autumn leaf?'

Our first vintage was just one wine with all the grape varieties blended together so the decisions were easy – well, easier than today. We now make eight different wines in different bottles with, of course, different labels.

Because of the fixed number of bottles per pallet I had to order two pallets of a total of 1,350 brown hock-shaped bottles, together with the best quality corks I could get, a box of capsules and, after several meetings with the printer selecting a typeface, colours and paper, 1,500 main, neck and back labels. I had agonized over the design of the labels. It had to be classic in style and simple and it had to be obviously English. At last I was all set.

Now we use modern bottling equipment which bottles at a much faster pace. My first bottling saw Ruth and me sitting on wooden boxes filling the sterilized wine bottles with the help of a clear plastic hose.

'Is this St George's?' said a large man with a cockney accent in blue overalls with an ancient cigarette glued to his lips. He didn't wait for a reply: 'Had a 'ell of a job findin' you. Got some bottles for a . . . Mrs . . . Buddleston.'

I walked back to the gate with him and there it was – a huge articulated lorry.

'You won't be able to get that in here,' I gasped.

'No sweat, lady.'

'But . . .'

He had already jumped in the cab and was roaring in with a quarter of an inch to spare at the gate post. I closed my eyes.

'Right. Where?'

'Oh, just here will do. They've got to go into my winery.' I pointed, feeling quite proud.

'Bit small, innit? How d'you get your fork lift in and out?'

'Fork lift? . . . you mean?' It suddenly dawned on me. 'Oh no.'

'Don't tell me you aint got one?' His cheery voice suddenly got colder.

'No . . . can't afford . . . in any case I only have a small winery.' My pride had taken a knock. 'How do we . . .? Well I suppose we'll have to take them off by hand,' I suggested weakly. 'I'll get some help. Ruth!'

'Only you two women, then?' the driver asked. I began to sense a note of chivalry creeping into his voice.

'Oh yes,' I smiled my weakest smile. 'We have to manage this place by ourselves. We don't even earn enough to employ a man.'

'Come on then, ducks,' he said, throwing the chewed unlit cigarette to one side. 'Let's get cracking. I've got to get 'ome tonight sharpish or me missus will 'it the roof.'

'Wait a minute.' I had a brain-wave. 'Isn't the front loader on the tractor?' I asked Ruth.

'I think so. Why?'

'Why don't we use that to lift the pallets off. Are they on the edge of the lorry?'

He was miles ahead of me and was already checking. 'You're in luck.'

The thought of unloading every one of the 1,350 bottles by hand and re-stacking them did not please any of us. And since they were sterilized and each pallet sealed all over I didn't want them handled.

'Oh God,' said Ruth, 'why didn't you think of this?'

'I can't think of everything,' I snapped. 'Anyway we can't afford a fork-lift truck. You're talking ten thousand pounds.'

As I got the tractor in position with the front loader's forks poised to edge under the pallet, it was obvious my little Massey was not man enough for the job.

'Wait,' I said to the driver, who had put another cigarette in his mouth and was looking at his watch. 'I won't be long.'

I ran to the phone.

'Mike,' I said cheerily, 'can you help? I need to unload two pallets of wine bottles off a lorry and . . .'

Within ten minutes Mike's son Stephen was driving in on a huge Ford tractor with enormous wheels, a glass cab and a great big hydraulic fork in front.

'I've never moved wine bottles with a tractor before – but I'll do my best,' he said.

Getting the first pallet on the fork took a while. Stephen was worried about breaking the bottles and moved the tractor and front loader very gingerly.

Ruth had made the driver a cup of tea and was softening his irritation with a digestive biscuit.

As the pallet with 675 bottles gently rocked on the fork Stephen began lowering it carefully to the ground. He was sweating with anxiety. I guided him to the entrance and he lowered the pallets right to the ground.

'Phew!'

Half an hour later the driver from Chapman's was speeding up the lane as though he was driving a sports car, Stephen was on his way back for milking, and Ruth and I were both relieved.

'Another close one,' Ruth said.

It took us three days to fill the bottles and put the corks in using a hand corker. We got merrier as the work progressed since we thought we deserved a glass or two. We ended up with 1,164 filled bottles!

I had borrowed a capsuling machine and bought some more capsules from another vineyard. The evening we finished bottling I applied labels and capsules to two bottles.

Ruth brought Adrian and the children up to the house at 8 p.m. just after Peter got home.

'What's this all about?' Peter asked.

'Don't tell me,' Adrian said. 'You're selling up and moving to Italy to start a spaghetti factory?'

'Sit down,' I insisted, 'and just wait.'

Ruth put her hand up to her mouth and blew a fanfare as I unveiled the two bottles which had sat unnoticed on the dresser. I repeated the fanfare. Ruth and I beamed.

'Great!' said Peter.

'Terrific . . . can we taste it?' asked Adrian.

'Is that really our wine?' asked Stuart.

'Yuk,' said Alexis.

I poured four glasses.

'A lovely nose,' said Peter.

'Complex . . . oozing with fruit,' smiled Adrian.

'And that's just Gay and Ruth,' laughed Peter.

It was dry, light in colour and had a very flowery bouquet. It tasted green, a bit too young, but we expected that so soon after it was made. But coming through was the clean, refreshing, fruity taste of the grapes.

'It's really rather good,' said Peter.

'It's smashing,' said Ruth.

It was a unanimous decision. Everyone agreed that, beyond any doubt, it was the best wine we'd ever tasted!

CHAPTER TWENTY-THREE
Happy New Year

'Ding dong merrily on high, in heaven the bells . . .' sang Peter, Alexis and Debbie, all with tinsel wrapped around their riding hats and around the horses' manes, tails and headcollars.

Debbie had organized a carol-singing ride to raise money for disabled riders and the three of them were to join other riders to visit pubs and houses around the area. Debbie was on her own horse, Peter on Laddie, looking festive and handsome with silver and red tinsel, and Alexis, who had started to learn to ride earlier in the year, was on a borrowed pony. She was growing up fast and suddenly mad about horses. Off they went on Christmas Eve morning singing slightly off-key.

We all arranged to meet at the pub at lunchtime, dogs and horses as well. Several of the villagers were there and since it was dry we stood outside singing with the riders, Peter leading the way but confusing the others by singing either the wrong words or the wrong notes. He had been offered a drink at most of the houses he visited and judging by the way he was trying to stay on Laddie it was lucky our village was the last on the route. There were about ten horses, an assortment of dogs and about thirty people.

One of the local traditions at Christmas is a performance by the Mummers. They are a group of men all dressed from head to toe in bright-coloured costumes made from strips of material. Like moving rag rugs, I always think! They roam from pub to pub giving a performance which dates back centuries and is steeped in tradition and superstition. When they saw we were there they performed the 'St George and the Dragon' playlet. But like the riders they were now getting quite merry. Not that anyone cared. Everyone was happy. Elsa was barking at the Mummers and Honey and Blue joined in the spirit of things.

The move to Cross Farm had not only changed our lives but also our Christmases and the first few were like no others any of us had ever experienced, especially when we had all the cattle, pigs and other animals.

Since Peter and I had married we had had a Christmas in Kenya, in the Canary Isles and in Jamaica. The rest of the time I had entertained the family. In London we had started a family tradition of dressing up for the Christmas feast, which we made extra special and extra long.

At Oaklands we wore evening dress and the feast lasted three to four hours with lots of different wines and a four-course gourmet lunch. We would then play games, including billiards on the old table left by the owners of our first house. On the last Christmas at Oaklands, after we had built a tennis court, we spent most of the morning playing tennis. Opening the mountain of presents underneath the tree took over two hours since that also was a ritual – one present per person at a time!

But Christmas on the farm was different. We still had to milk and feed all the animals and, because it was winter, muck them out. We gave them all an extra helping of food or special treats. The horses had a bottle of Guinness each in their feed, the donkeys extra apples, carrots and Polo mints, Joycey and Crystal some extra nuts and apples, the pigs had more nuts and certainly more cream because we didn't make any extra butter or yogurt. And so it was Christmas for everyone – except the Christmas goose!

One year everyone enjoyed goose as a change from turkey – everyone except me. It was one of ours. That Christmas was my first as a vegetarian!

'Grab the bird by its legs with both hands,' the book said. 'Keep the back of the bird away from you. Lower the head to the floor and get someone else to lay a broomstick across the neck, just behind the head. Tread on both ends of the broomstick and pull the legs upwards until you feel the neck break.' The book added: 'If you hold the tips of the wings as well as the two legs the bird will not flap after it is dead.' That was the theory.

When Peter proposed to kill one of our younger geese for Christmas I was horrified.

'Well what are we keeping them for,' he asked, 'if not to be self-sufficient?'

'We might as well have one of ours as someone else's,' Ruth reasoned.

'I don't care whether it's our goose or our turkey as long as I don't have to kill it,' declared Adrian.

I was outnumbered.

Nora and Christie had not long left us with instructions on how to do just about everything, including the way – the Irish way – to kill geese, chickens, ducks and even pigs – which we definitely were not going to tackle.

'To be sure, be-Jesus,' Christie said often, 'what else are the beasts for?'

Peter's mother was born in the middle of nowhere overlooking the River Shannon near Ennis, County Clare and Christie was her sweetheart until she came over to England to earn some money for her family. But she stayed in England and married and did not return to Ireland until Peter's father had been dead many years.

Shortly after Peter and I married she went back for a holiday and a few years later married Christie, who had been a farmer all his life and a widower for several years. The trip to Cross Farm was his first outside Ireland and all he wanted to see was farms, beef cattle, cattle markets, other farmers, tractors, machinery – in short anything to do with farming. But being

Irish he had different ways of speaking, of doing things, of farming – and of killing.

He laughed at me.

'Sure, missus,' he said, 'what'll ee do with 'em if you don't eat 'em!' He always calls me missus and not Gay.

Christie had his own method of killing a goose and it was not the way the book described. He didn't have much time for such books. One day, when I was out, he killed a chicken to show Peter what to do. He plucked it, de-gutted it and Nora had it cooking almost before it had gone cold!

So a few days before Christmas there was Peter, having selected the unfortunate goose, at the ready to show that at least he was prepared to be totally self-sufficient. Ruth was on standby to help and I only stayed to make sure it was done quickly with no pain.

'Are you sure you want to go through with this, you two?' I pleaded.

'Oh Gay, it's had a good life,' said Ruth.

'It's ridiculous if we can't eat one of our own,' said Peter.

I had made sure George and Bettie and the other geese were in another field and could not see what was to happen.

Amid quite a bit of noise, Peter grabbed the goose by the wings with one hand and with the other held its head by the beak to stop it biting.

'You're the last person I thought would do this,' I said accusingly.

He sat on a wooden box outside the cowhouse and forced the goose between his legs with his head facing away.

'Have you got the knife, Ruth?' He waved his free hand.

'Here. Be careful, it's very sharp!' she said.

'I can't bear this.' I had to walk away.

'Don't be silly,' Peter said. 'I'll be so quick, the way Christie showed me, it won't feel anything.'

As though he had done it a million times before, Peter bent the head down and drew the knife deeply across the top. The blood spurted all over his face and down the overall he was wearing.

'Oh my God,' I said, feeling sick.

'Call yourself a farmer,' he said.

I had to walk away. Never would I eat goose again.

'Well, I don't care what you say, Gay,' Adrian was rubbing his stomach, 'that goose was delicious. And the stuffing was lovely. You killed – '

'Adrian,' shouted Ruth, motioning with her eyes in the direction of my mother who hadn't registered what Adrian had said.

But Dad said: 'I prefer turkey, or better still beef, any day. Was the goose your own?'

Mum stopped joking with Stuart and said: 'Was it?'

'No, of course not,' said Ruth looking at me and shooting a severe look at Adrian.

'What did you think of the wine?' interrupted Peter hastily.

The highlight of the Christmas meal after our first harvest had undoubtedly occurred right at the beginning when, with great ceremony, we opened a bottle of our wine. It was treated with the reverence it deserved.

Dad said proudly: 'I never thought I'd live to see the day when I'd be drinking my daughter's wine from her own vineyard.'

'Well we had a hand too,' laughed Ruth.

'This is great,' said Peter, 'our own wine, our own vegetables and our own goo—'

'Yes,' yelled Adrian to drown the end of Peter's sentence.

We had also had several other bottles. Because we have always made it a long affair Peter has always opened several different bottles of wine. So far we had drunk two bottles of our own wine, three different red wines to compare, all made from the Cabernet Sauvignon grape – one from the Lebanon, one from Australia and one extra special, a Château Latour which Peter had nurtured for a number of years.

We were, to say the least, all feeling rather merry. And there was more to come with the Christmas pudding. But, as I said, Christmases were not the same. We had to stop halfway through the Christmas dinner because it was beginning to get dark. It was milking and animal feeding time.

'Hardly seems worth getting all dressed up,' said Adrian.

'You know what I think?' said my mother. 'I think you're all mad.'

'Oh come on,' said Ruth. 'The quicker we go the quicker we'll be back.'

'In any case,' I said, 'it will give us a chance to make room for the Christmas pudding and Mum a chance to clear the dishes!'

Because it was barely light we all decided there was no time to change into our working clothes. So off we all went, Peter still in smart trousers, white shirt and bow tie; Adrian in the new trousers Mum had given him, and new shirt and tie from Alexis and Stuart. Ruth was in a new longish dress Adrian had bought her together with a new necklace and I was in a not-so-new but smart black velvet dress, black stockings and green wellingtons!

'Landed gentry,' laughed Dad, 'doing the mucking out in a bow tie!'

Armed with more Polo mints and special horse candy Peter was on his way. Ruth and Adrian put on their wellingtons. It was much colder outside, almost frosty so we all wrapped up in our dirty old work coats.

Peter and Adrian fed the cattle, the sheep and the horses and made sure they had enough water. They were fooling around all the time and from the cowhouse Ruth and I heard singing and laughter.

Ruth and I started giggling, realizing that we must look ridiculous all dolled up and milking.

'Just think, Gay,' Ruth was serious for a moment, 'would you have thought we'd be doing this on Christmas Day?'

'No,' I admitted, 'and when the cows go it will be different again. But that's life.'

As we finished and said good night to all the animals it really was dark and getting icy cold. We raced back to the warmth of the house and Christmas pudding flamed in brandy. As soon as we walked in, the heat of the log fire hit us.

'I can't wait for my pud,' said Adrian, as we all queued to wash our hands.

'What's that awful smell?' asked Mum who was about to set light to the pudding. 'Has the pudding gone off?'

'Oh my goodness,' said Dad.

'Oh Adrian,' we all laughed. 'And on his new trousers too!'

'Oh sh—' started Adrian.

New Year's Eve followed Christmas quickly and as usual the family celebrated it together. It was another excuse for me to do some real cooking and I preferred it to the Christmas dinner. No goose would be sacrificed.

Peter as usual chilled two bottles of champagne to be opened at midnight and until then and after dinner we played Trivial Pursuits, the general knowlege quiz game, in front of a huge log fire surrounded by Elsa, Honey and Blue and all the cats. We could just about hear the celebrations in the village pub and at 11.50 precisely Peter opened the champagne and finished pouring us all a glass by the first stroke of midnight.

We all went outside into the courtyard and looked up at the church. A dim light was on which showed up the stained glass window through the branches of the trees in the churchyard. And the Waldron bellringers started their New Year peel.

'Happy New Year, everyone,' Dad called.

'Happy New Year,' we all chorused and toasted each other.

'What's your New Year resolution, Gay?' asked Ruth.

'Don't tempt fate,' Adrian laughed.

'To spend more money,' Peter grinned.

'To plant another vineyard and produce our own champagne so that New Years in future will have some style!' I replied.

'Oh no,' everyone groaned, 'not more work.'

'Happy New Year . . . wine lovers,' I smiled and raised my glass.

CHAPTER TWENTY-FOUR
Goodbye Old Friends

The wine had turned out well and it spurred me on. But I had to face facts. I was forty-one. There was no time to waste. It was time to plan the whole operation all over again – on a larger scale and with a better knowledge of what I was doing. I couldn't do this and keep all the animals as well.

I was lucky enough to find someone local to take both Joycey and Crystal. One of the women in my riding class, Jill, said she was looking for a couple of good milkers. She wanted to start rearing calves. Perfect, I thought. Perfect. She loved animals and already kept goats and chickens. She'd give Crystal and Joycey a good home. She was just down the lane so I could always go and visit them. Perfect. I went straight back and told them they were going off on holiday. They had nothing to worry about, I'd be down to see them in a few days. Crystal, I'm sure, was suspicious but Joycey seemed quite excited at the idea. So excited she actually kicked over a whole churn of milk before I could rescue it.

The following Wednesday I got the horse trailer out and off we all went. I took their halters with them so they would feel at home. Again Crystal seemed hesitant. But Joycey bounded out of the trailer as if she was ready for a new adventure.

I showed them their new home which, in fact, was much smarter than the one I had kept them in. They would have a purpose-built cowshed and milking parlour with plenty of drainage. They had a deep bed of golden straw which, I couldn't help thinking, reminded me of some glorious Sauterne. They had plenty of fields and lots of company. I was happy for them, although I admit, after I left them, I was driving the Land-Rover and trailer with tears in my eyes and a lump in my throat.

It was the end of an era. I don't care what people say – to me they were wonderful friends. They taught me a lot. They brought me lots of pleasure. It seemed somehow wrong to be saying goodbye to them like this but at least they were in good hands.

Finding homes for the rest of the animals was just as heart-breaking as saying goodbye to Crystal and Joycey.

Everyone else was glad to see the back of George. He and Bettie and the other geese we had accumulated went to a smallholder in Burwash who was going into goose eggs. He also took the chickens and ducks so I didn't feel too bad. George would still have his old companions to dominate.

My last two bronze turkeys went to a little boy who wanted them as pets.

All my calves were now bullocks. All the Sussex and Herefords were bought by a neighbouring farmer. He said they were the best he had seen and was not surprised since he knew how well they had been looked after.

The other bullocks, six Charolais crosses and two Friesians, went off to market. The auctioneers asked me if I would be attending. I said no. I don't think I could have stood it if they had all been bought by one of the big butchers – I would probably have bought them all back again. I thought it better to be ignorant.

It was a sad time for me and even now I miss them all. But we kept the sheep, the donkeys and, of course, the horses, dogs and cats.

With the animals gone the farm seemed quiet but we set about Operation Clean-up. Ruth and I got all the feeders and hayracks and cattle crushes together. The trouble was, everything had its memories.

'Do you remember the problems we had with Crystal and Pina Colada?' Ruth would say.

'And the flower pots we put on the calves,' I would reply.

'And the time . . .'

Dennis helped shift all the tons of straw and manure from the pens. We spread the manure every winter in the vineyard. He was able to use the tractor in the big open barn and the barn we wanted to turn into a shop. The cowhouse and the calfhouse we did by hand. I had lots for Wendy to do. She still came in mornings and evenings to look after Laddie, although she was costing me a fortune in woodshavings. She had just been given some Arab horses to look after and was now determined to be a professional trainer and jockey.

I kept meeting people who told me about all the animals who had gone.

'Jill is so happy with Crystal and Joycey,' Sheila told me at the stables. 'She absolutely loves them.'

Then one day in the post office: 'Got a good price for your calves didn't you, Mrs Biddlecombe?' said the auctioneer. 'Everybody knew if they were yours they must be good value. Shame you decided to sell.'

I took Elsa, Honey and Blue for a walk along the public footpath and across the fields at the back of the church. Just as we were coming back through the churchyard we met Lydia.

'Just heard,' she said, 'about the cows. How sad. The village won't be the same.'

'Yes, well you see . . .'

'Always remember the time I saw you walking them through the village to the fields and that American stopped and took your photo. Always remember that.'

'Yes. And he gave me five pounds,' I laughed. 'Thought we were country yokels.'

'It won't be the same any more,' she said sadly and wandered off into the church.

Next door, on one of the rare evenings I was in the pub,

Verity said to me in one of her stage whispers: 'Don was in the other night. Said he's got some of your bullocks. Said they were the most gentle he's ever had. More like pets.'

'I suppose they were really.'

'Said they give him so many problems.'

'Problems? Why problems?'

'Well he says because they're like pets, he can't herd them round the fields or get them into lorries. They just stand there looking at him, except for one which he says is a killer.'

'A killer? What do you mean, a killer?'

The whole pub suddenly went quiet, the way it does when you don't want it to.

'Well,' she paused with dramatic effect, 'the other evening he said he called all the cattle in and this big bullock came charging up the field. Straight at him. Then when it was just inches away from him, it reared up on its hind legs and tried to kill him.'

'Kill him?' I laughed. 'That's Pina Colada. That's his way of saying hello. He always did that, even when he was a kid – if you see what I mean.'

'Yes. But it must have been frightening.'

I suddenly felt like being alone. My poor calves, I thought. I could imagine them happily standing around instead of getting into the lorry. And poor Pina Colada. He was only being friendly. He didn't mean to kill. Kill. Oh no! They couldn't have . . . I was already wishing I had not sold them all.

The following morning I was dying to see Crystal and Joycey. I got in the Land-Rover and was about to drive out when a big furniture van swung in.

'Missus Biddlecombe?' said a broad Irish accent.

'It is.'

'I have some souvenirs for you. From the Emerald Isle.'

Souvenirs? I didn't order anything.

The whole furniture van was packed full of wonderful old farm implements from Christie. There were great big cart-wheels, a genuine old Irish dung cart, five or six ploughs, a tumbling Paddy for gathering in the hay, a real old Irish butter-maker, lots of old forks and even an Irish silage cutter. They were fantastic. I could see them scattered around the barn when Dennis had finished work on it and all over the gardens and mini vineyard when I finished planting them and laying them out. The cartwheels would need painting. The dung cart would probably need rebuilding. The tumbling Paddy and all the ploughs would need sanding down and painting. But they would add a lot of atmosphere and decoration. It was a marvellous collection. I remembered that Christie had mentioned all his old implements and I had jokingly said that I would love to have them.

We unpacked everything the Irish way.

'Well now, Mrs Biddlecombe, dee yee see that old cart there? We had the very same cart ourselves, dee yee see. 'Tis the very same. And the days we would spend in the fields . . .'

'Yes. Yes. Very interesting. Can you put it over there. No! Not there! There.'

'And these rakes and forks. Why, I remember 'twas a fine summer's evening. We'd been in the fields all day . . .'

'No. Leave them there. I'll sort them out.'

'This butter churn. Well, my dear old mother used to spend days at the very same churn. Glory be to God, the butter she made. 'Twas too good for the angels themselves. . . .'

'Careful! Don't do that! You'll . . .'

'. . . even if I say so . . .'

'. . . break it.'

'. . . myself.'

Then just as we were unloading some milk churns, an old saddle and some harnesses, Wendy arrived. She now had ten Arabs to train and race and had taken on two girls to help her.

'But they don't know how to muck out,' she complained. 'The amount of woodshavings they use, they're costing me a fortune.'

'Serves you right,' I said.

By the time we finished unloading the Irish lorry and Wendy and I had had a chat with Laddie, who celebrated her arrival by giving her some more mucking out to do, it was too late to visit Crystal and Joycey.

The same thing happened the next few days. I would get ready to go then something would stop me. First Dennis wanted some help in the big old tithe barn. I had wanted to convert the barn by the side of the road into a shop but it was going to cost too much. Instead I decided to turn a small section of the big barn on the left of the doorway into a shop. It wouldn't be as big but it could still look as pretty. It had obviously been used as some kind of workshop by the previous owner who had put in a chipboard ceiling and walls. The old ceiling needed pulling down and a new one putting back. Lights had to be fitted. There was a gaping hole in the outside wall that had to be repaired. Dennis was going to block it up with any old bricks but I insisted he used the same materials – sandstone rock. Of course, it took a long time to find rock that would look as old as the rest of the building. And the new mortar had to match the colour of the old. 'Use cow dung,' a farmer I knew told me once. 'It makes everything look old . . . hums too!' Crystal and Joycey, I thought. Now I had to go and see them – with a bucket! (When I finally tried it, it worked. You learn something every day.)

Then Wendy took Peter and Laddie racing up Lewes Race Course. She had two of her best Arabs she wanted to try out. Laddie was a former race horse and they wanted to give him a taste of the old days.

'Don't be long,' I said as they went off in the horse box. 'I want to visit Crystal and Joycey.'

'Righty-ho,' Wendy replied.

But, of course, they didn't get back till late. Another day was gone.

Finally, one day I was free. It had been pouring with rain and the ground was soaking wet but the sun was beginning to break through the clouds. Ruth had the day off, which was obviously why it had stopped raining. Dennis was out looking for some old oak beams which we needed to restore the small barn. I had two hours to spare. I decided to go and visit Crystal and Joycey.

I rang Jill and told her Elsa, Honey and Blue and I were coming. She said she would be out but no problem. She was sure they would love to see me. And how!

As soon as I opened the gate to their field and called out to them, they came running down to see me. Crystal was at the top of the field with her head buried in a mass of long grass. Joycey was in the middle of a clump of bushes. As soon as they heard my voice, they looked up. Crystal twisted her head at an angle. Joycey just stood stock still. I called again. You could almost see them thinking, 'Is it? It can't be. It is.' A huge lump came to my throat.

Then they both turned and slipped and skidded down the slippery field to where I was standing. It looked a bit like the start of a Harrods sale. Both were now old ladies. Both a little shaky on their legs. Crystal had dark round eyes and moaned gently like a caring aunt. Joycey was much more the happy-go-lucky mother who loved nothing better than playing with the kids.

They both nudged and knocked me and pushed and butted me. I'm sure they wished they could talk. Elsa sat there in amazement at this odd family reunion.

'Now how are you doing, my treasures?' I said. 'Are they looking after you?'

I scratched Crystal under her chin. It was like the first day she arrived at Cross Farm. She loved it. As for Joycey, I pulled her ear and she licked my hand in return. Still the same rough old tongue. Both looked on top of the world – their coats were shiny, their eyes were bright.,

'So do you remember the old days?' I asked. 'The times we spent together.'

They nudged me again. I know people say animals don't

remember but I'm sure that's not true. When Crystal and Joycey were at home they remembered their own stalls. All I had to do was open the door of the cowhouse and straight in they would go. Now I was sure they were trying to tell me about the old days.

The early days when we were still learning to milk and we chased each other round the cowhouse. The times they kicked the buckets over on the straw. The calvings. How once, I'll never forget, I got back from market and found Joycey happily wandering around the paddock with two legs sticking out and how I panicked and called the vet. How he told me not to worry, if often happened. Then lo and behold, about two hours later she rolled down on the grass and out came the most marvellous calf you've ever seen. Crystal turned round now and flicked her tail at me and I couldn't help but remember the flower pot. How Christie had shown us how to tie a flower pot over her calf's mouth so he could stay with Crystal in the field and the sheer amazement on both their faces when he tried to sup some milk and they both realized something had gone wrong.

And, of course, the scares. How once Joycey got milk fever and I had to nurse her and look after her and keep giving her lots of injections until in the end we got her better. How she stood on a teat once and tore it. And how she got mastitis in two teats and it took days to put it right. Then there was the time Crystal got a big gash in her side and I bathed it and stopped the blood and looked after her. The time she wandered off down the road after some idiot had opened the gate to her field and not closed it and we found her in a garden eating strawberries.

It was a shame, I thought, getting rid of them after all the time we had spent together, and tears came to my eyes. If I stay any longer, I thought, I'll either burst into tears or smuggle them back home with me in the back of the Land-Rover. After all, it wasn't their fault I wanted to plant a vineyard. They were quite happy having their feed in the morning, being milked, then spending the day pottering around munching grass, having their chins scratched.

Joycey gave me a nudge. And another. Then she ambled off towards their new cowhouse. Were they inviting me and the dogs in to look round? Crystal and I strolled along behind her.

Inside they each had their own stalls. Both were full of the same deep Sauterne-coloured straw. It smelt lovely and fresh and warm. I sat on the wall between them. Elsa snuggled into the straw. Honey and Blue just sat in the doorway wondering what on earth all the fuss was about. I told them everything I had been doing at the vineyard, which I think surprised them because when they were with me it was more a farm.

I told them their old cowhouse had been cleaned up; the open barn was now empty and all the other animals had gone, except the horses and sheep. Crystal, I noticed, shot one of those glances at Joycey that seemed to say, 'Why do horses always get special treatment?' And I told them all about my plans. Crystal rested her chin on my knee until I mentioned the horses. Joycey stood looking at me with those deep, soft, round eyes, wagging her head and flicking her tail.

Eventually it was time to go. It felt like leaving elderly aunts alone in a nursing home. You know it's the right thing to do. You know they are better off there. But you still feel guilty.

'Goodbye, old girls,' I said. 'We'll come and see you again.'

On the way back, I stopped the Land-Rover by Ron Delves' big field about a mile from home.

'Why did I get rid of them?' I said to Elsa. 'They were so nice and friendly. They were never much work really. Why didn't I let them spend the rest of their lives with me?'

She nudged me in the ribs.

'Don't worry,' I said, 'I'll never get rid of you.'

Honey barked. Blue frowned.

'Or you two.'

★

Dennis had a lot of work to do making our little shop in the tithe barn. Some of the timbers were rotten and had to be replaced. Rain was still coming through the roof and there were problems with the electrics to be sorted out.

My mother was busy making dried flower pictures and cakes to put in the shop.

'Might as well make a bit of money. It will help your shop look, well, look countrified.'

Ruth and I were even busier in the vineyard now we were preparing for the second harvest and I was still making plans to increase the acreage. We had bottled all of the first wine and most of it was capsuled and labelled ready for selling. It was also ageing well in the bottle so that every time we tasted it, it had improved and had more character.

The cats were now big game hunters. Practically every morning I was coming down to the kitchen and the breakfast room to find some kind of remains. The dogs didn't like it at all. But Honey went one stage further. One morning she sidled up to me with her mouth closed. She kept it closed until I realized there was something odd about her. When she finally opened it for me a frog leapt out and stared at me glassy-eyed. Our ponds, which Honey loved, were overrun with frogs but she obviously didn't know what to do with one when she caught it! When it leapt out of her mouth she darted backwards, turned her head slightly and looked puzzled.

And poor Françoise, the donkey. About three o'clock one morning, after a particularly hard day, Ruth telephoned me on the internal phone.

'Françoise,' she said. 'I think . . .'

I put on my old coat and ran out to the stables. It was pitch black. Ruth was there with Adrian, Stuart and Alexis. Françoise was lying in the pen making the most awful, piercing and moaning noises. Hardy, her daughter, was standing over her. Obviously she knew something was wrong.

'I've called the vet,' Ruth said. 'He said he'd come straight away.'

I shone the torch on them. Ruth was comforting Françoise by stroking her gently.

'You opened the gate?'

'Yes.'

Françoise then seemed to scream. A horrible scream. Then nothing. Silence. She was gone. Hardy nudged her a couple of times. Then, probably sensing her mother's death, hobbled off into another corner and just stared at the wall. We all waited until our new vet came.

'Cancer,' he said. 'She didn't have a chance. Don't worry, there was nothing you could have done. She must have been thirty or more years old.' He packed all his equipment away. 'You'd better get the Hunt to come and collect her.'

That morning none of us felt like doing any work. I walked the dogs and we mucked out. All the time Hardy just stood in the same corner of her stable staring at the wall.

'I wonder if she knows?' Ruth kept asking.

'What do you think?' I would reply.

People say horses and donkeys don't know but I'm sure that's not true. If two donkeys or two horses are friends and you just take one out for a ride and leave the other in the paddock, they'll usually play up. Especially the one left behind in the paddock. It must be the same if one of them dies. Mum and daughter must have been together twenty to twenty-five years or more. We really didn't know their ages. Hardy must have realized something had happened.

I hated the idea of calling in the Hunt. Apart from the fact that I was – and am – anti-blood sports, the idea of her being cut up for dogs to eat or even just being torn apart as practice made me feel ill. I couldn't face it.

'Maybe we could dig a hole in the field for her,' I suggested.

'Nonsense,' said Peter. 'It would have to be a very large one and even then the fox might dig her up. And we'd have to drag her over to it.'

I didn't fancy that either.

In the end Ruth telephoned the Hunt who came and collected Françoise in a large van with a winch and a hydraulic platform. We made sure Hardy and the horses didn't see or hear anything by putting them in the furthest field.

When Dennis had finished repairing the tithe barn and making our little shop ready we covered the floor with rush matting.

When we lived at Oaklands we had taken most of the huge painted pine cupboards and drawers out of the old kitchen but we had not thrown them away. Instead they had been installed in the garage and when we moved to Waldron we brought them with us and fitted them in the garage here. One of the pieces was a huge sideboard or probably the base of a kitchen dresser. I decided to strip the paint off it using an acid bath. It came up looking beautiful. So I now had a nice old pine base as our 'counter'. I had also bought an old pine dresser which I thought the wine would look good on, so the shop was beginning to develop an atmosphere of its own.

I also had some old oak barrels. One day, without any warning, a large lorry had driven up, loaded with barrels and half barrels.

'Now look 'ere, lady,' said the driver. 'I'm doin' you a favour.'

'Oh yes!' I joked. ' Don't tell me – you're going to give them away!'

'Yer, y' right!' he smiled. 'At my price, I am givin' 'em away. To you, a tenna for the 'ole ones and six nicker for the 'arves.'

'How did you know I was here?' I asked.

'I didn't. I just cum through. I stopped an' asked this geezer – well he was a gent really – where the brewery was. He told me 'ere.'

I laughed. 'I'm not a brewery but it doesn't matter. I'll take two.'

'What! You must be jokin'! At that price! Come on, ducks.'

As he drove away over a hundred pounds richer than when he arrived, Ruth and I put the barrels in the barn and spread the half barrels around outside what was becoming my entrance.

'It gives the place character,' I said. Then, noticing the wording stamped on the base of one of the barrels, 'But we'd better hide that! We can't have Scotch whisky barrels in an English vineyard!'

So the shop began taking shape. I used some St George's flags to make it attractive but it did look rather empty with just our wine, Mum's pictures and cakes.

Soon after I found my first shop assistant – or rather, she found me.

'Now don't you say another word, my dear,' she purred. 'It would be awfully nice.'

'But there's no heating,' I stressed.

'Not another . . .'

'It will be cold.'

'. . . word. That's decided,' said Joan Chidson, a wonderful, fragrant elderly lady whom we came to nickname Lady Bracknell. She was offering to be my first shop assistant.

Well, I thought, it would be like coming to a village shop and finding Harrods.

She lived in a cottage in the grounds of the convent and I had bumped into her quite a few times. She always took an interest in what we were doing and usually ended the conversation with her very correct voice saying: 'Well I've been in business most of my life, so I know what it's like, dear.' Peter had become quite friendly with her since she was a Catholic convert and he met her at mass every Sunday.

She was very elegant with white coiffured hair and just a hint of make-up. She always wore expensive clothes and with a wave of her hand would say things like 'At my coming out . . .' or

'When I was presented at court . . .' or 'When one had servants
. . .', so she gave the impression of being from the aristocracy
without ever really mentioning specific details.

I remarked once that she always looked very smart. She
proudly announced that the green Chanel suit she was wearing
at that moment with a matching green and cream silk blouse
was just ten pounds at the Oxfam shop in Heathfield.

'My dear,' she said in her precise well-educated voice which
was often a little theatrical for effect, 'all the best people give
their cast-offs to Oxfam. Sometimes they have only been worn
once, and I buy all the best names. There are lots of rich people
around here, you know.'

We decided not to advertise the wine or the shop since we
really didn't have much to sell. But it is still amazing how news
travels in the country. I started getting calls from little old ladies
and from housewives all trying to sell me whatever they made
at home, from dried flower arrangements and pot-pourris to
marmalades and chutneys. A local artist brought some paintings
and asked if he could hang a few in the shop on a sale or return
basis with me taking a 15 per cent commission.

'Darling, you might as well take it all,' said Joan, 'providing
it's the right sort of thing and good quality. Any money you can
make will make it worthwhile.'

CHAPTER TWENTY-FIVE
An Order from the PM

'Oh I say. This is really rather good. Dennis, come and taste this.'

In front of millions of television viewers there was Mrs Thatcher praising my wine. And getting Dennis to give it his expert seal of approval as well!

With my first vintage finally in the bottle complete with corks, capsules and labels the real excitement began. I was determined to produce the very best English wine. After four years' hard work, I thought I had produced it. But what did the market think? Would other people agree? Would they drink it? More importantly, would they buy it?

I had no problems locally, especially with our weekend shop and Lady Bracknell. The problem was London and then all the other big towns and cities in the south-east. During the summer and autumn of 1984 I made numerous telephone calls. I banged on doors – in fact I became a door-to-door salesman. I had meeting after meeting with wine merchants, restaurants and hotel managers. And tasting after tasting. Invariably the routine was the same. I would arrive complete with chilled bottles of wine, a selection of glasses, a corkscrew and a mass of typed information about the vineyard. At first, the conversation was a bit slow and stilted. I faced mild amusement at the prospect of English wine and equally mild amusement because I didn't look like Michael Broadbent or speak like Oz Clarke – although I suppose, in fairness, there would have been even more amusement had I looked like Oz Clarke and spoken like Michael Broadbent. Then the initial hesitation and jokes about the extent of their insurance cover before the actual taste. Then, of course, the sheer unalloyed joy when they realized how good it was. Looking back, I don't know what I would have done if I had received really large orders!

One evening I was starting to get supper and give the dogs their dinner when Peter switched on the television. It was the news. Minutes later, on came Margaret Thatcher. I didn't hear the introduction but my ears pricked up when I heard her saying: 'We should support our industries more. You don't have to buy foreign goods when our own industries make top quality products.'

'Hear, hear,' I said. 'And what about English wine?'

'I buy goods made in this country,' she went on.

'Oh yes?' I interrupted. 'You don't buy my wine! Come to think of it, Peter, I bet none of them up there drink English wine. I bet it's all French and German.'

'Fix it then,' said Peter as he was laying the table.

'I will,' I said, 'I will.'

All through supper I was thinking about it.

'If anyone should support British industry – and the English wine industry in particular – it is the Government.'

'Fix it,' Peter kept saying, more interested in the Horse of the Year Show which was now on.

After we had finished I ran upstairs to my office, uncovered our new electric typewriter and inserted a piece of our posh new letterhead. I wrote a whole page on why I agreed with Mrs Thatcher and hoped that she – and the Government and for that matter the House of Lords – would agree with me and stop drinking foreign imports now they could drink my English wine.

When Peter read it, before I folded it in three and put it in an envelope addressed to Mrs M. Thatcher, The Prime Minister with a copy addressed to 'The Wine Buyer, Houses of Parliament', he laughed. 'That just about tells them.'

I was opening the post one morning the following week in our little office when the phone rang. Ruth answered with the now familiar, 'St George's Vineyard. Can I help?'

Silence. She was waving at me frantically.

'Yes, she is here. Would you hold on, please.'

She covered the mouthpiece and excitedly whispered: 'It's the House of Commons!'

A stiff secretarial voice said: 'Mrs Thatcher has passed your letter to the Refreshment Department and we would like to see you to taste your wine.'

The following week I was in a small dark office with green velvet curtains and green leather chairs embossed with the famous gold portcullis.

Mr Smillie was obviously a busy man. I was wondering whether to joke about his name and John le Carré's book, but thought it would not be the correct thing to do – although he pointed to a press cutting on his wall which had done just that. He smiled broadly and said how interested he was in my letter! Here goes, I thought.

I started my lecture on why the top people in England should drink English wine and support this young and exciting industry.

'Well, let's see just how good it is, shall we?' he said gently.

I opened the chilled bottle and handed him a glass. He looked at it. Smelt it. Twirled the glass a little so the wine whizzed around. Smelt it again.

His face lit up. 'Nice nose. I suppose I shouldn't be surprised,' he added, 'but it is rather good.'

I glowed.

'And you're quite right,' he went on, 'we should be drinking English wine.'

I glowed even more.

[335]

'Okay, you've got yourself an order,' he said. Just like that. Then it suddenly struck me. I was looking at the gold portcullis on the leather writing set on his desk. Nothing ventured, nothing gained.

'May I go a stage further,' I suggested, 'and print a special label – House of Commons English Wine – in green and gold with the portcullis?'

'If you can do it in two weeks, yes.'

I was staggered. I felt like kissing him. As I left his office I wanted to jump for joy. I had the most enormous grin on my face, and as I walked out the security policeman at the gate said: 'You look happy!'

I rushed to the nearest phone.

'I've got it! I've got it!' I shouted at Peter who, as usual, was taking two phone calls at the same time.

'Got what?' He was talking to me, then suddenly he was talking to the other phone, 'I can fly over tomorrow . . . yes . . . I'll . . .'

'Got what?' He was with me again.

'An order from the House of Commons,' I said.

'Can I call you back?' I heard him say. I heard a bang.

I got in a taxi and went straight over to Dave Gilmour's office near Marble Arch. Dave did a lot of design and artwork for Peter and was a little surprised to see me. I explained and begged: 'Can you do it by tomorrow? Please!'

The artwork was done by the following day. I went up to London again, took a photocopy and having made an appointment went to see Mr Smillie. He was surprised but pleased. Within five minutes he agreed the design and off I went.

My printer is used to rush jobs and last minute panics, but when I gave him the House of Commons label I laid it on the line. 'It *must* be done in five days or I'll lose the order and you won't get paid! I've bloody well got my first wine order, and I'm doing a special label for the House of Commons.'

'Great!' he said.

Within the two-week deadline I was driving my little white Mini-van proudly through the security check at the House to deliver ten cases of House of Commons English Wine. Ruth and I had labelled them by hand to make sure they were perfect.

Several weeks later I was going off to see Crystal and Joycey when the phone rang. It was Mark Andrews from TVS, our local television station. Mrs Thatcher was visiting their new studios in Maidstone in a couple of weeks' time. They wanted to have an interview that somehow linked the region and Westminster going on in the studio while they showed her around. Would I come and be interviewed about supplying the official English wine to the House of Commons?

'You bet,' I said, 'but how did you know about it?'

'I've tasted it. I had it at the House. Jolly good stuff.'

This was an opportunity not to be missed. I was going to be on television! Just about every member of the family was informed. The ratings would shoot up that day! Out came my best suit and a trip to the hairdresser was called for.

When I got to the studios – late because the lane was blocked with sheep when I left – everybody seemed jumpy and nervous. The security was enormous. I was searched three times before I even got to the floor of the studio. Thinking ahead, I had brought several bottles of chilled wine, some with the House of Commons label and others with our own St George's label, a bottle opener and six glasses. When I got into the studio I suggested I pour out a few glasses.

'That's a good idea,' said the twitchy producer, 'help create the atmosphere.'

Since they had lots to think about they left me alone while I placed bottles everywhere and glasses of wine on the table where I was to be interviewed.

'Now sit there and don't move,' I was told by the studio manager. 'Whatever you do, don't talk to her unless she speaks to you. Okay?'

'Okay,' I said.

'And don't offer her a glass of wine. She won't like being seen drinking alcohol.'

I was then wired up for the microphone so that even if I had wanted to move I couldn't.

'Relax,' they kept telling me. In fact, I think I was the only relaxed person there – *I* was having fun.

Mike Debbens, the interviewer, then arrived. He sat down opposite me. My bottles of wine were out on the table. I'd left them in my chill bag as long as I could.

'The Prime Minister is arriving at the front entrance,' the announcement came over the loudspeakers. It couldn't have been more reverential had it been the Second Coming. We all held our breath.

She was first taken to the new control room to watch me being interviewed so she could see how programmes are handled and transmitted. She would be seeing me and my wine at different angles on twenty screens!

Mike Debbens started the interview. I think he was more nervous than me.

'How would you describe your wine?' he asked.

Having poured out several glasses, here was my opportunity.

'See for yourself,' I said. I was enjoying every minute. I like television work, I thought to myself.

'Okay, Mike,' a voice came over the loudspeaker. 'The Prime Minister is coming into the studio.'

There was lots of shuffling, stroking of hair and straightening of ties. And there she was, much smaller than I imagined, in blue. And what a stroke of luck – Dennis was with her and obviously more eager to taste my wine than shake the line-up of hands at the entrance to the studio.

He came straight over to me and took a glass. 'Must try this,' he laughed. 'Here, Maggie,' he said, 'have a glass.'

Wonderful, I thought, keep going, Dennis.

The cameras and microphones followed her and she joined Dennis and me and sipped the wine.

'This is very good,' she said, turning to me. And she started asking me questions. To hold the cameras on us I took a long time to answer and, whenever I could, mentioned the name 'St George's'. She kept saying that it was delicious.

Fantastic, I thought. I was willing her to say more and she did. We chatted for several minutes.

As she walked away she turned and said: 'Why don't you supply Number Ten? Cut out the middle man and supply me direct.'

'You're on,' I called back. And it was all picked up by the cameras and microphones. Brilliant. Thank you, Dennis . . . and oh yes, thank you, Maggie.

That day I was everywhere – on the lunchtime news, on the magazine programme *Coast-to-Coast* for ten minutes and on *News at Ten*. I even came on briefly just before midnight. No other English wine had had such publicity. St George's English Wine was well and truly launched.

That night, when I got home, the phone didn't stop ringing. All my friends and relatives rang and there were a number of calls from complete strangers, all more or less saying the same: 'Well done. Keep the English flag flying.'

The following morning I rang Number Ten.

'You heard the Prime Minister,' I said. 'She would like some of my wine!'

We had calls from restaurants, hotels, wine merchants. We had calls asking about special labels. And we had calls from people all over the country asking how they could obtain a bottle of St George's English Wine.

We even had a call from Holland – did we export?

At the weekend our little shop was actually busy. Elsa was delighted with all the fuss made of her. Peter, riding out on Laddie, couldn't believe there was a queue.

'But I've only got seventy cases left,' I said as Ruth was wrapping a bottle in tissue paper for a young couple.

'You'll just have to make more,' Peter shouted as he trotted off.

Ruth smiled. 'Well, you've got what you wanted. Now you'll have to plant more vines!'

Suddenly St George's was on the wine map.

14'

40'